APRIL 2012
Dedicated to
Ferry
1/8/03 - 4/22/12

HOW
THE
DOG
BECAME
THE
DOG

Marly

HOW THE DOG BECAME THE DOG

FROM WOLVES TO OUR BEST FRIENDS

MARK DERR

OVERLOOK DUCKWORTH

NEW YORK • LONDON

This edition first published in the United States
and the United Kingdom in 2011 by Overlook Duckworth

NEW YORK:
The Overlook Press
Peter Mayer Publishers, Inc.
141 Wooster Street
New York, NY 10012
www.overlookpress.com
For bulk and special sales, please contact sales@overlookny.com

LONDON:
Gerald Duckworth Publishers Ltd.
90-93 Cowcross Street
London EC1M 6BF
www.ducknet.co.uk
info@duckworth-publishers.co.uk

Library of Congress Cataloging-in-Publication Data
Derr, Mark.
How the wolf became the dog : an epic tale / Mark Derr.
p. cm.
Includes bibliographical references.
ISBN 978-1-59020-353-8
1. Dogs--History. 2. Dogs--Evolution. 3. Wolves--Evolution.
4. Human-animal relationships--History. I. Title
SF422.5D47 2011   636.709--dc22   2010052278

A catalogue record for this book is available from the British Library

Design and typeformatting by Bernard Schleifer
Printed in the United States of America

1 3 5 7 9 10 8 6 4 2

ISBN 978-1-59020-700-0 US
ISBN 978-0-7156-4301-3 UK

For Katie and Harley

CONTENTS

Part IV: Running with the Dogs

Part V: The Classics Rock

CONTENTS

LIST OF ILLUSTRATIONS

Travels of Early Dogs and Humans from the Near East through the Last Glacial Maximum

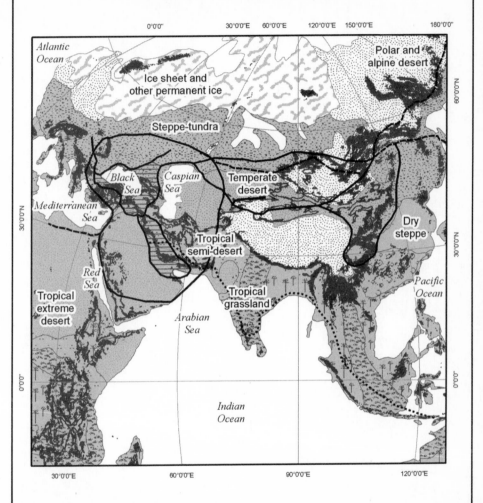

—— Human and dog routes before 16,000 years ago

---- Later dispersal routes

••••• Dingo route

▤ Predicted primary areas for early differentiation of dog from wolf

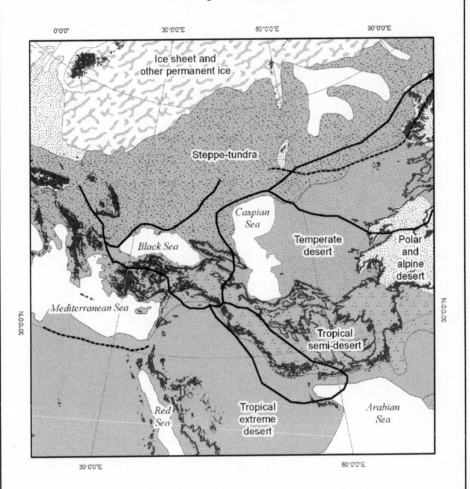

Areas of Interest for Initial Differentiation
of Dogs and Wolves

Ice sheet and
other permanent ice

Steppe-tundra

Caspian
Sea

Black Sea

Temperate
desert

Polar
and
alpine
desert

Mediterranean Sea

Tropical
semi-desert

Red
Sea

Tropical
extreme
desert

Arabian
Sea

—— Human and dog routes before 16,000 years ago

------ Later dispersal routes

HOW
THE
DOG
BECAME
THE
DOG

PREFACE
Dog 2 Dog

A couple of years ago a young editor at The Overlook Press tracked me through cyberspace to ask if I would consider writing a book about how the wolf became the dog, or in the shorthand of digital communication, "Wolf 2 Dog," compressible to "W2D." Having studied the question for more than twenty years, I had no illusion that the actual transformation could be so neatly distilled, but I welcomed the chance to examine what was known and suspected against what was possible in the world at the time of the various periods in question. The task is complicated by a difference in scale between geologic time, measured in tens of thousands to billions of years, and biological time, counted in years and decades. Whatever genetic mutations were involved in W2D appeared and were isolated within several generations, and despite continued tinkering in some places by human breeders, those changes have persisted over geological time.

In the past two years, a number of new scientific papers have rocked, if not overturned completely—yet—the prevailing view that the dog was derived from a self-taming group of garbage-dump grazing, juvenilized wolves during the Mesolithic Age, when our forebears, beginning in the Near East or Southeast Asia or both, renounced their big-game hunting migratory ways for exploitation of a more diverse, local food base, including more aquatic life, game of different sizes, and nuts and grains. In fact, about the only certainty left by the fall of 2010 was the identification of the gray wolf as the wild progenitor of the dog, the two being closer genetically than are the races of humans.

Dog remains dating from around sixteen thousand years ago in the Ukraine, twenty-seven thousand years ago in the Czech Republic, and more than thirty thousand years ago in Belgium were identified. The finds firmly established Europe as the continent with the oldest dogs on record, even though no expert believes that dogs originated there, and more definitively established the dog as a creation of hunting and gathering people on the move.

Increasingly sophisticated genetic analyses have suggested that just a few mutations with large morphological effects—reduced size, dwarfed legs, and brachycephalic, or punched-in, snouts, for example—account for the physiological and, perhaps, the behavioral differences between dog and wolf. For example, a 20-pound animal with bowed, dwarfed legs and a broad, flat nose, like a Pekingese, is going to see and move through the world far differently from a 150-pound mastiff, or a 50-pound Sloughi with its long straight legs capable of speeding close to thirty miles an hour.

Moreover, despite evidence that the little Middle Eastern wolves might serve as foundation stock for the dog, the most sophisticated and thorough genetic survey to date by researchers in the laboratory of Robert K. Wayne, an evolutionary biologist at the University of California at Los Angeles, failed to point to a place where the transformation occurred. Rather, it appears that several types of dog were consolidated from the mixing of Middle Eastern dogwolves with those derived from other wolves.

The question of the dog's origins becomes even more complicated by the association of wolves with hominins, most notably *Homo erectus* and *Homo neanderthalis,* who preceded the arrival of our species among the hunters of the Pleistocene. Did they have socialized wolves and even dogwolves? Without firm evidence of the hominins' direct as-sociation with wolves, I suggest that even if they did, their animals do not figure in the evolution of the dog in human society. Nonetheless, the hominins cannot be ignored, since they were full members of the Guild of Carnivores, the big predators who fed on the migrating herds of rein-deer and horse. To keep them in proper perspective relative to their other guild members, I often refer to them as "furless bipeds," because they lacked their own fur.

I also use the term "socialized" rather than "tamed" wolves to emphasize that the animals were active participants in the process and that their behavior and adjustment to humans went far beyond simple "taming." In cases where socialized wolves existed in sufficient number to form reproducing groups in human camps, I call their offspring "dog-wolves," or "doglike wolves," a descriptive I find more accurate than the traditional "wolfdogs," or "wolflike dogs." These names represent a world of difference. Dogwolves are wolves that genetically and behav-iorally are dogs; we know this because their genetic profile more closely aligns with dog than wolf and because they reproduce and live in human society, looking out on their wild cousins. But these dogs do not appear in the fossil record with the physiological changes that archaeologists consider essential to calling an animal domesticated, including an over-all reduction in size and robustness and a shortening and broadening of the muzzle that forced crowding of the teeth before they too became smaller. That size reduction, shortening of the nose and jaws, and other physical changes increasingly appear caused by specific genetic muta-tions that arose in particular dogwolf lines and became highly desired because of their uniqueness and utility.

Seen in that light, there was no identifiable domestication event; rather, mutations were captured and passed on for reasons of utility or desire or amusement or lassitude in certain populations of dogwolves. It thus becomes more accurate in many ways to speak less of how the wolf became the dog and more of how the dog became the dog—W2D becomes D2D. The change reflects the way natural and artificial selection have worked to create the dog since the earliest encounters of humans and wolves. The small dog itself, long the standard marker for dogs, could owe its distinctive size to its ancestor Middle Eastern wolves, some of which are in the twenty- to thirty-pound range.

My operating premise throughout is that the dog is inherent in the wolf, and the dog lover in all humans—that is, members of the human genus—making the emergence of the flesh-and-blood dog an evolutionary inevitability. Essentially, among the broader population of Pleistocene wolves and humans were individuals who by virtue of extreme sociability or curiosity, or both, became best friends and compatriots after encountering each other on the trail. That connection could have happened on any trail and anywhere that anatomically modern humans met *Canis lupus*—puppy, juvenile, or adult. The question then becomes why some of these relationships continued to grow and flourish while others perished.

My goal is to identify those mixing zones complete with wolves and humans and to show how they represent an early step in the process of domestication that is in certain fundamental ways only now drawing to a close—in a way that sometimes does disservice to both dogs and people. I have attempted to reconstruct the types of environments and ecosystems that our forebears would have encountered in their migratory-game following, especially the refuges during the Last Glacial Maximum (LGM) when people and animals would have mixed. The dog, I suggest, arose from the mixing zone of the ancient Near East among a group of anatomically modern humans, with a lot more mixing and matching between then and now.

The dog finally is a biological and sociocultural creation that has in turn affected its human companion—albeit to a less physical and psychological degree. The wolves and people who took up together tens of thousands of years ago could not have foreseen the many divergent paths that they have followed, much less what they have become. They did not even ask. They simply took to traveling with each other and never stopped. The relationship takes many different forms, to be sure. Too often, ignorance, prejudice, and fear substitute for knowledge and compassion, but that situation applies to people as well as to their dogs and other animals.

It is perhaps more important for everyone involved with dogs to consider that wolf and human were drawn to each other by their great sociability and curiosity, and they stayed together because of their mutual utility. Each benefited from the relationship in various ways. Arguably our obligation today, when we and our dogs grow increasingly distant from the world of our forebears—to the extent that it sometimes seems we live on a different planet—is to think about whether on this journey, we are doing right by our companion every step of the way.

I hope that in some way, this book contributes to that conversation. For now, I think it best to let the story unfold, after one final stylistic note. In order to illustrate specific points, I have created scenarios that are clearly designated as such in the text running up to them and by the italics in which they are printed. They are true to their time, insofar as I was able to make them. Otherwise, the material in this book is factual, recognizing that facts in the study of the distant past—where evidence is often less than pieces of bone and fragments of DNA, which is to say nearly nonexistent—are finally provisional. Yet from these fragments it is possible to weave something approaching a coherent narrative, or at least an attempt at one.

—MARK DERR
April 21, 2011

PART I
Lurking in the Shadows

The dog is what we would be if we were not what we are!
—*Dreamtime Aboriginal saying*[1]

ONE
The Cave

*The elusive first dog—is it an image in Plato's Cave,
a human desire posing as reality? Or is it the wolf
next door—the dog who always was?*

There is something disconcertingly familiar about the tracks that appear abruptly deep in Chauvet Cave, an ancient many-chambered rock art gallery cut high into the limestone of a gorge overlooking the prehistoric bed of the Ardèche River that rushes out of the rugged, volcanic Massif Central in south-central France. The footprints belong to a boy about eight years old and just over four feet tall, walking through a bestiary where images of giant animals line the walls or emerge abruptly from crevasses, wavering in the dancing light of the torch that he holds in one hand for balance and light. Beside him glides a ghostly presence, a four-legged shadow that can project itself into another realm and then rematerialize in the blink of an eye, looking as if it had gone nowhere, as if its absent self were a figment of our imagination. We assume that the boy and the creature have names, though neither is known to us. They could have walked through the cave yesterday or last year, but they passed through twenty-six thousand years ago. Whether they came here to explore a place that they had just discovered or to revisit a sacred ground is also unknown. The footprints simply appear and then vanish.[1]

It is unlikely that the boy added any art to the cave galleries, perhaps already twelve thousand years old when he viewed them, and doubtful that he knew anything more than that they were the work of ancients—if he knew that much. After all, they portrayed the animals his own people hunted—horses, aurochs, megaceros deer, reindeer, and moose—as well as those with whom they sometimes contended for food and shelter—bears, jaguars, dirk-toothed cats and scimitar-toothed cats, lions, other wild dogs, and several species of hyenas. They also portrayed an owl, known widely for the ease with which it navigated the night and for its sagacity, or wisdom, to which many people aspired. Inexplicably, nearly two-thirds of the paintings in Chauvet Cave portray these predators, as well as two large animals that people tended not to hunt—mammoths, rhinoceroses—although they opportunistically took the young of each.

At the time the boy and dogwolf visited Chauvet Cave, bone-aching cold and deepening ice were advancing across Europe, disrupting the biannual migrations of animals and people. The plants—grasses, fruits, berries, and nuts—that both relied on were dead or dying, replaced by other plants that they could not, or would not, eat or by glaciers. Seeking food and shelter, people and animals moved south toward the Mediterranean, or they found refuge in the north in pockets of warmth that persisted through the most bitter cold. They congregated along the Ardèche and other rivers flowing out of the Massif Central or followed them to the Rhône River and ultimately to the Mediterranean Sea. Animals and people were hungry and on the move. The boy might have been one of the migrants, or he might have called this land and cave his home and counted himself among the chosen ones to live in a place where the herds still grazed and nuts and berries were abundant. The challenge lay in getting them before the animals, who seemed always to strike and strip vines and trees bare the moment the fruit reached its peak.

The Chauvet Cave rock paintings are the oldest yet found, the first in a tradition that flourished in southwestern France and Spain until around seventeen thousand years ago when artists—they may have been shaman or graffitists, but since they produced art, I will call them artists—painted the crowning glory of Paleolithic art, the Grotte de Lascaux. By that time, the cold had broken and the ice sheets had begun their long retreat. Warmth-loving plants and animals were recolonizing abandoned lands and new territory so rapidly that it appeared as if they were racing one another to a land's end that no one could see. Resuming the migratory hunting life of their ancestors—following reindeer, bison, horses, and aurochs—some groups moved northward from the south of France, while others turned northeastward. Wherever people went, it seemed that they met strangers coming from other directions, many of them with dogs.

Doubtless the cave artists had stories, along with their images, to explain why they followed the herds of big grazers, while many neighboring groups hunted them only when they passed by their caves on their long migrations. These storytelling artists must also have had tales about how the ancients first encountered the dogwolves that later hunted with them and guarded their camps against predatory people and animals.

The Chauvet Cave artists stenciled their handprints on the wall, like signatures, but they did not draw humans, wolves, or dogs, although alone or together they were the most ubiquitous predators around human dwellings at that time. Artists at other caves did not depict humans or canids, either—not even those at Lascaux. The artists might have believed that self-revelation would bring them harm, the way many American Indians believed that a portrait captured living people's spirit and caused a bad fate to befall them.

Or perhaps the Lascaux artists believed themselves born of the union of woman and dog, or woman and wolf. The first mother appears in terra-cotta as a wide, fecund body, often referred to in our age as a fertility goddess or "Venus," but the dogwolf remains absent, perhaps because of taboos, like those in Judaism and Islam, against creating images of the deity.

The search for the first dog seems always to lead to more questions, to dissolve into a ghostly visage leaping just out of grasp. The dog remains a hint, a whispered rumor in the genetic code, an inexplicable fossil, before it seems to arrive full blown upon the scene, a gift from the gods or a god itself—or more. The Aboriginal people of Australia said: "The dingo is what we would be if we were not what we are." That is why the impressions left in Chauvet Cave's soft mud are so tantalizing in their intimation that twenty-six thousand or so years ago a boy and a dog walked there, just like they would today. That is why not everyone will agree, even when standing in front of the impressions, that what they see is a dog as opposed to the illusion of a dog.[2]

But suppose the tall, lean animal shadowing the boy is not a dog but rather a wolf—a socialized wolf nearly as old as the boy. What distinguishes it from a socialized dog? What brought the boy and the wolf to this cave and where did they go from here—physically and metaphorically? Most discussions of domestication focus on physiological, behavioral, and genetic changes that mark the advent of a domesticated animal, whether it's the dog, the horse, the goat, or some other animal. These changes are the manifest clues that let archaeologists and paleontologists distinguish between the remains of wolves and dogs—as well as other wild animals and their domestic kin—but their appearance does not necessarily mark the moment of domestication, as it were, nor the reason for it.

How then, do we learn about the origins of the dog, the animal who shares our lives more intimately sometimes than members of our own families? That is the signal question underlying this book. The answer is simultaneously straightforward and convoluted due, in large measure, to the animals involved—human and wolf—highly social, tactically minded, pack-hunting global wanderers.

That the Dog is a Wolf modified by nature, wolves, and humans is as nearly beyond dispute as an evolutionary line of descent can be. Geneticists, paleontologists, archaeologists, evolutionary biologists, and animal behaviorists, who normally agree on little else, have confirmed that finding repeatedly. The primary lingering questions are: Which wolf subspecies or population gave rise to the dog? And did the dog evolve more than once in different locales, following different paths from among different wolves?

Georges-Louis Leclerc, better known to history as Comte de Buffon, the great eighteenth-century French natural scientist who anticipated Charles Darwin by nearly a century, believed the wolf bore the dog, but was frustrated in his attempts to breed a shewolf to a greyhound in the hope of producing fertile offspring that would prove his theory. Buffon had raised the two together specifically to encourage their mating once mature, but the wolf repeatedly rejected the greyhound's advances and attacked him. Finally, frustrated, the greyhound killed the wolf. More often than not, when such experiments have been tried subsequently, results have gone the other way, with the female wolf killing the male dog, often after copulation. That's why the more common cross is male wolf to female dog.

Buffon never caught on with the English-speaking public partly because he was French and partly because his perfectly lucid predictions were negative. Darwin preferred to ignore his work, and subsequent Darwin scholars tended to follow his lead, until recently. Buffon by now has received credit for suggesting common ancestry for humans and apes, as well as dogs and wolves, donkeys and horses, and other animals. Buffon also believed that characteristics developed by an individual in response to the environment were passed on to the organism's offspring. Jean-Baptiste Pierre Antoine de Monet, Chevalier de Lamarck, developed that idea into a theory of evolution based on the inheritability of acquired physical and behavioral traits. Although once discredited, Lamarckism is enjoying a revival among some environmental and evolutionary biologists studying the ways in which environmentally triggered mutations in the genomes of individuals can be passed on to their descendants but because they wish not to be identified with Lamarck, they call their field "epigenetics."

Buffon also believed that species tended to degenerate from the parent form, not to improve. For Buffon, the sheepdog was the "ur-dog," the closest to the original wolf stock in terms of brains and talent. Breeds or types of dogs that followed were lacking in one or more essential characteristics of the wolf. Buffon engaged in a heated debate with Thomas Jefferson over his assertion that humans and animals in the New World were degenerate versions of those found in the Old World. Jefferson convinced him otherwise.

Charles Darwin's progressive metaphors suited the nineteenth-century zeitgeist in America and England much better, and his language did not require translation. Unfortunately, although Darwin got much right about many topics, including dogs, whom he loved, his observations and theories about their origins were wrong. He observed that northern wolflike dogs were so different from southern pariah dogs that they had to have separate parent species—wolf and jackal respectively. Then and now, the jackal was considered a garbage-grubbing scavenger, fit largely to be killed on sight, while the wolf was all that was wild and free—and, of course, the enemy of livestock.

Konrad Lorenz, the Austrian founder of modern ethology—the study of animal behavior—embraced Darwin's erroneous notion for most of his long career, which is to say for much of the twentieth century. He changed his mind and accepted the wolf as the sole progenitor of both northern and southern dogs after listening closely to the respective vocalizations of jackals and wolves. Unfortunately, Lorenz's initial error had appeared in his 1949 bestselling book, *Man Meets Dog*, which has long outlived his later correction. In 1967, John Paul Scott, coauthor with John L. Fuller of the classic study of dog development, *Genetics and the Social Behavior of the Dog*, declared that behaviorally the dog could be descended only from the wolf. Dogs are capable of all wolfish behaviors except when humans have altered their physical and behavioral responses through breeding.[3]

Put another way: Human breeders have by design and accident made some dogs more wolflike than others. For example, dogs and wolves are gregarious, sociable animals who communicate through physical posturing, scent marking, and a variety of vocalizations—howls, including harmonized howls; growls; chirps; chortles; yodels; shrieks; snorts; whines; whimpers; sighs; and barks. Wolves are said to bark little, and then only in defense of their dens, but that is an exaggeration. They will bark at a bear or lion they are encouraging to abandon its recent kill for what appear to be the same reasons some dogs will bark at livestock they are herding—to disrupt its thought process, get and hold its attention, and help control its movement. I say "help" because additional actions, like snapping teeth and bluff charges, usually accompany the wolf's barking. Dogs, on the other hand, have developed barking into a high art, a fairly sophisticated, and frequently maddening, form of communication that humans with a little effort can understand.

But humans, primarily through selective breeding, have altered the appearance and physical capabilities of some dogs in ways that sharply curtail their ability to communicate. Floppy ears lack the mobile expressiveness of prick ears. Excessively long hair prevents other dogs and humans from looking into an animal's eyes in order to read its intentions, while docked or naturally shortened tails deprive dogs of a whole range of significant communicative gestures. The individual animal's size, shape, and other physical characteristics clearly affect its speed, stamina, strength, and relationship with the world.

More important, in terms of the origins of the dog, both wolves and dogs can become well socialized to people and other animals during a crucial developmental period that begins at three weeks of age. That period lasts until around eight weeks for wolves and fourteen weeks for dogs, after which both enter a "fear period" that works against forming close bonds to people, although both are capable of forming adult friendships. That extended socialization period and delayed fear response in puppies appears to lie at the heart of the difference between dog and wolf, although how and when the dog came to possess it are still unclear.

For some years, biologists have tended to say that the transformation occurred at a time when humans were giving up their hunting and foraging ways and settling into more or less fixed villages. Wolves joined the army of other scavengers working the midden heaps on the edge of the villages. Over time, the dump-diving wolves tamed themselves— that is, made themselves less fearful of humans. The observant humans chose the best of them to tame further and turn into dogs. A major problem with this theory is that the accepted archaeological evidence says that the human groups with the first dogs were hunters and gatherers, not proto-farmers. A second problem is conceptual: Why would early humans want to bring into their lives and homes a sniveling offal eater? Even if the humans themselves were as rank and dirty as they are frequently portrayed in docudramas, that they threw garbage— waste—in specific places suggests that they perceived it as categorically different from what they kept. There is scant evidence that they did not view scavengers hanging around their middens the same way. From all indications, early humans did not take in and tame hyenas, who were the primary scavengers among the animals found at many early human sites. Dogs rank among the best scrounges in the world, but it does not follow that their progenitor wolf had to become a garbage-dump beggar before humans could accept it and then bring forth its true talents, rescuing it from the trash heap and turning it into a hardworking, lovable companion.

Many students of dog evolution have largely failed to match proposed dates derived from genetic analyses with what was happening among wolves and early humans, including human ancestors, at that time in the place or places dogs were said to have first appeared. In the pages that follow I aim to pick a path through an often bewildering, sometimes contradictory, mass of information to examine how, why, when, and where these two species—human and wolf—got together and produced the dog. I will begin with a review of what has already been proposed and then offer my own explanations, based on what we know and can reasonably conjecture.

Genetic analyses conducted since the late 1990s have placed the origins of the dog as early as 135,000 years ago. That remains a tantalizing date, but most researchers into dog evolution have chosen to ignore it as too early. Scientists have divided into two camps, one placing dog origins around 40,000 to 50,000 years ago; the other, around 12,000 to 16,000 years ago. An additional proposed date of 27,000 years ago, based on nuclear DNA, came out of the completed sequencing of the dog genome.

Proponents of the older dates favor the view that dogs arose in multiple locations and for some time thereafter were frequently crossed with wild wolves—a practice that continues, although the number of dogs is so large that the wolves now leave barely a trace in the overall dog gene pool. Even in their own corner of the world, such hybrids soon pass back into dog except, perhaps, for a few variations on genes that might or might not help the local dogs improve their strength or intelligence or endurance or looks. Reflecting the human cultural bias that sees dogs as debased wolves, wildlife biologists tend to view dog genes that find their way into depleted populations of wild wolves or booming populations of coyotes and their hybrids as detrimental.[4]

Groups supporting a more recent origin following the Last Glacial Maximum diverge regarding time and place. Many favor the Middle East and other locations in Europe and Asia. In 2009, a team of Chinese and European geneticists stated with certainty that the dog originated from a population of several hundred wolves south of the Yangtze River, no earlier than 16,300 years ago. Virtually all of the world's dogs belong to one of six clades, defined by similarities in their mitochondrial DNA, that originated in this region around the same time.[5]

In domesticating wolves, a group of people in that region sought to create a more palatable and manageable entrée, the research team said. The dogs were raised in cages, undoubtedly with their canines and carnassials broken off to prevent them from chewing their way to free-dom. The people south of the Yangtze also began raising guard dogs. In quick order, the descendants of these dogs spread to all corners of the globe, developing new talents and traits as they went. In effect, these early dogs transformed themselves from dinner to consumer of game that they helped hunt, kill, and carry to the pot, which they still some-times occupied. Odder conversions have happened in history, to be sure, but this one is a little hard to digest because it assumes not only that a top predator can be made a prey species—that is, livestock—but also that the results can be reversed and extended in the opposite behavioral direction. The docile prey species can be remade into a pred-ator for the benefit of another species.[6]

Dates derived from DNA analyses rely on a number of assump-tions regarding such "facts" as when one species split from another—say the coyote from the gray wolf—and a regular rate of mutation in specific regions of the genome. Maternally inherited mitochondrial DNA is traditionally used for such studies because it has its own genome, which is considerably smaller and more easily sequenced than the full genome. The Y or male chromosome often provides dates that diverge markedly from the mitochondrial DNA, and until recently has not been commonly looked at by researchers attempting to sleuth out the dog's origin. The same goes for the complete dog genome, which researchers finished sequencing in 2005. Using sophisticated computer software and specially manufactured chips that allow them to survey all of this genetic material from large numbers of animals, geneticists have begun producing new studies of wolf and dog evolution with sometimes surprising, and apparently contradictory, results. Statistically those results might be unassailable, but no group has produced the physical evidence needed to clinch its case. Whether such evidence exists is an interesting question—it might not.

Proponents of a southeastern China origin for the dog, in attempting to explain the absence of fossil evidence supporting their thesis, argue that archaeological sites have either not been excavated or were excavated without regard to whatever canine bones might have been found. (That claim is made around the world and has the ring of truth: Dogs are ubiquitous in texts but are not indexed, because they are animals; so, too, canids abound in many archaeological collections but have largely gone unsorted and uncataloged.) But they fail to show why they have chosen the area south of the Yangtze River above other places in China and Asia more likely to have served as a place of origin for the dog. In most parts of the world, the first dogs appeared in the camps of hunters and gatherers following the migrating herds of reindeer, horses, and other big game. Evidence suggests that dogs were camp guards, hunters, companions, and, perhaps, draft animals.

China covers a vast territory with the Huang He (Yellow) River, well north of the Yangtze, taken as the traditional ecological, agricultural, and cultural divide between the wheat-producing north and the rice-growing south. During the last glacial advance, northern China and neighboring Mongolia formed a region of open steppes and tundra that harbored large ungulates and the animals who hunted them, including humans and wolves. From all available evidence, this area is more likely to have figured in the creation of the dog than southeastern China, where wolves were in short supply and no dog remains more than ten thousand years old have been found. The country itself was more rugged and forested than the steppes, with a great diversity of animal life for hunters to exploit. Even accepting for the moment that dog meat is as fine a delicacy as its proponents claim, there is a difference between sacrificing the occasional puppy from a larger pool and raising large numbers of those puppies as food. It is hard to see, for example, why people would choose to domesticate for food an animal that could potentially harm them and would have produced scant caloric return for the amount of effort spent in capturing, holding, and breeding it in fairly large numbers. Gastronomic logic suggests that given the rapid spread of dogs, if serving as dinner was their primary purpose, more people around the world would be chowing down on them now. More likely, the wolf who became dog helped find, hunt, haul, and guard the large meat on the hoof that its human companions preferred.

An argument in favor of a one-time domestication event flies in the face of a growing body of scientific literature showing that domestication of a species invariably occurred at several different, and often widely separated, locations and involved several different populations or subspecies. The Middle East, Europe, and Southwest Asia have all produced dog fossils dating to about 14,000 years, but finding earlier physical evidence for the dog has proved difficult. Specimens are rare and often of a sort that can make distinguishing dog from wolf difficult. Dated to 31,700 years ago, a canine skull found in Goyet Cave, Belgium, in the 1860s, and then tossed aside as uninteresting, was recently declared a dog on the basis of its shortened muzzle, believed a sign of domestication, and its mitochondrial DNA, which does not match that of any known wolf. It does not match other dogs', either, but that does not bother the animal's human supporters.

Skeptics say that wolves from that period were as variable as early dogs and so the Goyet Cave dog might actually be a wolf—such are the difficulties involved in finding evidence for an evolutionary split that might initially have been imperceptible.

Similarly the mud-preserved paw print in Chauvet Cave was declared that of a dog because the animal seemed to have accompanied the boy on his journey and the print more nearly resembled that of a dog than a wolf. But expert animal trackers admit that distinguishing dog from wolf prints, assuming the animals are of similar size, is at best difficult even when the print is fresh and clear. When the prints are twenty-six thousand years old and belong to animals that may no longer exist, the task is that much harder, even if they are immaculately preserved.

Still, the evidence suggests that the flesh-and-blood creatures at the Goyet and Chauvet caves were large socialized wolves who served as camp guards, hunters, haulers, and fellow wanderers. Their appearance is arguably the strongest physical evidence for the early dog and for the hypothesis that what is commonly called "domestication" of the wolf occurred in several different places, and involved different subspecies or populations. The paucity of older fossil evidence does not arise from a lack of looking on the part of contemporary archaeologists and paleontologists, nor does it absolutely mean that the early animals called dogs are indeed phantoms, that there were no dogs at that time horizon. But it does suggest that although there may have been socialized wolves, they were not dogs. The lack of physical evidence can be due to many reasons, not the least of which is that the dog existed genetically before it did phenotypically, and I can say that because the dog is fundamentally a wolf still capable of looking like a wolf. But archaeologists want a canid that looks like a dog—large or small—before they will admit its existence.

In this regard the archaeologists claim an inherent advantage because they deal only with physical evidence, but for that reason they have failed collectively to deal with the genetic evidence, which has its own standards. I have chosen to reject neither the genetic nor the archaeological evidence and to focus on two periods—the first covers the initial encounter of humans and wolves, currently set around one-hundred and fortly thousand years ago, and the second runs from around forty to fifty thousand years ago to the dawn of the Neolithic Age ten thousand years ago.

This period encompasses the rise of art and culture, weaving, invention of new and more lethal weapons, long-distance trade, the extinction of Neanderthal, and the dramatic retreat into refuges to escape the most recent glacial lockdown of the planet. The Last Glacial Maximum reached its peak around twenty-four thousand years ago but lasted from twenty-seven thousand to nineteen thousand years ago, or possibly shorter. The period ends with retreating ice, and human and dog population explosions out of those refuges to retake a world growing warmer and wetter.

Any number of explanations for how the wolf became dog concentrate on this period, particularly the end of the Last Glacial Maximum, because that is when the first dogs appear in human burials. They are smaller than the wolves of the region in which they are found, we are told, and further distinguished from wolves by an overall slighter build, shortened and broadened nose that initially is too small for their teeth, which show clear evidence of crowding, and other physiological changes that, taken together and in the context of a burial with a human or humans, spell "dog." Those size differences are explained as the results of malnutrition at the time of domestication, an argument based on the assumption that a free wolf ate far better than a scavenging camp follower. Or the smaller size could be due to a biological process called paedomorphosis and broadly defined as early sexual maturation and delayed physical and mental maturation relative to the parent species. The paedomorphic dog, in short, looks like the juvenile wolf.

Whatever their cause, those changes have long been interpreted as the inevitable result of domestication and thus proof of it. According to the two most popular lines of thought today, domestication happened because humans adopted puppies from the ranks of garbage-eating, self-taming wolves hanging around their villages; or because humans adopted and raised wolf puppies on a regular basis, and over time enough of them were hanging around the camp and tame enough that something happened and they became dogs.

Neither explanation seems satisfactory—that is why there is no consensus—and so in an effort to provide a new way of looking at the problem, I decided to change names a little. I call the wolf who takes up residence with a human a "socialized wolf," rather than a "tame wolf." I use this term because *tame* is a word tied up with *domestication* and *meekness* or *subservience*, and the wolf who befriended an early human was not that. Rather it was an animal capable of forming an active friendship with a creature from another species.

Individuals in a band of hunters and gatherers could have socialized wolves in small numbers for years and generations, and no doubt did. But in other cases, a band's socialized wolves would breed with each other and in so doing become what I call "dogwolves," to denote animals that are doglike wolves rather than wolflike dogs or "wolfdogs."

We don't currently know beyond a doubt what natural and cultural events led groups of "socialized wolves" in several locations to integrate so fully into human society that they stopped being wolves, but I think we have to assume, absent proof to the contrary, that the association between socialized wolves and humans was consensual and mutual, and in response to the needs and desires of both species, as well as to exigencies of rapidly shifting environmental conditions. They helped each other out, and they adapted together to a changing world.

Arguably, both wolves and humans made a conceptual leap to "dog," a wolf who cast its evolutionary lot with humans and thus ceased being a wolf in physical and cultural terms. In prehistory and early history, captive wolves could have been restrained tightly with wood and sinew or woven fabric or leather, but could not have been kept that way easily and securely for long periods unless their teeth were knocked out. Until the advent of metallurgy thousands of years later, which allowed humans to produce stronger collars, chains, and cages, an unwilling wolf could not be routinely tied up or restrained in a less-than-sturdy stockade or a deep, covered pit. But by that time, animals clearly recognized as dogs were widespread, so factors other than force must have been involved in the wolf's ancient and ubiquitous presence in and around human encampments.

The dog could have arisen only from animals predisposed to human society by lack of fear, attentiveness, curiosity, necessity, and recognition of advantages gained through collaboration—notice I say "gained," not "to be gained," because while not everyone will agree that wolves or dogs can project ahead in such a fashion, few would argue that dogs do not recognize when an action brings immediate benefits; dogs also know how to split when it does not. Many discussions of domestication generally proceed as if humans and animals were clueless ciphers under the control of genes or of natural or supernatural forces. But those animals were not biological Audio-Animatronics born with a preprogrammed response to people, lions, scimitar cats, dirk cats, hyenas, bears, or any number of other familiar and unfamiliar situations and creatures that had somehow to be overcome in order for them to join the anthropocentric world as domesticates. The humans were neither actors in a cosmic farce nor the chosen lords of the world, nor visionaries—except perhaps in their own minds.

It is fair, I think, to say that the humans and wolves involved in the conversion were sentient, observant beings constantly making decisions about how they lived and what they did, based on their perceived ability to obtain at a given time and place what they needed to survive and thrive. They were social animals willing, even eager, to join forces with another animal to merge their sense of group with the others' sense and create an expanded super-group that was beneficial to both in multiple ways. They were individual animals and people involved, from our perspective, in a biological and cultural process that involved linking not only their lives but the evolutionary fate of their heirs in ways, we must assume, they could never have imagined. Does that thesis project too much self-awareness into the past? I doubt it. Powerful emotions were in play that many observers today refer to as love—boundless, unquestioning love.

But love seems too limited in its meanings and applications to describe such a relationship. The American painter George Catlin visited forty-eight Indian tribes between 1832 and 1839, when many of them still had strong links to their cultural traditions and their only domesticated animals were the dog and the horse. Some tribes called horses "big dogs," because prior to their arrival with Spanish conquistadors, they had never seen one and thus had no name for it. Indian dogs were known not only to resemble wolves but also to interbreed with them. There was nothing refined about them, and for that reason Western observers often wrongly devalued them—unless they needed them for something or, like Catlin, they opened their eyes to see how these dogs lived and interacted with their people. "The dog, amongst all Indian tribes is more esteemed and more valued than amongst any part of the civilized world," Catlin wrote in his account of his journey. "The Indian who has more time devoted to his company, and whose untutored mind more nearly assimilates to that of his faithful servant, keeps him closer company, and draws him near to his heart; they hunt together, and are equal sharers in the chase—their bed is one, and on the rocks and on their coats of arms they carve his image of fidelity."[7]

I will argue, too, that domestication is a continuing process aimed at bringing an animal or plant to the point where the human controls all important aspects of its life, including its reproduction and freedom of movement from birth to death. Seen in that light, the formation of modern breeds and the war against free-roaming dogs during the past two hundred years more nearly resemble a domestication event than does anything that happened before in terms of limiting genetic diversity and gaining greater control of the dog.

TWO
Proper Naming

*The Confucians knew that proper naming was
the first step to knowledge and understanding.
What should we make of people who want
the dog to be other than the wolf it is?*

ew taxonomical designations are as contentious or confusing as
those for wolves and dogs. Officially the gray wolf is *Canis lupus*,
a wolf of the dog genus, and the dog is *Canis lupus familiaris*,
a household wolf, or the wolf who stayed and hitched its evolutionary
fate to that of a furless biped. The Integrated Taxonomic Information
System, a major adjudicator of proper biological names, delivered its
opinion on the issue twenty years ago and then surrendered without
adjudicating the continuing debate. While many biologists, ecologists,
and taxonomists agree that the dog is at its genetic core a gray wolf,
they disagree with the man-altered canid's official name. Because the
dog occupies a far different ecological niche than the wolf—that is,
the human-built rather than the natural world—these scientists favor the
traditional designation of the dog as a separate species, *C. familiaris*

or *C. domesticus.* Both convey the sense of the dog as to the household born, as well as of the dog as household servant or slave, a proposition any number of Anglo-European dogs would doubtless dispute, if asked.

Assigning separate species status for the dog based on the notion that its ecological niche is human society fails to recognize that the dog knows no boundaries, that it is found in nearly every terrestrial habitat—from the densely peopled city to wilderness—and even successfully works the land-water boundary. The faux-Solomonic solution to this taxonomic disagreement has been to declare *Canis familiaris* and *C. domesticus* synonyms for *C. lupus familiaris* and *C. lupus domesticus*—just another way of not deciding, since they clearly are not synonymous.

Conceptually, there is a significant difference between a domesticated wolf and a domestic dog that is not easily bridged. For people raised to believe that humans will eventually unlock all the mysteries of the universe, the dog can be an unwelcome paradox, an ambiguity they can neither fully define nor control and thus one whose close proximity they cannot abide. Dogs share our lives more intimately than any other creature, and according to some studies have been selectively bred over thousands of generations to pay attention to people—at least Anglo-European dogs have been—yet at the same time they dwell in a perceptual and physical universe far different from our own.

For all the refinement that breeders have brought to the dog's appearance, the purebred dog still has paws, claws, and a jaw. They may not be as powerful or efficient as those of the wolf, but they are there, and they define the way the dog approaches its world. The dog's place in the zoological firmament is just one of the areas of disagreement surrounding the origins and nature of our putative best friend. Bound by cultural definitions of *dog* and *wolf, tame* and *wild, domesticated* and *feral* and *free,* humans studying dog evolution might be looking for an animal that matches their unconscious vision of the earliest dog rather than the animal that existed. As a result, they might be overlooking or misinterpreting valuable evidence.

In short, the chief differences between a socialized wolf reproducing in camp and raising her offspring there and a female dog doing the same are defined by humans, and those distinctions have changed over space and time since the two species started their evolutionary tango. Saying that, I include the phenotypic and behavioral changes that pass from parents to offspring and thus can be called *fixed*—reduced size, including the skull, brain, jaws, and teeth; piebald coat; curled tail; floppy ears; sociability around humans—that are believed to be the inevitable products of domestication. Instead, they might be the inevitable by-products of mixing and matching those fixed mutations in different ways in an effort to achieve particular effects, or of constrained breeding of any sort that is done within a context that provides basic food, shelter, and security for an animal.

A view currently popular among individuals who like simple answers to complex problems holds that the phenotypic changes are an inevitable by-product of natural and artificial selection for tameness around humans and other animals. The assumptions—not really scientific hypotheses—underlying this argument are almost too numerous to count. For now, I will simply point out that in common English, a tame animal is a domesticated animal, and a domestic animal is a tamed one. In many scientific papers, however, a tamed wolf is not a domestic wolf, but a wolf that has been raised with humans from very early age and is able to curb its wild instincts enough to live in human society. A domestic wolf, on the other hand, is a dog who possesses and passes on a whole suite of behaviors and physical attributes associated with domestication, particularly tameness.

In this view, natural selection worked successfully to make wolves scavenging village middens tame and tamer, so they would be acceptable to the humans producing the garbage. As the wolves got tamer, they also became cuter, more juvenile-looking, and attracted the attention of humans, who adopted the cutest, tamest ones and, through directed breeding and culling, converted them into dogs—basically juvenilized wolves subject to human selection. Although the process of domestication was different for other animals, it, too, is said to rely on increased tameness with attendant morphological changes.[1]

A five-decade experiment with silver foxes in Siberia is the primary, often the only, evidence cited in support of this hypothesis. Working with a long-established colony of silver foxes, Dmitry Belyaev, a geneticist at the Institute of Cytology and Genetics in the Russian Academy of Sciences in Novosibirsk, began breeding in 1959 for a single trait he called tameness. After thirty-five years of intensive breeding, tame foxes were producing tame foxes that looked and acted like small dogs. They whined, licked hands, solicited attention. Many had piebald coats and curled tails, along with early estrus. But rather than being slightly smaller and more gracile than wild foxes, they were larger, a deviation from the expected result that, like others, was minimized.[2]

For some evolutionary biologists, the results coming out of Russia for the past twenty-five years have resembled a gift-wrapped key to the mystery of domestication. The dog became the offspring of a sniveling, self-domesticating, whining, excrement- and garbage-eating wolf. Almost no one questioned publicly any aspect of the study, although there were abundant grounds for the sort of healthy skepticism that lies at the core of the scientific method. Belyaev and his team claimed a foolproof scoring system, as if such a thing existed, that shifted all kits into one of three categories: fearful avoidance of humans; open solicitation of human attention with hand licks, whining, and submissive tail-wagging approach—that is, tameness—and ambivalence. The overtly solicitous foxes were bred to each other until fox became dog—or doglike. The beauty of the experiment is that it provides an apparently simple solution to the problem of how the wolf became a dog.

A number of researchers eager to find the genes responsible for specific behaviors believe the code lies in the whining foxes, and they might be right. For example, Susan Crockford, an evolutionary biologist in British Columbia, proposed in 2002 that changes in thyroid levels are responsible for increased submissiveness as well as for changes in rates of development that account for paedomorphosis and related processes that define how the dog looks and behaves. Absent hard proof, all anyone has are theories of varying degrees of plausibility.[3]

For now nagging questions about Belyaev's foxes that seem to undercut many of the conclusions of his successors at the institute and fans among American scientists, geneticists especially, need to be answered before his theory moves into the realm of the plausible. Much of the information has dribbled out of Siberia in papers on other topics. The selection criteria have been changed at least once, ostensibly to make the measure of tameness more precise, but changes in scoring on their face alter the terms of an experiment and, at the least, require explanation. It has never been clear what controls, if any, were applied during the selection tests to guarantee that researchers were not basing their decisions on some subtle shift in appearance or demeanor in addition to tameness.

Among other cautionary notes, it turns out that foxes in the discard population—those being bred for no particular behavior or look—are also producing kits with piebald coats, floppy ears, curled tails, and the other characteristics of foxes selectively bred for tameness, albeit at a slower rate. That would indicate that some other factor or factors are involved in the transformation of the farm foxes and probably inherent in captive breeding. In fact, many different wild animals when subjected to captive breeding over long periods of time tend to produce animals with the same phenotypic changes as the foxes—particularly in the jaws, overall robustness, and early sexual maturation It is assumed that animals with these characteristics are selected against in the wild, killed by their own kind or by some genetic ailment that accompanies the phenotypic change, but no one is certain. Female reproduction is suppressed one way or the other by the reproducing female in natural circumstances, primarily because of the costs of feeding the newborns.

But young subordinate females in a pack may come into first heat at an earlier than usual age if the matriarch is killed. As an article of faith, captive breeding programs designed to rescue endangered wild animals, select against, not for, the type of tameness toward humans that Belyaev wanted in his foxes.

Nor do wild wolves lend support to Belyaev's theory. In Abruzzo, near Sienna, Italian wolves have scavenged municipal dumps for generations, even sharing them with free-ranging dogs, without becoming dogs, and the same is true of the wolves of the Negev Desert in Israel. These wolves suggest that some mechanism other than self-selection for tameness was involved in the transformation of wolf to dog.[4]

Belyaev's successors also created a group of aggressive foxes who, among their other attributes, bark in doglike fashion and attack their human handlers. There is no evidence that aggression was bred out of early dogs—barking certainly was not. But the Russian researchers reported that their tame foxes do not bark, even though barking is the primary language of dogs and a common one among wolves, especially for close defensive work or offensive feints, or as attention grabbers, if nothing else.[5]

Feral animals—cats, cattle, horses, pigs, and dogs—present another class of problems for the farm-fox model, which is a better description than the word *experiment,* since the results of the experiment are taken as proof of its general validity, instead of, more conservatively, as showing that selectively breeding silver foxes for a characteristic called tameness over the course of half a century produced foxes that look like and act like whiny little dogs. Feral animals are free of any dependent relationship with humans and so can as easily seek to avoid people as to approach and obey them, perhaps more so. Since proponents of the farm-fox model consider tameness around people the behavioral pattern primarily selected for in the process of domestication, it is strange that it should be among the first to be lost, unless it is little more than an inclination, a fragile stretching of tolerance for a creature other than the self, and a delay in the onset of fear of the new and strange that can spring back when domesticated animals go feral.

There is scarce evidence that early dogs were selected for tameness and a lack of aggression. Evidence abounds, however, that socialization toward humans or other species—the ability to deal with them without fear and with real affection—is crucial in the dog. A number of studies conducted in the mid-twentieth century showed definitively that the wolves, even adult wolves, were quite capable of becoming socialized to humans. "Socialization is possible at any age provided the affective components of fear can be brought under control," Jerome M. Woolpy and Benson E. Ginsburg, two behavioral psychologists who raised and trained wolves, wrote in 1967. The time before the onset of fear is lengthened in dogs, and the critical socialization periods for newborns and juveniles are expanded—all within the parameters of what already exists in wolves. I would suggest that the wolves in which the capacity for socialization was strongest were the ones who joined human society. When they became concentrated enough or isolated enough that they bred primarily with each other, they produced offspring more likely to possess their strong social inclinations and delayed flight response than to run and hide in fear and distrust.[6]

Romanian sheepdog puppy

THREE
The Cultures of the Dog

People imagine the dog, define it, and then set out to find it. They succeed to a remarkable degree in creating the dog of their desire, even if it is not the one they want—such is the paradoxical nature of the beast.

Rapid advances in genome sequencing in recent years have focused so much attention on the biology of domestication that its equally important cultural dimensions have at times been overlooked. Part of the reason lies in convincing genetic evidence that most domestications occurred in more than one place at one time. In fact, multiple domestications sometimes occurred at widely distant locations nearly simultaneously. We know too little about the cultures of Neolithic people to speak definitively about their motivations, and even less about people from an earlier age who were responsible for the dog. It is tempting to say that they shared a common knowledge of how to socialize a wolf, but it is at least as accurate to say that the wolf showed humans the way.

The wolf as dog has already proved itself one of the most successful colonizers of territory in the animal kingdom—second only to humans in its ability to reach and occupy nearly every terrestrial ecosystem of the globe. Dogs live in every habitat, human or natural, from densely peopled urban centers to wilderness, from suburbs to farms, from forests to grasslands, from frozen tundra to tropical deserts.

Although it has formally been banned by treaty from Antarctica, ostensibly to protect seals, which explorers fed to their dogs in vast quantities through the 1950s, the dog has made its mark at both poles. Dogs carried Robert Peary and Matthew Henson to the North Pole in 1909, and two years later they were at the South Pole with Roald Amundsen and two companions. Preferring his own power, Amundsen skied to the South Pole, leaving his companions to manage the dogs and sleds.

The dog also beat its human companion into space, although there, as so often has happened on Earth, humans failed to uphold their end of the bargain. To overcome limitations on the amount of food that could be carried on sleds, polar-expedition dogs were routinely overloaded on the run to their destination, then killed and eaten by the explorers, the other dogs, or both, on the way back, whether they had reached the Pole or not. Laika, a Moscow street dog, was chosen to be the first creature to orbit Earth, because it was assumed that, as a female, she could urinate while strapped down in the space capsule. She successfully orbited Earth aboard *Sputnik II* on November 3, 1957, and after her oxygen ran out, she died there, the Soviet Union's space agency having made no provision for returning her to Earth.

For more than fifteen thousand years, subjected in different times and places to all the kindness, evil, attention, neglect, opprobrium, and love that humans can provide, the dog has done more than endure, if not quite flourished. It has proliferated. Aligning itself with the furless biped, the wolf gained access to a relatively steady supply of food that freed it from many of the burdens of puppy rearing for prolonged periods after the pups are weaned, reproductive freedom for young females, and greater ease and efficiency in hunting. That the biped was not always true to its words or beliefs is another matter. The biped gained a hunting partner who greatly increased its take, a guard against the dangers of the night, a guide in life and death, a beast of burden, a traveling companion, and a lap dog.

With females free to reproduce when ready, with the burden of hunting for food to feed those puppies alleviated by the availability of garbage, scraps, offal, and whatever they could scavenge or kill in vicinity of camp—everything from snakes to big game like deer, bison, and gazelles—with guard duties shared and protection provided, the dog has proliferated, while its undomesticated compatriot has suffered such relentless persecution and habitat destruction throughout its vast range that it sometimes seems to have become the dog's wild doppel- gänger, rather than its living cousin. (double of A living person)

The worldwide population of wild wolves is estimated at 300,000, compared with an estimated 550,000 wolves or wolf-dog hybrids held as pets. But from another perspective in spinning off the dog, the wolf effectively inserted itself into human society as a hedge against extinc- tion in the wild. The world is home today to an estimated one billion dogs, with seventy-seven or so million in the United States and some of the greatest densities in urban Africa, where they are part of the land- scape, as poor and malnourished as the people. Contrary to a popular view in the West, the vast majority of these dogs are owned, although it is not the controlling style of ownership one finds in the developed world. It is more like an association with or an accounting for, a way of saying that this dog calls this house home and guards it, noisily, if not al- ways aggressively.

Since World War II, human societies throughout the world have changed in ways and at a pace that are nearly unfathomable, not least in terms of the explosion in human population and the movement of people and their dogs from the countryside, where many of them lived in village societies more medieval than modern, to burgeoning megacities. In country after country, populations shifted from 80 to 90 percent rural to 80 to 90 percent urban. The sorry plight of dogs and people in the developing world's megacities results more from a breakdown of traditional society than from anything inherent in or missing from the relationship of dogs and people. Without traditional support networks or some satisfactory replacement, animals and people often wander alone and alienated. Unmoored, the dogs, like their human counterparts, can form troublesome roving canine gangs.

For people who value their dogs as if they were members of their families—spending more on a single veterinary procedure than many people around the world will earn in a year—it is difficult to conceive of the life of dogs in poor regions of the world, or sometimes even to think of those animals as the same wolf subspecies as their dogs. Charles Darwin proposed his now disproved theory of dual descent from jackal and wolf to explain the difference. With the wolf established as the sole wild face of the dog, a more recent twist on the jackal/pariah connection argues that because pariahs live by scavenging offal and excrement, these dogs are direct heirs of the self-domesticated garbage-grubber who evolved from a group of sniveling, self-domesticating scavenger wolves who made themselves extra useful by barking at strange animals and people. These dogs are sometimes thought to be of a different kind, one that is less tractable or trainable, more "primitive," more like the dingo than the more refined and biddable Anglo-European purebred dog. Sometimes they are also referred to as feral or semi-wild or free ranging, these terms being used synonymously. Whatever its designation, this transitional animal exists to date largely in the minds of its creators and believers who have produced no tangible evidence in support of it, other than the common human desire for explanations to be clean and simple. But like dogs, they seldom are.

The Canaan dog, for example, is derived from and refined through human-directed selective breeding of the Bedouin dog, often considered a pariah, even though it lives and works in close association with people. Genetic analyses suggest that the Bedouin dog represents one of perhaps a dozen ancient types of dog still extant in the world. In many ways, it resembles the dingo, whose forebear it might be, but it also looks like the Japanese Shiba Inu, a purebred dog. Whether the refined Israeli and American version of the Canaan dog is more trainable is unknown, but evidence would suggest that the original Bedouin dog needed little help from scientific breeders to prove its worth. Its value is proved in a negative fashion whenever Israeli soldiers enter a village of Bedouin to relocate them into more permanent domiciles on a reservation, much the way American Indians were forcibly resettled in the nineteenth century. The first thing the Israelis do, according to reports, is shoot the dogs.

Any comparative test would require proper socialization and training of a number of dogs from both the Bedouin and the Israeli lineages, and such tests are so costly that they are not conducted. That said, a more tractable or trainable dog in contemporary terms is not necessarily smarter; it is just more malleable to human desire, more subject to having its behavior shaped by its human companion. The Bedouin dog might be more independent. To train it, a person would have to understand its motivation, and that requires closer study than most people give their dogs.

More generally, the Canaan dog represents the belief that purebred dogs are more trainable and talented than their freely breeding forebears because of the refinements made by human breeders. This particular mythos is woven into selective breeding of dogs, but it took hold of the popular imagination during the rise of kennel clubs in the nineteenth century and became received wisdom following World War II, when purebred-dog ownership exploded and breeding became a commercial enterprise. Overlooked is the simple fact that for most of the dog's history, it has bred relatively freely and been judged on its working ability and personality, not its pedigree. I say *relatively* because female dogs do make choices, and people affect the gene pool through culling and forced breeding of specific dogs. But when dogs breed without human interference, they make do with what is available locally and so take on certain local characteristics to form landraces, autochthonous breeds, adapted to the demands of their natural and human-made environments. They begin to breed to type—that is, to a certain broad look.

Those types are products of mutations arising in the wolf genetic stew that created the dog that appeared with or soon after the allele for smallness produced the first dogs unmistakably different from wolves. Tracking down the founders of each type and their relative contributions involves a certain amount of guesswork, but the results are surprisingly consistent with older approaches that relied on phenotype alone. I believe these basic types were the northern spitz, with their distinctive, tightly curled tails; the wolfish husky, or Arctic dogs, who followed their own evolutionary path; the dingo/pariah; the heavy-boned mastiff/mountain dog, which is sometimes split; the fleet sight hound; and a raft of little dogs and mutant dogs. The rustic shepherd dog or cur is a puzzlement because it seems so essential and fundamental, but I suspect it involves a mix of dingo/pariah and spitz, occasionally with a touch of mountain dog and sight hound.

Humans took a role in their dogs' reproduction by trying to select mates—tying a female's hind leg up when she was in heat had the effect of forcing her to sit down when a male mounted her. Bitches themselves actively chose which dog or dogs would copulate with them. Dogs were also controlled, to a degree, by confinement or with leather or rope leashes, but they can chew through organic material, eventually, and escape. To prevent that, their teeth were sometimes knocked out or broken off. The discovery of iron and steel created a new level of restraint, but only after thousands of years of dogs and people living together.

Looking back at all that has happened since those wolves cast their lot as dog with humans, all we can do is marvel at what a "long, strange trip it's been." More than any animal—cats not excepted—dogs have made their way with humans through wars; pestilence; cultural, political, and socioeconomic upheaval; and open persecution, and have lived with us in everything from caves to transportable encampments, from seasonal fishing and hunting camps, villages, and farms to towns, cities, and sprawling suburbs. Well, rats have made the move, too, but they are a different story. Indeed, the *Oxford English Dictionary,* that bastion of late-nineteenth-century British civilization, equates domesticating an animal —habituating, or taming, it to live in or near human habitation—with civilizing it. In this context, *civilizing* means making the dog fit for bourgeois society through breeding and training. Like a proper human, the truly civilized dog had to have a pedigree and deportment.

Through breeding, humans sought to make at least their "sporting dogs" more biddable. That is a word many animal behaviorists dismiss as imprecise, but here we use it to mean more attentive and trainable or tractable—obedient. Human breeders also softened the dog's appearance to the point of infantilizing several breeds, and bred others for extreme brachycephaly, their noses flattened, their eyes more frontal and forward to give them a more human, civilized appearance to match their more "decent" behavior. Other dogs, especially gundogs and retrievers, the dogs of sportsmen, were made mesocephalic, with a shortened snout and domed head—to signify intelligence and slavish devotion. This drive to civilize the wild out of the dog was part of a more far-reaching effort to cleave wild nature, including "primitive" people, from proper human society. Without that clear split, there was no justification for slaughtering the wild stock as sport, while promoting the domestic variant as "man's best friend."

Clearly, there is an epistemological problem here that goes way back and insists on cleaving the natural and wild from the built and domestic, such that moving from one to the other is seen to involve a "state" change—a shift in the animal's essential nature. Thus, the wolf is subject to natural selection while the dog is a creation of artificial selection by humans seeking to capture and perpetuate specific behavioral and morphological traits. Natural selection is a deeply conservative process, tending to reject the odd and aberrant, while preserving the possibility for change and adaptations. On the other hand, human breeders often have favored "freaks of nature" or "hopeful monsters" not only because they are different but also because they are often believed to concentrate and enhance certain general wolf behaviors and talents. Thus, sight hounds like the Saluki are faster in the chase than wolves, while the mastiff is more massive and powerful, although less mobile.

The confounding difficulty with the dog is that it defies categories; thus, the dilemma over pariahs versus wolves. For all the change that humans have wrought in the dog's appearance and behavior, it retains the capacity to hear and heed the "call of the wild," as Jack London so aptly put it. Other domesticated animals also have this capacity to revert relatively quickly to a wild state—cats, pigs, cattle, horses, donkeys, goats, sheep, and some chickens. Perhaps among domestic animals, only the rodents—guinea pigs, hamsters, mice, and rats bred for generations for use in laboratory experiments—lack the ability to live free of human intervention.

But as a top-order predator, the dog presents a more significant problem even than the cat, which lacks the size to take livestock. Dogs do not lack size, nor do they have to be feral to kill. Years ago, I had a thoroughly urban Dalmatian who, during a visit to the country, killed and started to disembowel a sheep in front of its owner. She could legally have shot my dog, she said, but she did not want the sheep anymore anyway. (She did take some money in compensation for it, as I recall.)

A few researchers have attempted to characterize the different types of social and cultural relationships dogs have with people throughout the world and in specific regions, primarily as a way to deal with public health problems that free-ranging dogs present. Common categories used to sort dogs include: household dogs that are under restraint at all times—fenced, leashed, or kept in the house; free-ranging dogs, who have homes or at least people who feed them but basically roam as and where they will; stray or truly ownerless dogs, often found in conjunction with free-ranging dogs, who survive largely off dumps and handouts; and feral dogs who live independent of the human world.

Free-ranging and stray dogs are somewhat easier to assimilate intellectually, if not from an animal welfare perspective, because they do not violate categories. Often the difference between them is happenstance; the stray has come unmoored but could return to human company any time someone takes it in. In urban areas, where populations of dogs and people are dense, stray dogs, as they are known, seldom form packs, and the males do not appear to assist in raising the pups, a clear violation of wolf culture—indeed, of most canid culture. These groups of dogs are perpetuated through recruitment into their ranks of other strays. Free-ranging dogs in rural areas of America and Western Europe appear much the same but are not very numerous compared with those in other areas of the world—a result of fence, leash, and licensing laws adopted in almost every locale since the 1960s.

The relatively few studies of free-ranging and stray dogs that have been conducted show that their level of hunting in any given area is related to the amount of food that people give them and the availability of small game or accessible livestock, which is often related to their place in their world. Their social organization also takes different forms. In Bengal, India, free-ranging male dogs cooperate in tending their puppies, and in many parts of the world, including Alaska, feral dogs are known to form self-perpetuating packs.

In Bengal, researchers established three broad categories of dogs, determined by the zone in which they spent their days: village dogs, who stayed in the built environment; farm dogs, who occupied the boundary between cultivated lands and wild grasslands; and herding dogs, who traveled daily with livestock throughout those grasslands. All of them ate food provided by humans and hunted, usually snakes, birds, and small game. The farm and herding dogs also scavenged livestock carcasses. By comparison, in the Basque region of Spain, free-ranging dogs prey primarily on livestock, especially sheep, although wolves are commonly blamed.[2]

Praised as [hu]man's best friend—and in more than a few cases more intimate with their human companions than are other people—praised, as well, for their sagacity, loyalty, courage, tenacity, devotion, and capacity for love, dogs are also damned by public health officials and wildlife managers as major threats to human health and endangered species of birds and mammals. Dog bites on people are deemed a public-health epidemic, with some breeds—in this case, types of dogs, since technically their pedigree cannot be proven—condemned as inherently dangerous. Dogs also spread rabies through bites.

Dogs have generally been slaughtered to eradicate rabies or clear city streets of marauding packs of street curs. Before the advent of mobile refrigeration and the relocation of stockyards from central cities to suburbs, packs of dogs routinely harassed people and killed livestock being driven to market. Until the Pasteurs identified the source of rabies in the nineteenth century, and even for some decades after that in many parts of the world, rabies was called hydrophobia. Overheated dogs frothing at the mouth from thirst on hot summer days or wildly slopping water while trying to drink were routinely declared rabid and killed.

Since the advent of the environmental movement in the last decades of the twentieth century, officials have added killing and disrupting wildlife to the list of crimes dogs—and, in this case, cats—allegedly commit. The policy, as I have said, is a direct reflection of the absolute divide many people, academics among them, draw between the wild and natural and the domesticated and human-built.

No one should be surprised that the dog bridges these worlds;

indeed, the dog lives in the border zone between states. That is a major reason dogs are so valuable in our lives—they connect us to a world outside ourselves and our categories. Yet ours is not a society that deals well with ambiguity, ambivalence, paradox, and border zones, and so the tendency is to cleave the dog from its wild side and lament the contradictions we have created. It is enough to drive a dog to ruin.

Between the nineteenth century and the date the socialized wolf became dog, lie thousands, if not tens of thousands, of years, during most of which time the lines between wolf and dog remained blurred in areas where they mingled freely, like the Arctic. That does not mean they engaged in abundant interbreeding; rather, it means that the dogs in those areas remained more wolfish in appearance and behavior than those subjected to more intensive human-directed breeding. The point is that Middle to Late Pleistocene wolves had scant reason to fear the furless biped, despite its spears and flames. Even today, after intense persecution, wolves have no inherent reason to fear humans. Left alone—I should say, left unpersecuted—they will live in proximity to human settlements, if not within them.

The wolves of Isle Royale National Park in Lake Superior have, we are told, become tame, which is to say, not fearful of human visitors to the island's campground. The wolves stand watching the campers, waiting for food, perhaps, or simply observing, but people are told not to feed them or interact with them for fear they will become acclimated to humans and cause conflict—believed the inevitable result of a wild animal becoming tame or acclimated to humans! Dingoes—the dingo is by any measure a dog who remains close to the wolf and exhibits none of the so-called paedomorphic traits said to be common to all dogs—did the same on Frazer Island, Australia, only there one of them apparently absconded with and ate a child, as they had been known to do when the Aborigine roamed the continent.[3]

Not all wolf or dingo encounters lead to conflict, any more than all dog encounters with strangers do, but for wildlife—and increasingly for certain breeds of dog—zero tolerance is the rule, and the justification for that rule becomes the absolute moral imperative to separate the wild from the human and domestic. In the case of pit bull terriers and other "biting" breeds, *aggressive* becomes synonymous with *outlaw* and *wild,* as in, not civilized or domestic. The system of categorization is self-reinforcing.

That dogs in much of the world live in squalor is unfortunately true, that they are neglected, brutalized, persecuted is also undeniable, but their people are generally little better off, a fact that a number of evolutionary biologists overlook in trying to read the past from the present. The problems are especially acute in societies under stress from outside forces to abandon their ancestral ways without any viable alternatives and in societies undergoing deep internal changes. That is happening on Bali, where the Bali dog, an Akita/chow/dingo type has been genetically isolated for approximately twelve thousand years—twice the length of time that the dingo has ranged across Australia or the New Guinea Singing Dog has hunted pigs in Papua New Guinea.[4]

When Hinduism became an overlay on Bali's animist culture some five hundred years ago, the dogs had been residing with the indigenous people for more than ten thousand years. Islam also has influenced the culture to create an intricate multilayered relationship between dogs and people in the countryside. The dogs roam freely, but among the Hindi Balinese nearly all are associated with a temple or home that they guard in exchange for food put out to feed evil spirits. The dogs also scavenge garbage and excrement, which adds to the problems people have in categorizing them. Among some of the indigenous animists, dog is considered a delicacy, and in some Hindi rituals, dogs are sacrificed, while at the same time praised for their loyalty and devotion as guides.

Despite that long history, the dogs have been alternately declared pariahs or feral by successive imperialists. Most recently, animal welfare workers representing Western values have conducted sterilization campaigns to cut what they see as an overpopulation of dogs that leads to disease and early death. But the reaction to dogs on Bali is a microcosm of our multifaceted, ambiguous, and paradoxical relationship with dogs, which sees dogs in various contexts as food, the eating of which at times verges on cannibalism; as objects of worship for their steadfastness; as sacrifices to appease outraged deities; and as creatures to be coddled, ignored, cared for, reviled, and celebrated. But the greatest current problem for dogs on Bali is common to other developing regions—habitat destruction and sociocultural dislocation. Urbanization on the island has demolished long-established social ties and conventions, leaving animals and people to face the mean streets of their new circumstance with scant support and fewer resources. Bali's rulers should pray to all their gods that dogs and exploited people do not reconfigure ancient alliances.[5]

These island dogs are aberrations in most regards, but because they managed to remain relatively isolated genetically and socioculturally for so long before being colonized, they can provide useful glimpses into a distant past and the way ancient humans and our humanlike, hominin forebears might have interacted with their socialized wolves and emergent dogs, if there was a difference. As helpful as they can be, islands can also lull people into a false sense that they have found a living fossil rather than a cul-de-sac that history only appears momentarily to have bypassed.

There are other tools from paleontology, anthropology, archaeology, genetics, evolutionary ecology, and history for examining the epochal event when Wolf became Dog, and I have attempted to deploy them all to present a more than plausible account for the sudden change in a long-running relationship. Along the way, I attempt to answer a basic, seldom asked question from the perspective of the wolf, *What's in it for me?*; the dog, *What's in it for me?*; and the human, *What's in it for me?*

Those are central questions in the quest to explain how Wolf became Dog and just what that dog is. By most calculations, the numbers of people and animals involved in that process was vanishingly small by today's standards. It was an inevitability that might never have happened, yet as an inevitability, it could have happened only when it did.[1]

PART II
Staking Claims

Great numbers of wolves were about this place and
were verry jentle. I killed one with my spear!
—William Clark, May 29, 1805[1]

Study of a Wolf or Dog

FOUR
Joining the Guild
of Carnivores:
The Benefits of
Membership

A Guild of Carnivores shadows the big mammals of the
Pleistocene throughout Eurasia, living by tooth and
claw. Wild dogs and wolves choreograph the hunt.

he Late Pleistocene was the crowning age of big mammals and
the "big hunt," a final bash before glaciers retreated, and, like
dinosaurs before them, giant warm-bloods toppled into the trash
bin of extinction. That happened when the world's warmth-loving plants
and animals were spreading out to all continents and islands—except
the big ice patch that is Antarctica. As yet there is no consensus as to the
question of whether the extinct animals fell to human hunters over-
whelmed with a bloodlust not seen in them before, or, boxed in by
advancing forests, failed to slingshot into the future off the latest climatic gyration in an epoch marked by wild swings of global weather.

Whatever reasons finally account for it, the end of the Pleistocene
some ten to twelve thousand years ago brought a massive dying of

the largest terrestrial mammals—mastodons, wooly mammoths, rhinoceroses, giant deer, long-horned bison, aurochs, musk ox, horses and reindeer, short-faced bears, two-ton glyptodonts, giant Irish elk, hippopotamuses, and hulking vegetarian cave bears, among them. Some of them for hundreds of thousands of years had grazed their migratory routes deep into steppes and tundra, grooved mountain passes. Their constant companions in life and death were the carnivores—including giant spotted cave-skulking hyenas, smaller spotted hyenas, dirk cats, scimitar cats, jaguars, panthers, lions, tigers, cheetahs, raptors and huge scavenging condors, dire wolves, wild dogs, dholes, wolves, and Neanderthal (the big bipedal meat eater).

Excluding small cats and foxes, those animals formed the Guild of Carnivores, the collection of bone crushers, slicers and dicers, stalkers, slashers, bushwhackers, pouncers, scavengers, and long-distance pursuit artists who shadowed the herbivorous ungulates on their migrations. The big cats sat atop the Guild. Nothing could match them one on one, yet some of them, like the scimitar cat and dirk cat, were so highly specialized that they had virtually no ability to adapt to dramatically changing conditions. Nor could the hyenas, prime scavengers of Pleistocene encampments for thousands of years. who seemed unable to alter their behavior or temperament in response to exposure to several different species of early humans—although there is no evidence that any human group tried to befriend them.

This period in the world's history is a tumultuous one filled with various animals unknown in the world and barely recognizable today, but which a few adaptations of nomenclature might bring into sharper focus. Following the emerging convention, I use *hominin* to refer specifically to members of the genus *Homo* who rank as our most direct ancestors but are not of our species. I also sometimes refer to members of all human species as naked bipeds, to keep them in their natural context as members of the Guild of Carnivores, as another species of hunters who nonetheless were different from other animals.

The naming system Swedish botanist Carl von Linné established in the eighteenth century to bring uniformity and order to the babel of names for the various representatives of life on Earth is essentially binomial. Each organism is assigned a species and genus name by which it is formally known, and subspecies and specific population designations are added when necessary to recognize unique genetic, ecological, or behavioral characteristics of a smaller group that might be on its way to forming a new species. Genus and species names lie at the base of a hierarchical chain of categories and subcategories. The system is old and clunky and favors splitters—people who want to name a new species every time they find individuals that are different in appearance from the description for that species, even if the description is of only one or two individuals. That is the way dog breeds are sometimes identified, but it is a narrow, restrictive view , especially when applied to wide-ranging species.

Despite its flaws, taxonomy provides uniform descriptions and definitions that allow people in different parts of the world to communicate in a meaningful fashion. Here are the taxonomies (only major categories provided) of three members of the Guild of Carnivores: cave hyena, scimitar cat, and Arabian wolf, the only generalist in the group and the only one of the three to survive the Late Pleistocene extinction, is categorized as follows:

Class: Mammalia
    Order: Carnivora
    Family: Hyaenidae
    Genus: *Crocuta*
    Species: *C. crocuta*
    Subspecies: *C. c. spelaea*

The scimitar cat is:
    Class: Mammalia
    Order: Carnivora
    Family: Felidae

Genus: *Homotherium*
Species: *H. latidens*

The Arabian wolf, a subspecies of the gray wolf, is:
Class: Mammalia
Order: Carnivora
Family: Canidae
Genus: *Canis*
Species: *C. lupus*
Subspecies: *C. l. arabs*

The order Carnivora has 23 families with 118 genera and 287 extant species. Families include Ursidae (bears), Mustelidae (weasels), Proccyonida (raccoons), Ailuropodas (pandas), Otariidae (eared seals), Odobenidae (walruses), Phocidae (earless seals), Felidae (cats), Viverridae (civets), Hyaenidae (hyenas), and Canidae. The Family Canidae is comprised of foxes (Vulpes); South American canids; the maned wolf and bush dog, which are not included with other South American canids; a group of ancient fox lineages made up of the island-gray fox, the gray fox, the bat-eared fox, and the raccoon dog; and the wolflike canids.

Carnivorans, as members of the order *Carnivora* are known in order to distinguish them from carnivores of different orders, like *Homo sapiens,* have binocular vision and specially adapted carnassials—the last premolar in the upper jaw and first molar in the lower jaw—like for shearing and tearing skin, muscle, tendons, and bone. They are possessed of a minimum of four and a maximum of five toes (the fifth toe on the forefeet of many is the vestigial dewclaw), relatively large, thick-boned heads with generally well-protected brains, and a pronounced preference for meat, although the giant panda is a bamboo-chewing vegetarian, who only occasionally indulges in eggs, insects, and fish; and raccoons and bears, except the polar, are omnivores. Cats and dogs walk on their toes; bears go heel first; and seals, sea lions, and walruses waddle with their flippers in lieu of walking. Carnivorans teach their offspring how to find, kill, and protect the food they need to survive. The absence of such teaching has long been a major impediment to the success of captive breeding programs intended to reintroduce predators to the wild. Those animals did not have a clue how to survive because no one had taught them.

The catlike and doglike carnivorans are believed to have originated some forty to fifty million years ago in North America as miacids—ferret- to fox-sized animals with distinctive carnassials who gave way to larger five-toe hyenas (creodonts). Around thirty-five million years ago, *Hesperocyon* walked on its toes to found the Hesperocyoninae subfamily of Canidae and spawn two more subfamilies, Borophaginae and Caninae, both of which manifest a distinctive and crucial mutation in the lower carnassials that makes them versatile enough to rend flesh, tendon, and bone, or to grind fruits and vegetables. The Borophaginae remained in North America, crunching their way to extinction, while the Caninae went walking. From *Hesperocyon* also came the long-nosed *Leptocyon*, who gave rise to foxes five million years ago.[1]

The true dogs began with *Eucyon* five to seven million years ago, contemporaneous with the secession of South American canids, among which there were a few "hypercarnivores." Weighing more than forty-five pounds, the hypercarnivores of the Pleistocene rose and fell in population and territory according to the rhythms of glaciations, which affected the amount of prey available to fuel their appetites. They were creatures of the cold because of the huge ungulates it supported. *Eucyon* headed for Asia and Europe and down into China, creating along the way the first Holarctic explosion of wolflike species.

Canis appeared in the form of *C. ferox* and *C. lepophagus* five to six million years ago in North America and almost immediately headed west and south, crossing Siberia and coming off the steppes, the same way Mongol horsemen would slingshot into Europe millions of years later. *Canis* burst upon Eurasia at the end of the Pliocene and, mixing, matching, radiating new species in all directions, joined the Guild of Carnivores.

Prehistory is a sand painting subject to constant revision by scholars, fossil hunters, and time itself. A great mystery revealed one day is forgotten the next. A paucity of physical evidence at many sites—for many periods, a shortage of *sites*—makes all species counts and timelines provisional. In a recent revision, the start of the Pleistocene was moved from around 2 to 2.58 million years ago to include all the major glacial events of the last Ice Age. Because of the persistent and insistent cleaving of humans and human activities from natural events, geological time—in this case, the Pleistocene—covers natural events and all organic activities, except those related to humans, which are considered to have occurred in the Paleolithic, or Old Stone, Age. A major problem with this approach becomes apparent every time a natural disaster or an environmental catastrophe affects all life and reshapes the landscape. In an attempt to avoid confusion, I will use Pleistocene throughout, except in those cases that absolutely demand use of Paleolithic.

Many species of wolves rose and fell before the Pleistocene yielded to our own era, the Holocene, around twelve thousand years ago, most notoriously *Canis dirus,* the dire wolf, a hypercarnivore among hypercarnivores, and a whole group of previously unknown wolves recently unearthed in Alaska that liked to crunch bones of horses and bison. They are a powerful reminder that in many cases, we do not have a clue how much of the story of life we do not know, much less how its discovery would alter what is known. Other significant animals might still be buried in the permafrost or submerged with the ancient coast awaiting discovery and excavation, or lying among the unnamed fossil fragments in a long-forgotten collector's neglected cabinet of natural history.

But based on what is known, for wolves—and for hominins—the last third or more of the Pleistocene was a time of diminishing species diversity and pulsating demographic expansions and contractions in response to the dance of glaciers. Nonetheless, the main canid species we know today slipped into place long before the Pleistocene ended: *Canis adustus* (side-striped jackal), *C. aureus* (golden jackal), *C. lupus* (gray wolf), *C.s latrans* (coyote), *C. mesomeias* (black-backed jackal), *C.s simensis* (Ethiopian wolf), and, perhaps, *Canis rufus* (red wolf). Scientists in India recently suggested that their indigenous wolves—*C. lupus pallipes* and *C. chanco*—played no role in the creation of the dog, despite a strong supposition among many paleontologists that both might have been involved, and also differed enough from the gray wolf to deserve separate species status.[2]

All the extant wolflike canids have 78 chromosomes and could be classed in the genus *Canis*, but two are not: the superpack-forming red dhole (*Cuon alpinus*) of India and Asia, and the patchwork-coated African wild dog (*Lycaon pictus*). They are assigned their own genera largely because of habit and peculiarities with their feet—they lack the vestigial fifth toe, and the middle two toes are fused, a characteristic that turns up in *Canis lupus arabs* as well. The dhole, like the wolf, was a member in good standing of the Pleistocene Guild of Carnivores, as was a larger wild dog, *Xenocyon lycaonoides*, also counted as *Canis lycaonoides*. For some time on both sides of a million years ago, *X. lycaonoides* and a smallish wolf, *Canis mosbachensis*, appear in tandem at caves in Spain, Italy, Greece, Germany, and the Levant. The reasons for this are unknown, since *lycaonoides* was primarily a courser of the steppes, not a scavenger of caves. The wild dog decamped for Africa around 700,000 or 800,000 years ago and is there still in the different, smaller form of *Lycaon pictus*, but until then it seemed to cap the size of prey that *C. mosbachensis* pursued at deer.[3]

Whether precursors of *Canis lupus* or evolutionary dead-ends, the various wolves that rose and vanished during the first million-plus years of the Pleistocene were, with the exception of North America's dire wolf, not the biggest dogs in the Guild of Carnivores. Paleontologists call them mesopredators, or middlin', down at the bottom of the list in terms of size and thus, according to modern scientific calculations, too small to bring down game much bigger than a deer. Certainly, that appears initially to be the situation with *C. mosbachensis,* who would have had to compete with larger carnivorans, including its running mate, *Xenocyon lycaonoides,* for bigger game. Often mentioned but not much discussed or described, *C. mosbachensis* is variously referred to as the size of a small wolf, like the Arabian wolf, or of a coyote or a medium-sized dog.

Once *Xenocyon lycaonoides* dropped into Africa, *Canis mosbachensis* turned to larger game and began to grow and evolve into *lupus*—or so runs one theory. Similar arguments are made today concerning deer-eating the coyote or coyote-wolf hybrid that is colonizing the Eastern United States. The gray wolf was different from the start, a leggy, wide-ranging, devoted carnivore with catholic tastes who nonetheless showed a pronounced preference for bison in England, reindeer in northern Europe, and reindeer and horse on the Mammoth Steppe—predilections it shared with hominin hunters. *C. lupus* had the added advantage of being highly adaptable through changes in shape and behavior to a range of ecosystems. Subspecies include the 24- to 50-pound Arabian wolf who tends to hunt singly or with one or two partners, when it is not scavenging dumps, and the 150-pound tundra wolf running in packs of twenty or more, pursuing the downsized megafauna that survived the Last Glacial Maximum.

What distinguished wolves, dholes, and wild dogs behaviorally— and still does—was their pronounced, we might even say exaggerated, ability, relative to other carnivorans, to run and attack together. Spotted hyenas also hunt in packs but they are not renowned for their social cohesion or toleration for long hunts. The wolflike canids were constantly aware of the position of everyone in the pack, spatially and temporally, as if they projected themselves into spatial comprehension. Pack-running hounds do get lost, usually because they surrender to their noses and eagerness in pursuit and as a result forget to recalibrate their positions. Once contact is lost, other demands take charge. But anyone who has hiked with a dog in the woods understands the phenomenon of the disappeared animal who suddenly materializes at their side and looks at them as if to say, "I knew where you were all along." The ability of wolves to communicate over distance and act in concert amplified their strength, so that together they could drive all but the largest, most obstinate bears from their prey, or bring down animals considerably larger than themselves, like moose or giant elk. Wolves also adapted their hunting style to suit the prey a capacity that helped them through rough times.

Gray wolf

FIVE
Hoofing It

*When did this affair between long-distance
wanderers begin? When the first furless bipeds
hiked out of Africa and kept walking? Did wolves
teach successive newcomers how to hunt the big
herbivores? Or did it work the other way?*

S ome 1.8 to 2 million years ago for reasons unknown, bands of
furless bipeds with opposable thumbs crossed the last few kilo-
meters separating Africa from the rest of the world and walked
right into and through the Guild of Carnivores. The first of them,
called *Homo erectus*, appear to have pushed through the Levant and
around the Caspian Sea before turning east across Asia. They then
turned south to Indonesia. Another group went north into the Balkans
and west along the northern Mediterranean coast to Spain. Although
identification is unsettled, that European group is probably *Homo
erectus* but is by custom and habit called *H. ergastser*, who became
H. antecessor, who begat *H. heidelbergensis* about 700,000 years ago,
who begat *H. neanderthalis* between 400,000 and 100,000 years ago.
H. sapiens, or anatomically modern humans, replaced Neanderthal in

Europe, the Levant, and central Asia by around 30,000 years ago, although relict populations appear to have persisted for another 5,000 years in Spain and the Balkans. By about the same time, in eastern Asia, *H. sapiens* had effectively relegated *H. erectus* and its 1.8-million-year reign to the boneyard of prehistory. A person today can go mad trying to sort out the hominins and still be proved wrong by the next significant paleoarchaeological find; indeed, in the six months to a year between the time I write these words and the time this book is formally published, the above genealogy, rough as it deliberately is, probably will have changed. In recent years, a species of little people, *H. florensis,* has been identified on Flores Island in the Indonesian archipelago, and in 2011 researchers reported that a fossilized pinkie finger found in a Siberian cave and dated to 40,000 years ago belonged to a new species of hominin.[1]

What seems clear is that the furless bipeds who colonized Eurasia had new, broad, Acheulean stone blades good for the kind of chopping and scraping needed to process meat—I should say that they traveled with the knowledge and ability to make those tools when needed, since hauling rocks was probably no one's idea of fun. Some paleontologists believe that, at least initially, these hominins lived primarily by scavenging and foraging leftovers from other large carnivores, especially scimitar cats and dirk cats, who abandoned considerable amounts of carcass uneaten because their teeth prevented them from getting to it. But those hominins more likely were foragers, hunters, and opportunistic scavengers because subsequent sites of human occupation show, with few exceptions, that the furless bipeds ate before the carnivoran shadows—bears, hyenas, and wolves—got their turns. These hominins did not move through the world motivated by fear of the new and unusual.

The first among the "shadows" were wolves, although sometimes spotted hyenas probably filled that role. The earliest hominins into Europe, their remains found in Dmanisi Cave in the Georgian Caucasus and dated to 1.77 million years ago, encountered *Canis etruscus*, who was apparently supplanted on a transcontinental scale by *C. mosbachensis*, who first appears in the fossil record about 1.5 million years ago at 'Ubeidiya cave, Israel, within spitting distance of the Sea of Galilee. The new wolf apparently had come out of North America, where at least one expert has suggested it was the parent species of the red wolf (*C. rufus*), the indigenous wolf of the southeastern United States that may be a hybrid between the gray wolf and the coyote.

The U.S. Fish and Wildlife Service, which has run the unsuccessful red wolf recovery program for more than twenty years, has embraced that view, while the red wolf seemed content whenever released to the wild to seek the company of coyotes. The hybrids did quite well, but because they were not pure representatives of a species that may never have existed as anything other than a hybrid, they were killed by wildlife officials. The official red wolves are kept on a coyote-free peninsula where they, like all the people involved, are bound by an eighteenth-century system of classification of animals and a consensus definition of species that have always been too rigid to represent populations in flux due to migration, hybridization, and other causes.

Other wolves appear at other prehistoric sites but *Canis mosbachensis*, often grouped with the generic, because unidentified, *C. variabillis*, is so commonplace that it arouses the suspicion that hominins and wolves must have known each other as more than opportunistic hunters and scavengers—or that contemporary paleontologists are using it as the generic name for several small, coyote-sized wolves. I shall call it the small wolf and observe that it would have taken more effort for it and the resident hominin *not* to recognize or show curiosity about each other than to have some interaction.

Indeed, some kind of alliance would have made sense given the nature of the carnivorans in whose company hominin and wolf found themselves. For example, at Pirro Nord, a cave on the southwest coast of Italy, hominins lived and hunted 1.3 to 1.7 million years ago along with dirk cats, scimitar cats, cheetahs, hyenas, and small wolves. The dirk cat (*Megantereon cultiridens*) was a dagger-toothed bushwhacker, while the 800-pound scimitar cat (*Homothereum crenaditens*) yielded to nothing. Foxes and bears joined the mix at Cal Guardiola, Spain, around 1 million to 800,000 years ago. Jaguars, lions, and dholes were also members of the guild in good standing.

It is commonplace even for many scientists to speak about the predators in the Guild of Carnivores as if they competed for the same prey species, but that view may be overly simplistic. Analysis of predator and prey remains from a site near Granada in southeastern Spain dating to 1.5 million years ago show that predators tended to specialize in certain types and demographics of prey, with some overlap. Heavily muscled, powerful dirk cats and leopards worked the forest edge, ambushing horses and deer from cover. Despite its size, the scimitar cat chased down young mammoths, young giant hippopotamuses, horses, and bison—a suite of species that put it at the top of the guild in that region. The big wild dog, *Xenocyon lycaonoides,* contented itself with medium-sized ungulates like deer and goats, which in turn tended to keep the small wolves from pursuing them. The giant hyena seemed to prefer stealing from them all.[2]

Prey choice varied from region to region, indicating, among other things, that some places were more hospitable to certain predators than others by virtue of the other guild members who were present and the available prey. In England, the resident small wolf was a deer hunter, but its successor, the gray wolf, followed reindeer and bison on their migrations. The gray wolf was larger and stronger than *Canis mosbachensis* and had the coursing field much to itself.

How the various predators ate was in the long term as important as what they ate. Wolves, including wild dogs and dholes, shared the hunt and the spoils of the hunt, something not even pack-forming hyenas did. Cooperation and submission not to a rigid hierarchy but to the well-being of the pack are crucial to its social cohesion and success. Thus the pack, including the father or leader or alpha male, may defer at certain points in a hunt to a younger member, even allowing it to make the kill, if its talents have brought it that right. Such an individual will soon be out looking for a mate and establishing its own pack.[3]

During the Middle Pleistocene, about 700,000 years ago, with *Xenocyon lycaonoides* gone, *Canis mosbachensis* was a Holarctic wanderer, showing up everywhere hominins went. The wolf ranged from England, through Spain, Belgium, France, Germany, the Caucasus, and the Balkans to Siberia, Mongolia, and China and then back through southwest Asia to the Mediterranean. During this period, perhaps because of climate swings, species diversity declined, at least for wolves and, it appears, for humans, while remaining species, if they were robust and ambulatory, became more widely distributed. *C. mosbachensis* maintained its standing as the most common wolf for another 200,000 or more years, when it morphed into, or yielded to, the gray wolf, who changed the game.[4]

About that time, 500,000 years ago in Bolomor Cave, Spain, a hominin was scavenging bones picked over by another carnivoran, although whether they initially had been brought there by the ubiquitous *Canis mosbachensis*, hyena, or some other carnivoran is difficult to determine. Starving, the people doubtless took the first thing they could find to eat without compunction. The fossil record contains other evidence of humans scavenging from other animals, but it is far more common to find animals scavenging human sites. Humans might have eaten what the guild ate, but they clearly understood that they were a different kind of creature. They cooked their meat and processed bones for marrow; moreover, they ate first—while other members of the guild watched.[5]

That notion of being a different order of beast would become more meaningful if these hominins had consciousness and some form of communication and culture. Like many people who have considered the question, I assume they did, but it also seems that they were not as sophisticated in those areas as their successor, our own species, would be. That is a more convincing working hypothesis than one born of the thoroughly ingrained, too often unexamined, belief in human exceptionalism, holding that hominins were simply more clever bipedal apes, who lacked the brains to know, much less to understand, what they did. Without language, they could never be said to be fully human.

Human exceptionalism is entrenched in the Western Judeo-Christian tradition and holds that God has given humans dominion over the earth and all its assets, including animal. We are different—we are chosen—and because of that we have minds and culture and reason and language and have tasted of the fruit of the tree of knowledge of good and evil. If any other species had those things, it would have to be considered our equal, and we have no equals on this planet—that is the essence of human exceptionalism, and unless it is dismissed, it will continue to distort everything we see and experience. Often, scientists who do not consciously believe in human exceptionalism nonetheless hide behind it when there are issues they do not wish to discuss, like the prehistoric Ice Age bonds that might have formed between hominins and wolves. Yet at nearly every turn, behaviors or inventions believed unique to anatomically modern humans have proved not to be—spatial organization of living areas, travel by boat, control of fire, and creation of art. Neanderthal, it is now said, probably had some form of language, an ability once loudly denied the carnivorous cave dweller. More upsetting to human exceptionalism is the finding that Neanderthal and anatomically modern humans mated and produced viable offspring that became anatomically modern humans. We are all part Neanderthal and who knows what else. That list of challenges to human exceptionalism does not even address animal emotion, consciousness, or volition. Life does not fall into neat, discrete boxes and categories in which generalizations become facts or absolutes. Life proceeds along multiple continuums of the possible.

Feist, common small dog of the American South

SIX
What About the Wolf?
Canis Who?

The long-distance wanderer becomes a
homebody sometimes. Wolf is prime mover as
alliance builder; adapts as dog to settling down.
Was Canis mosbachensis *the first socialized wolf?*

French sculptor Antoine-Louis Barye named his snarling bronze wolf *"Loup Défendant Sa Proie,"* "Wolf Defending His Prey," but it is also known as *"Loup Qui Marche,"* "Wolf Who Walks," and *"Loup Marchant,"* "Wolf Walking" or "Walking Wolf," as if to moderate its fierce visage. It is a beautiful, purposeful wolf of the imagination and of some observation; nineteenth-century scientists and artists puzzled over such a creature's relation to the dog, and the place of wild things in the civilized world. That we are asking nearly the same questions a century and a half later indicates that they are more difficult to answer than we imagined—assuming we are even asking the right questions. It certainly shows that the fault line created in the Anglo-European world between wild and domestic continues to underlie many of our assumptions and attitudes, despite having been well exposed and discounted in recent years. Until all preconceived notions are laid aside, I posit, we will not gain a clear understanding of the nature of the animal who fills so many different, frequently contradictory roles in quite different human societies.

Like the hominins with whom they mingled, some prehistoric wolves adopted the nomad's way and followed the massive herds of reindeer on their long migrations—indeed, some North American wolves appear still to follow the caribou on their semiannual travels along routes their ancestors laid down when our human ancestors were still following reindeer half a world away in Eurasia. Other wolves tended to stay in their home territories, switching prey with the season, just like the bands of stay-at-home hominins. Whether they stayed or went, among them were wolves of great curiosity and need of attention, for the proximity of a warm body, and when one or more of those hooked up with a human of whatever species, age, or gender who had the same craving, a friendship was likely to be born.[1]

"It is my experience that if you put your hand into a pen with newborn wolves, a certain percentage will come immediately and never want you to leave," experimental psychologist Benson Ginsburg told me in an e-mail in 2009. "They are so hypersocial that if you were to take them and put them in isolation, they will become withdrawn and depressed. Some may die. Other pups will run away and still others will be stuck in avoidance-approach. As adults, the social ones can still become sociable to humans but it takes much longer and is more difficult." With the wolf we know today, socialization must be steady and daily from birth or at least three days of age, with the more handling the better. The same goes for dogs—the more handling the better.

It has always seemed to me that these questions of sociability and lack of fear of the other—or should I say, the ability to moderate or control the fear response in the face of the new and the other, the alien being—lie at the root of Wolf's transformation into Dog. It is also at the core of the human and dog relationship. That does not mean that the dog or person has to go up and lick everyone on the face as a sign of slavish affection. But it does mean they have to be able to make a leap of friendship, if not faith, with a creature who is clearly not the same.

I have tried thus far to look at the way ancient hominins, the forerunners of our species, might have interacted with the wolves all around them. But that approach has severe limitations based on a profound lack of information about those hominins. Like other writers faced with the dilemma, I could try fiction, a novel filled with drama and characters of my creation, but it seems to me that trying to shift back through the obscuring fog to understand a process that was simultaneously global and intensely local is ultimately more satisfying even when thoroughly provisional.

self evident

To start with what is known: It is nearly axiomatic among dog scholars and wildlife biologists that the structural similarities between wolf packs and human hunter and gatherer bands made it easier, even natural, for the two to get together. But no evidence exists to suggest that hominins kept company with socialized wolves, tame hyenas, purring cats, soaring raptors, or any other animals, although we assume they must have. In fact, there is insufficient evidence to do anything but wonder what was going on between hominins and wolves. That they could have cohabited for hundreds of thousands of years *one by one* without doing more than gnaw each other's bones in seriatim seems more unlikely than that there were among them individuals who became socialized to each other to some degree, or that neophyte hunters learned a few tricks from wolves—and later returned the favor. People who have lived close to wild animals know that many of them will, over time, become habituated to a nonthreatening human presence to a considerable extent, with some growing quite friendly, even tame.

Wolves may possess the capacity for sociability with humans to a greater degree than other species. and in the Early Pleistocene *Canis mosbachensis*—to Europeans *Canis lupus mosbachensis*, a subspecies of the gray wolf—was the wolf and various hominins were the human for around a million years. That is five times longer than our own species has been around and twice as long as *C. mosbachensis*'s successor, *C. lupus*, has ruled the world of wolves and the diminished Guild of Northern Hemisphere Carnivores.

For more than 200,000 years of the epoch's million-year run, *Canis mosbachensis* was top canid, free to hunt prey of its choosing rather than settle for something smaller, like it did when *Xenocyon lycaonoides* was around. It does not seem to have been in competition with humans even where they hunted the same species. In some areas around the Mediterranean, wolves focused on deer and ibex. While humans hunted them as well, they showed a predilection for larger animals, like horses, aurochs, and red deer. Farther north in Eurasia, wolves joined humans and other members of the Guild of Carnivores in eating horses and reindeer. The high-protein diets must have suited both species because wolves steadily increased in size and strength, while the energy-hogging human brain grew. Humans also developed more sophisticated and productive, even profligate, hunting strategies that allowed them to kill many animals at once. Significantly, even where they pursued the same prey species, humans targeted mature adults while wolves and other carnivores preyed on vulnerable individuals—the young, old, and infirm.[2]

The pack-forming pursuit-specialist wolf, whose mode of operation was to run a herd or group or single big grazer to exhaustion, sometimes used a relay system that involved switching pacesetters—that being the most psychologically demanding and thus also the most tiring position—to keep as many pack members as possible strong for the slashing attacks on their prey's face, neck, flanks, and hamstrings with the intent of bringing it wounded and hemorrhaging to bay and then to its knees and death. It was hard, dangerous work that demanded cooperation.

Wolves would rather attack easy than hard prey, and they are more content opportunistically to run other predators off their kill than go to the dangerous effort themselves—who would not be? But they are also consummate hunters capable of strategizing and working together in ways that bespeak intelligence and profound tactical understanding.

I have read that the furless biped was an ambush hunter who attacked from within caves, whereas the wolf was a cruiser and pursuit hunter. The wolf was the more experienced hunter at the time it first met anatomically modern humans with full knowledge of the difficulty and risk of running amidst panicked grazers. It was also practiced at hunting by deception.

Take for example the little Arabian wolves in the Negev Desert a century and a half ago. The Bedouin would gather their sheep and goats close to their tents at night and place them under guard of their fierce dogs and camels. The wolves used a simple tactic to get past those defenses, placing a decoy on one side and an attacker on the other. The decoy initiated an attack and when the guard dogs responded, its partner rushed in to grab a lamb. In a bit of counter-strategy, Bedouin herders started leaving a collar of fleece on lambs they sheared, believing that the cushioning prevented a wolf from dispatching its catch quickly or grasping it tightly enough to flee very far very fast. The shepherds and their dogs would have time to react and rescue the lamb. I have seen no report on how many lambs were saved in this fashion.[3]

Gray wolves reportedly will sit staring at musk oxen circled in defense around their young in a way that would be called giving eye, were they border collies or kelpies. When one of the oxen cracks psychologically and breaks from the protective ring, the wolves charge. Its defensive shield broken, the herd scatters, and the wolves take their pick. They have been known to drive their prey over bluffs or into water, where the ungulates might temporarily gain an advantage, and charge herds in order to break the defensive walls adults form around their young.

The first of the furless bipeds entering the Guild of Carnivores as they passed through the Levant to Eurasia must eventually have observed and possibly learned from such tactics. In his 2008 novel *Wolf Totem*, the Chinese writer Jiang Rong provides several powerful fact-based descriptions of Mongolian wolves driving a herd of gazelles into a lake where, bogged down, they are slaughtered. He also describes a bloody wolf assault by night on a human-guarded horse herd that involves the deliberate sowing of panic among the horses, especially the stallions. Whether they developed those tactics on their own and then taught them to humans or the obverse, no one can say definitively.[4]

No matter who invented the technique, the upstart biped of the Upper Pleistocene with longer, looser limbs and a fondness for new approaches to old problems, as well as to new technologies, perfected hunting by stampede. It produced large amounts of meat, in many cases, it appears, more than could be gorged on quickly at the site, the way wolves ate. Human hunters grabbed some choice bites, then field dressed and hauled back to camp all they could. Even if everyone in the band joined the effort, and socialized wolves decided to carry their share, meat was left on the field for wolves (wild and socialized), ravens, vultures, and other scavengers at a time when wildly oscillating climatic conditions had finally driven the long-time scavenger king, the hyena, from Europe.

At Gesher Benot Ya'aqov in the Jordon River Valley, nearly 800,000 years ago, roughly the time *Canis mosbachensis* was assuming its new role, hominins were organizing their encampment spatially in ways that paleoanthropologists have long considered a sign of our own species' unique abilities and consciousness because such arrangements require communication and division of labor among group members. The hominin inhabitants of Gesher Benot Ya'aqov built hearths for cooking in specific locations in their encampments that, as if following some mysterious universal law, almost immediately became centers of group social activities as well. In so doing, they established the kitchen as the center of the home, and the communal fire as the focal point of the village. They also set aside areas for tool making and for processing the fish that were staples of their diets.[5]

The presence of the hearth and its central position in the life of the family group confirm that these hominins had gained control of fire. That puts an outer limit on an old argument over when hominins became fire savvy. Arguably they had knowledge of fire making a million years earlier, when they moved out of Africa and pushed into northern latitudes where fire would have been essential for warmth and cooking, but the sort of definitive physical evidence that archaeologists demand as proof has not yet been found.

It is hard to conceive of this one site as an aberration, a neat and tidy hominin nesting site that occurred once and then vanished until spatial organizing abilities became manifest in anatomically modern humans. It seems far more reasonable to say that these hominins were probably more human than not—inventive, adaptable, observant, possessed of some form of language, if only sign language. I say that because one current theory holds that a mutation in the FOXP2 gene that only occurred around 200,000 years ago was necessary for humans to develop the capacity for actual speech. Since there is no indication that the hominins at Gesher Benot Ya'aqov were hearing impaired, but plenty of evidence that they were behaviorally sophisticated in a way reserved for anatomically modern humans, I suspect they could communicate verbally in some fashion.

We might assume as well, based on the evidence from multiple sites, that at the least wolves were gnawing on bones humans had worked over, that they followed the human thieves back to their caves or encampments and took back, if they could, some of the meat they had lost. They waited in the shadows, watching, and it is understandable if now and then a bone was tossed their way. We can only speculate at what point the biped recognized that it was better to feed the wolf than be on constant alert against it stealing food or even an infant.

During this period hominins changed phenotypically, developing not only larger brains but also longer, leaner limbs more suitable for long-distance, ground-eating trotting. Moreover, the wolves had long since developed successful pack-hunting strategies for bringing down their preferred prey. They did not need to change that, but if the biped offered something new that might actually produce many more dead at once, then they might take note.[6]

I would like to say more than that. I would like to talk about how inventive those hominins were, how they developed the technique of stampeding herds off bluffs using fire. The surplus of carcasses produced in that way fed wolves, hyenas, and other carnivorans with minimal effort on their part. There are a few signs that *Homo erectus* did occasionally engage in mass kills, but we simply do not know enough about how its brain operated or about its behaviors to make anything more than a tentative guess about its plans. Certainly when not participating in a drive, hominin and wolf tended to hunt the same animals differently—if they hunted the same animals at all—so that they would not necessarily have found themselves in competition. We also know that killing a large animal, say, a horse, with a spear requires great luck, incredible skill—either to throw the thing with enough force and accuracy to bring down a three-hundred-pound animal, or to get close enough to stab it in succession in vital places—or a group of hunters. I can easily imagine a couple of wolves who bring a red deer to bay. The prey is so focused on the wolves that she fails to heed the bipeds charging in from either side until it is too late. When the first hunter appears, the wolves focus their attention on the young red deer.

Wolves and hominins also shared an ability to vary their diets to fit what was available, an omnivory they had in common with bears. They could hunt everything from rodents, like marmots, to fish to the largest ungulates, and eat fruit, nuts, and grass when necessary. That adaptability doubtless served them well in lean times. Notable exceptions to this omnivory among bears, wolves, and humans were the polar bear, *Ursus maritimus,* and Neanderthal, both single-minded carnivores as well as the dire wolf and other hypercarnivorous wolves.

This hypothetical relationship of hominin and canid is made more interesting by the possibility that *Canis mosbachensis* is the common parent species to the North American red wolf (*C. rufus*), the Holarctic Eurasian wolf (*C. lupus*), and the dog. Were that even two-thirds correct, it would suggest that the smallish Pleistocene wolf was a creature of resilience and talent, possessed of both highly developed social skills that would become its enduring legacy and a highly plastic phenotype—like dogs and humans.[7]

That kind of speculation is amusing, but speculation it must remain, part of the lore of *Canis mosbachensis* or *C. lupus mosbachensis,* who became *Canis lupus,* the gray wolf—the big, strong, shrewd pack hunter of the tundra, able to scale down for the hot desert climate. Thus, the gray wolf was born in the presence of Neanderthal, and much later would witness the birth of anatomically modern humans. What that means is harder to discern. Whatever deal *C. mosbachensis* and *Homo erectus* or *H. heidelbergensis* or *H. antecessor* or any of the other modern human precursors had struck, in what became Neanderthal country, in all likelihood ended when the species involved vanished. That is well before any trace of dog appeared in the genetic or paleontological or archaeological record despite their frequent revisions to accommodate new information and theories.

Homo erectus reigned in East Asia for well over a million years, and the most famous of its sites, Zhoukoudian Cave outside Beijing, was long associated with wolf remains dating to 400,000 years ago. That association was declared invalid in the late 1990s when the hominin remains were redated and the assemblage of bones was declared the work of natural forces. A more recent revision has placed the age of the Zhoukoudian hominin remains between 680,000 and 780,000 years ago and invited a reexamination of the other remains. Although the Chinese record for wolves, humans, and dogs is still little understood, current evidence suggests that Archaic or "Early modern" *H. sapiens* cropped up 300,000 years ago, and our subspecies finally arrived around 30,000 years ago.[8]

I do not mean to imply that those ancient hominins had no real interaction with wolves or other animals. Rather, I want to suggest that nearly a million years of interaction between wolves and humans had left members of both species with a range of available social behaviors toward each other and toward other animals. At one end of that range were individuals distrustful of anything they did not know; at the other end were those wolves and humans capable of embracing other animals. That suggests that the relationship between humans and wolves, was not founded in competition and enmity. Although given the subsequent persecution around the world of wolves it might be hard to accept that line of thought, the fact remains that hominins would have been no more likely than anatomically modern humans to take an enemy into their homes. If they accepted the presence of the wolf, it was as a friend. Even if those socialized wolves had become a self-sustaining population among a group or groups of *Homo erectus,* they would have had to outlive their human companions and/or contribute to the gene pool of their successors their disposition toward sociability. Hominins could also possibly have passed on knowledge of the wolf to their successor, although that possibility seems remote in this case, especially in Europe.

Anatomically modern humans had to learn about wolves on their own, without guidance from their forerunners. As climatic conditions deteriorated, beginning around forty thousand years ago, and other carnivorans dropped out of the European Guild of Carnivores, gray wolves emerged as the predators to fear, gaining the position before the Last Glacial Maximum peaked on any continent. It appears to have been a bumpy ascent punctuated by at least one sharp decline, but the wolf adjusted and ultimately flourished. At its Late Pleistocene apex the global gray wolf population was an estimated 33 million, with 5 million breeding females—less than half the number of dogs in the United States today.

I doubt a wolf would glamorize the hunt. The adrenalin rush might be refreshing, but often attacks fail, game is lost, and the cost

Artemis with hunting dog

in terms of energy expenditure or injury can be high. It is far better to let someone with a weapon do it. That raises one of the great unanswered questions regarding the alliance of human and wolf: When did they start hunting together, and what form did that cooperation take? Other significant questions would be: When did the socialized wolf assume watch duties and at what point did the simple enjoyment of each other's company enter the equation? There are other tasks to which the socialized wolf was put but arguably they are subsumed under these—flock guarding, for example, is simply territorial, and family defense and herding is a form of hunting. But is the wolf capable of such behavior?

Lupa, adoptive wolf mother of Romulus and Remus and protector of shepherds, was the model of wolf and human cooperation. Although the stuff of legend, she stands as a valued signpost pointing toward wolves with an affinity for people and, by implication, other orphans.

On July 26, 1930, *The New York Times* reported on a "lonely ewe" in Central Park. Rejected by her own kind at birth, "Queenie" had been named and hand-reared by the Central Park shepherd, Thomas F. Hoey. Her protector was "Wolf," the three-quarters wolf hybrid Hoey kept as a guard dog. Wolf and Queenie were inseparable. He was her main man; she, the object of his devotion. Wolf kept her safe for four months until someone abducted him, and Queenie went into mourning.

The world of Hoey, Queenie, and Wolf, in which sheep were used to mow and control the grass in Central Park under supervision of a shepherd and a wolf, is completely unknown to the vast majority of New Yorkers—and that was just eighty years ago. Despite being the time that our direct forebears stepped to the fore in human evolution and began to remake the world, the Late Pleistocene, or for the homocentric, the Upper Paleolithic, is considerably more profoundly remote than time alone can indicate. This epoch is conceptually distant as well, beyond our experience in nearly all regards but not beyond our belief that we can come to understand this and any other period or that we in fact could cope were we thrown into such circumstances. That existential optimism, even in the face of bone-crushing cold or mind-numbing depression—metaphysical pessimism —might be numbered among the distinctive human traits that pulled this particular furless biped through the Last Glacial Maximum and other hard times.

A corollary of that optimism is an openness to the new and different that can overcome the opposite tendency, deeply entrenched in many animals, including humans, to distrust the unsettled and unknown. Konrad Lorenz commented on the habit of dogs of jumping over a log in the path they walked daily even after the log has been removed. Like us, they are creatures of habit who map their world. But individuals with a capacity to explore can be found among any group of animals. For example, several years running in the mid-1990s, a young manatee spent its summers swimming thirty-three hundred miles from southern Florida to the northern end of Maine and back. Wolves are known in our current fragmented world to travel three hundred miles, or more, looking for a mate and place to start their pack. Reports over time from around the world indicate that left unpersecuted, wolves freely and openly will live close to humans—take up residence themselves even after thousands of years of relentless killing by those same humans.[9]

The gap between those ancient hominins, the prey they hunted, and the predators all around, not to mention smaller animals of every sort and birds, was vanishingly small. They were furless bipeds, even if clad in borrowed skin. They doubtless took in animals, the way people today take in animals, who in turn left or stayed as they matured, unless they were caged against their wills.

Arguably, wolves and humans have always been together, since humans were born into the world of wolves already familiar with furless bipeds carrying sharp sticks and flames. As ethologists Wolfgang Schleidt and Michael Shalter suggested, it was the wolf who trained the human, not the other way around. That is a far less radical proposition than the one contained in the myths of a group of ancients in central Asia who believed they were descended not from Wolf but from Dog.

SEVEN
Dogged Pursuits:
Neanderthal Agonistes
or Respect for Erectus

Neanderthal, the homegrown European meat eater,
becomes top carnivore but fails to make it into the
Last Glacier Maximum. Was he replaced, or absorbed?
The nature of the beast, or what about those wolves?

Whether spelled Neandertal or the more cosmopolitan Neanderthal, this unfortunate species has for some time been synonymous in the public imagination with the lumbering dullard, the grunting, muscular, club-wielding caveman. *Homo neanderthalensis* was a close quarters hypercarnivore, a not necessarily more sophisticated version of the dirk cat and scimitar cat, but ultimately no more successful at surviving the Last Glacial Maximum than its fellow guild members or the megafauna on which they depended. Neanderthal's first counterpart in eastern Asia, the durable *H. erectus,* might have persisted longer. With Neanderthal, *H. erectus* seemed poised to have a hand in making the dog, but then the focus blurred, as it always seems to when the mystery threatens to come clear. Out of habits dating back half a century, I tend to think of Neanderthal as Enkidu to *H. sapiens'* Gilgamesh—the brutish, brooding, loyal, misunderstood alter ego without whom the hero or heroine is nothing— Caliban to Ariel in Shakespeare's *Tempest*. The lumbering, ham-fisted brute to the long-fingered, gracile human. More pointedly, I see Neanderthal as always, chronically, "yesterday," an anachronism without creativity, a plodding unsightliness of an evolutionary failure, devoid of imagination and curiosity about the world outside his cave and his quest for meat.

More tellingly, Neanderthal seemed to lack the one attribute that set the upstart biped apart, more even than artistic talent: the capacity to trade, which requires, above all, an ability to deal with other beings, even strange beings, on an equal footing—because they have something you want, and you have to find something they want in return for it—and to trust untrustworthy people to do the correct thing under the proper circumstances for the appropriate payout. Simply put, the person stands to benefit more from completion of the transaction than from not delivering the promised goods or slaves or dogs. The trader —and, even more so, the solo wanderer—must be accommodating to others in a way not required of people who die in the clan and place they were born.

That bias makes it relatively easy to dismiss Neanderthal, but like most biases, mine has no factual base to stand on. It is a literary creation dating to discovery of the first Neanderthal fossil, one example showing how cultural attitudes that are passed to us through all the circumstances of our lives become filters we do not even know are on until forced to confront an image or idea or reality that profoundly contradicts us and tells us that what we thought was simple is the opposite. By now it should surprise no one that evidence made public in 2010 showed Neanderthal could have been a wanderer after all. Archaeologists displayed freshly discovered stone artifacts from Crete indicating that hominins, probably Neanderthals, had first reached the island by sea at least 150,000 years ago and then returned multiple times—astounding behavior for a species of human heretofore deemed, for no apparent reason, too primitive to build even a raft. That is on its face a strange assumption given that naturally occurring "rafts" in the form of tangled downed wood are a time-honored form of sea transport for otherwise nonaquatic species, and there is absolutely no reason to assume that hominins were afraid of water or couldn't swim.[1]

It was as a hunter that Neanderthal expressed his genius for organization, planning, execution, and cooperative and coordinated group efforts. Neanderthals appear to have hunted seasonally, pitching their camps in the middle of migratory routes of reindeer, bison, and their favorite game—horse. Neanderthal used box canyons, cliffs, and bogs in mass kills. In addition to horse, at least in northern France and Belgium, Neanderthal hunters specialized in mammoths and rhinoceroses, and when game was not migrating, they went after red deer, ibex, and saiga antelope. They targeted mature adults from big game because they provided the most food. Each group maintained its own large territory, making it, as ethologists Wolfgang Schleidt and Michael Shalter have suggested, a hunter in the style of the consummate social hunter, its *sensei* the wolf.[2]

That transcontinental loper who hopped over to the Americas before glaciers sealed them for a few thousand years and was at home from China to England was a resilient, adaptable, social, gregarious canid capable of planned assaults and sudden improvisations. Neanderthal appears to have been a more methodical disperser who came to range from Gibraltar to the Near East and Balkans, into the Caucasus, western Asia, and Siberia, and back across Europe to England. Neanderthal was a hunter, *Homo venator,* as close to being a total carnivore as any human species has come, late-twentieth-century American beef eaters notwithstanding.

Other highly carnivorous humans have appeared over time—in

what is clearly an adaptation to available food sources in the Arctic, Patagonia, the North American Great Plains, and the Asian steppes—but Neanderthal apparently outdid them, turning to cannibalism and perhaps to eating wolves and any other creature that could be said to be made of skin, muscle, and bones. In that sense Neanderthal was a failed evolutionary experiment in human specialization. Among the first of the late Pleistocene megafauna extinctions, Neanderthal exposed the limits of dietary overspecialization and in so doing, oddly enough, issued a warning on the hazards of trying to turn a generalist into a single track specialist. It is a warning modern, "scientific" dog and livestock breeders have chosen to ignore.

Few creatures great or small seem to generate as much disagreement as *Homo neanderthalensis*. It sometimes seems that everything about this muscular hunter is subject to constant revision, beginning with its dates. Not many years ago most official accounts said fully formed Neanderthals assumed their spot atop the Guild of Carnivores around 130,000 years ago and lost it around 30,000 years ago, curious numbers that like so many other number combinations are doubtless coincidental. These dates are eerily close to the estimated 150,000 years ago for anatomically modern humans exiting Africa; the 135,000 years ago indicated by early mitochondrial DNA surveys for the first dogs; and the 27,900 years ago for those same first dogs, derived in 2005 by the group of researchers sequencing the dog genome. By these three measures, Neanderthal came into existence with the gray wolf or the dog, or went extinct upon the appearance of the dog, meaning that despite the apparent contradictions, we cannot get to the dog without going through the enigmatic hunter.

I can almost see through the occluded lens of time three wolves lazing outside the cave mouth, watching where the river spreads out enough to slow all but the heaviest spring torrent. When two young men leave the cave, each carrying two spears, the wolves rise and stretch. They lope down the narrow winding trail in advance of the men. Near the bottom of the cliff face, where the trail suddenly steepens and narrows, one of the wolves doubles back through the trees, undetected by the humans until it reappears by their side. From a distance it appears gently to nudge the trailing hunter, who is favoring one leg, away from the ledge toward which he lists. When they reach level ground, the wolves proceed at a fast trot toward the river ford. . . . The men cut into the forest and are lost from view. A short while later, just where the forest fades to meadow, they attack from opposite sides a small group of horses and their colts. Two horses fall; their colts bolt into the meadow and jaws of three wolves waiting.

A small but steadfast number of ethologists and paleoanthropologists argue that these Neanderthals and wolves were together out of their mutual need to hunt and their recognition that they might help each other. All of the proposed, and often mutually exclusive, dates for the debut of dogs have genetic and/or archaeological support based on the calibrations of various clocks for dating prehistoric events, meaning most of the world's history. There is the genetic evidence pointing to 135,000 years ago; genetic evidence targeting 40,000 to 50,000 years ago; physical and genetic evidence for 27,000 and 30,000 years ago; genetic and archaeological evidence dated from 12,000 to 15,000 years ago in the Levant, Germany, and Siberia; genetic evidence and faith for less than 16,000 years in southeastern China, craggy country below the Yangtze River. The genetic clocks are calibrated to the putative time for divergence of gray wolf and coyote, but the range of possible years for that—700,000 to 4.5 million years ago—shows how provisional these dates are.

A 2009 paper on penguins in the journal *Trends in Genetics* argues that the standard practice of calibrating a mitochondrial DNA evolutionary clock to a speciation event produces an understatement of the age of the species or population in question by a factor of about five on average. Mitochondrial DNA, which lies at the heart of the cell's energy system, has long been used to show descent, even though it is known to present only a partial view of the animal's evolutionary history. If the finding that the mitochondrial clock is miscalibrated to a significant degree survives intense scrutiny, it may lend support to the oldest and most controversial date named for emergence of the dog. Conceivably it could go back even further.[3]

Although it is seldom used, the oldest date for the dog to split from the wolf, 135,000 years ago, has yet to be withdrawn or fully revised or refuted. That date places the first dogs, who would have looked like wolves, because whatever genetic changes had occurred had not yet become physically manifest, in the villages or caves of *Homo erectus, Homo neanderthalis,* or perhaps even archaic *Homo sapiens* during a warm period between major glacier advances. Perhaps all of them had dogs. No one knows.[4]

That is about the time that anatomically modern humans first successfully migrated out of Africa and headed south along the coast of India and east to Southeast Asia until they reached Australia some sixty thousand years ago without leaving any sign of dogs or socialized wolves. They also moved north along the coast into China. They were in the Eastern Levant, on the Mediterranean coast, and in the Jordan River Valley until roughly 75,000 years ago, when Neanderthal, fleeing intense cold, pushed them aside—figuratively if not literally. Between thirty thousand and fifty thousand years ago, Neanderthal vanished and anatomically modern humans again occupied the Levant. At least one group moved north and northeast beyond the Caucasus and Caspian Sea into Siberia and Central Asia, stopping in the region of the Altai Mountains and headwaters of the Amur River. Other groups could have crossed the Bosphorus into the Balkans before following the course of the Danube River east to the Black Sea or west onto the

Pannonian Plain, bound for central and western Europe. Bands of anatomically modern humans also moved into the Balkans and then west through southern Europe. By thirty thousand to thirty-five thousand years ago, they had reached western Europe.

Arrival of anatomically modern humans in western Europe, with qualitatively different technologies and behaviors, including, most profoundly, an embrace of long- distance trade, marks the start of the Upper Paleolithic Revolution or, more cautiously and perhaps more accurately, if less graphically, the Upper Paleolithic Transition. This time period is also crucial for the evolution of the dog. There is intriguing circumstantial genetic and mythic evidence that the group of humans moving out of the Levant north into central Asia may have started from the grand mixing zone between the Saudi Arabian Peninsula and the Zagros Mountains with a sizable collection of "dog-wolves"—a breeding group of socialized Iranian and Arabian wolves.

Dates for events in human prehistory, even the events themselves, are subject to more than the usual amount or revision, because they are so extensively studied and because complete genomic sequences for dogs and humans, among other creatures, are just now allowing more comprehensive genetic dating as well as revision of many previously "established" dates. Among the problems many people have accepting genetic dating are its challenges to standard histories with their underpinning of human exceptionalism. That is especially true in the case of Neanderthal where evidence for interbreeding with anatomically modern humans has long existed and for just as long been denied. In this case, hybridization means that the cultural explosion that occurred in Europe around forty to fifty thousand years ago marking the transition from the Middle to the Upper Paleolithic was not solely the work of the unique anatomically modern human but of a cross between it and Neanderthal—in short, of a mutt. If we were to shift the dates back a little, we could make the same case for interbreeding between archaic *H. sapiens* and *H. erectus* in eastern Asia.

These dates are best used as markers, signposts for navigating in a world too often lacking meaningful context. They present relationships and the sequencing of events in a way that make sense in our terms. That is to say they fit and support a credible narrative of an event or events about which we know little. Of course what we consider credible is shaped by our own experience and knowledge and may only have any relation to Paleolithic hunter/gatherers because we assume it does. Those are some of the unexamined facts by which we live, until something comes up that demands examination.

In many ways, Neanderthal, like *Homo sapiens* several thousand years later, walked into a ready-made world. Other hominins had mastered fire, stone tool and weapons making, living space design, even group hunting and carcass processing. But Neanderthals had to learn what to hunt and when, how to make it last, how to anticipate seasonal migrations—that is to say, seasonal change—and how to drive their prey into death traps. They learned to read the body language and vocalizations of animals. If this knowledge was not willingly passed on from one hominin species to another, it could have been stolen—liberated, as it were. Nearly every ancient culture had in its creation myths tales of obtaining fire or some other prize, from a tribe or group or person who did not want the newcomers to have it.

Arguably anatomically modern humans took from Neanderthals the most valuable item of all—their existence—either by pushing them over the precipice of extinction or consuming their genome in what might be called an act of genetic cannibalism. While doing that, they also learned enough of Neanderthal's hunting tactics to assume their role as top predators of the Mammoth Steppe. Although I doubt our forebears also stole Neanderthal's wolves, I cannot say absolutely they did not. It is hard to see Neanderthal without shadowing socialized wolves—there by mutual consent. I can even see those socialized wolves, protodogs, if you will, baying up a big bear, thereby providing time and distraction enough for the hunter or hunters to stick their spears up and under the ribs into the heart.

That is a more plausible scenario than one proposed by anthropologist Valerius Geist in 1980, which has one Neanderthal hunter grabbing the long hair of a wooly rhinoceros or mammoth and then holding on to the bucking animal while his mate tries to kill it with a spear. The first rule of most hunting for food is to aim at a stationary target whenever possible, since your odds of hitting it are dramatically better than if it is moving, especially if it is bucking madly in an attempt to brush off a giant insect and you are trying to dodge flailing limbs and gnashing teeth while mustering enough strength to power a spear into a vital organ.[5]

Conventional wisdom has held that Neanderthal had largely blinked out by thirty thousand years ago, with relict populations persisting in southern Spain, Croatia, and perhaps elsewhere for several thousand more years. Those were Neanderthal strongholds, places they returned to frequently as part of their seasonal hunting cycles. The caves that housed Neanderthal in Croatia from more than sixty thousand years ago to thirty thousand years ago contained in their fossil assemblages an astounding number of wolves in the most recent unearthed levels—from more than eighty to nearly two hundred in every one. Perhaps even more intriguing is the relative absence of spotted hyenas, who preyed on the same game as humans and who hunted, scavenged, and occupied the same caves for long periods. Located in northwestern Croatia in a well-drained area of karst limestone hills and bluffs, the caves back up to the Julian Alps on the west, and face the Pannonian, or Hungarian, Plain on the east. Paleontologists have recently argued that the area was less a refuge for animals fleeing the cold of the Last Glacial Maximum than it was a continuously occupied temperate ecosystem, an oasis in a desert of increasingly bitter cold waves, as it were. While that seems a distinction without a difference in many ways, the continuity could explain how Neanderthal apparently persisted there longer than in many other places.[6]

But it fails to explain what those wolves were doing there, unless, in fact, they were socialized wolves who in their non-refuge had begun to mate with each other, thereby fixing in their offspring their propensity to befriend the stocky cave dweller and the human who came to stay in its stead. A more interesting scenario is based on the old observation, freshly bolstered by genetic evidence showing extensive interbreeding, that the two species were intimately familiar with each other in some locales, perhaps even the Croatian hills. In fact, the Neanderthal remains from which the DNA producing those results was obtained came from Vindija, one of the most famous of the Croatian caves.

If Neanderthals and humans interbred—and the preponderance of evidence suggests that they did—so did their socialized wolves. That initially may sound far-fetched to those of us raised with the popular portrait of Neanderthals, even if it has been revised enough to accommodate an expanded view of their intellectual and aesthetic talents, but on reflection it begins to appear that the alternatives are more odd. Overcoming received wisdom is notoriously difficult even in science, where skepticism is said to rule. True to that observation, the same group of researchers who in 2009 announced that based on their reading of the Neanderthal's genome they had concluded that Neanderthals had not interbred with anatomically modern humans presented the most powerful case for the opposite view a year later and they reported that 1 to 4 percent of our genomes came from Neanderthals. Moreover, the interbreeding seems to have occurred considerably earlier than thirty-five to forty thousand years ago, when anatomically modern humans pushed into northwest Europe as Neanderthal was blinking out—although it could have

*Sexual
relations*

occurred then as well, without showing up afresh in the genome. That would put the time and place for the first miscegenation at eighty thousand years ago, when Neanderthals retreating south ahead of glaciers ended up in the Levant, the Old World's premier mixing ground, near the Sea of Galilee, where some might have found shelter in caves occupied by *Homo sapiens.* Before throwing them out, the Neanderthal interlopers might have found accomplices for love or victims for rape. To be fair, we can assume *H. sapiens* exacted vengeance somewhere else, because the evidence from the Levant says Neanderthals evicted them after impregnating a few of their women—an old tactic in war.[7]

This group of *Homo sapiens* appears to be the one that moved into the Zagros Mountains or the Saudi Peninsula in their own exile. That is where they hunted game the wolf also pursued—wild goats, sheep, and mountain gazelles. Making common cause with wolves who approached them, they realized that in their midst were adepts at learning the ways of the wolf.

Proponents of the view that *Homo sapiens* blew out of Africa 100,000 years ago and, bearing the consciousness and accoutrements of modernity. swept across Eurasia and Australia, replacing all the extant hominins purely by virtue of their superiority in all things human, are hard-pressed to come up with solid archaeological evidence in support of their arguments. In fact, the more researchers learn about the mix of hominins getting on in their patches of the world relatively well, the weaker grows the aptly named "replacement hypothesis." Invariably, the ancient hominins prove to possess qualities and characteristics formerly reserved for anatomically modern humans, forcing more critical examination of what if anything makes us special rather than lucky. In this case, as I have said before, there is at least one other species involved—possibly two, if *H. erectus* maintained its hold on eastern Asia—with different behaviors, motivations, and constraints.[8]

PART III
Into the Mixing Zone

Wolf Human Dog Wolf Man Wolf
Woman Wolf Child Wolf Dog Human Wolf

Tlingit wolf mask, Alaska

EIGHT
Old Places,
New Faces

*Homo sapiens usher in a revolution as Earth heads
for deep freeze. Dogs are present—almost—or
maybe—depending on your definitions. What's a
generalization to do in a world as big and varied
as this one? Trade and expanded horizons.*

Genetic evidence has long pointed to eastern Asia, southwest Asia, central Asia, and the Middle East, including the Levant and Arabian Peninsula, as places dogs might have originated, and researchers seeking the original dog or dogs have tended to focus their attention in those places. To their surprise, Europe vaulted to the lead in the first dog sweepstakes in 2008 when Belgian paleoarchaeologist Mietje Germonpré announced that he and his collaborators had determined that the skull of a large, relatively short-nosed canid found more than a century ago in Goyet Cave, Belgium, belonged to a dog. Dated to 31,700 years ago, it was the oldest dog on record—15,000 years older than the runner-up from a camp of Paleolithic hunters on Russia's Mammoth Steppe. The discovery was greeted with cheers from the dog community for finally providing fossil support for what DNA had been telling geneticists for more than a decade—that the dog was much older than the 15,000 years certified by the existing archaeological record.[1] Reportedly, a 27,000 year-old dog has surfaced.

Overlooking the Samson River, a minor tributary in western Belgium of the North Sea–bound Meuse River, Goyet Cave provided the sort of karst limestone shelter with a river valley view that ancient hominins, including Neanderthals, favored. From their perches, they watched the valley for movements of game or people, friendly or hostile, and they chose these locations with the consistency of long habit. Because such places were in demand, like prime real estate in any age, they would attract a number of families, if only seasonally—when reindeer migrated through, for example—meaning that the resident Neanderthals, *Homo erectus,* archaic or modern humans had the putatively modern ability to mediate social conflict and organize collective action.

Belgian geologist Edouard Dupont, who pioneered dividing archaeological sites into strata, or layers, for dating and analysis, excavated Goyet in the 1860s, looking primarily for human artifacts. He found the canid skull in a side chamber containing the remains of red deer, mammoth, lynx, and several large, unidentified canids, but since there was no sign of human involvement with the site's assembled fossils, Dupont laid them aside, largely unremarked.

Since for decades archaeologists routinely tossed unidentified and uncategorized bones into drawers, on the grounds that they were common and uninteresting, researchers have in recent years turned their attention on the museums with high hopes of finding an early dog or two, or other treasures. But they have found little of note. Germonpré and his collaborators focused on the short-nosed canid from Goyet and several other wolflike canids from nearby caves. Although the other canids from Goyet would have made for interesting comparisons, they were apparently not included in the study. Germonpré said that he wanted to test the theory that basic morphological changes associated with the dog—especially the shortened muzzle—occurred relatively quickly in the process of domestication. More than twice the age of the next oldest fossilized dog yet found, the Goyet Cave dog certainly appeared abruptly from a place—Western Europe—where few experts expected the dog to have originated.

In fact, Germonpré's genetic analysis merely shows that the Goyet Cave canid's genetic sequences do not match any of more than one thousand wolf and dog sequences in public databases. That does not translate into a dog, nor does a relatively short nose. More than a few wolves fit the description. Because of these and other interpretive problems, Germonpré's dog was greeted with a large dose of skepticism from many researchers, including geneticists, who suspected that it was a short-nosed wolf of a sort not yet categorized. Skeptical archaeologists observe that since no human remains or artifacts were found in association with the skull, there is no proof that the animal, no matter what it is, had anything to do with humans. Artifacts found in different areas of the cave have been attributed to the Aurignacian culture then spreading across Europe with anatomically modern humans. With new techniques for making stone tools, new burial rituals, sophisticated art and sculpture—the Chauvet Cave paintings date from roughly the same time as the Goyet Cave dog—and long-distance trade, the Aurignacian culture is often said to reflect the arrival of a different human consciousness, one qualitatively different from those of other hominins. But no human remains were found in conjunction with the Goyet Cave artifacts, leaving open the possibility that they were carried there or perhaps even made by Neanderthals, the only human whose fossils have been found in nearby caves.[2]

The lack of physical evidence notwithstanding, I think it fair to attribute the artifacts, the mystery canid, and the broader cultural period they represent to anatomically modern humans—even if they prove genetically to be mutts, the product of interbreeding between Neanderthals and eastern Asia's human stew. What these humans are genetically is less important for our purposes than what they did. The canid itself, I would call a socialized wolf of the sort that was common, if not overly numerous, from a previously unknown wolf lineage; however, given the dates it could also be an early dogwolf from a lineage that died out without contributing anything to the current dog population. Without a more solid context, it is not apparent at available resolutions, but the difference is significant.

Dogwolves were like second-generation immigrants in a community that clung to its old ways even while adapting to its new land. Born near humans, they were more likely than the first-generation socialized wolves to seek to reproduce in or near their human settlement, and more of their offspring were becoming more consistently socialized to humans, more familiar to human society. That was happening, I believe, around hubs where two or more major trade and migratory routes merged and people met to exchange goods, raw materials, and stories; in places where hunters regularly gathered to pursue their primary prey; and in remote hunting camps on the steppes where companionship and the opportunity to grab some extra food mattered. Prime examples of these areas are the ancient Near East, bounded by the Red Sea, the Mediterranean, the Anatolian Plateau, and the Dinaric Alps overlooking the Danube River as it flows across the Pannonian Plain toward the Black Sea; the Carpathian Mountains on the north side of the Pannonian; the Black Sea; the Caucasus Mountains; the Caspian Sea; and Zagros Mountains. Within that area are the Levant, the Fertile Crescent, and the Persian Gulf Oasis, now the Persian Gulf. A gap between the Caucasus Mountains and Caspian Sea was a major thoroughfare for people and animals coming and going from the Anatolian and Iranian plateaus, the Levant, Siberia, central and eastern Asia, the Zagros Mountains, Mediterranean Europe, central Europe, and western Europe, including England. In many ways, it was the master hub of the world, feeding trails to other hubs.

The south of France around the Rhône River Valley and its tributaries, with its abundant food sources and favorable climate, was a major refuge but not the hub that the Near East was. It was in the south of France that a boy and his wolf or dogwolf left their tracks some ten thousand years after the Goyet Cave dogwolf's death. Whatever they turn out to be, these animals, along with the recently identified 27,000-year-old Czech dog, are outliers whose existence restores Europe to the debate over where the dog turned its evolutionary path from that of other wolves. That is appropriate since the next four oldest dog remains are from Europe, not the Middle East or southeastern China.

The dogs are: one from Bonn-Oberkassel, Germany, at twelve to fourteen thousand years ago; two from Eliseevichi 1, a hunting camp on the Sudost River—a tributary of the Desna River, which feeds the Dnieper River on its run to the Black Sea through the Mammoth Steppe, now properly the Central Russian Plain—at fifteen thousand years ago; and two from two other Mammoth Steppe sites—Mezhirich on the Dnieper River, and Mezin 5490 on the Desna River just south of Eliseevichi 1—at thirteen to fourteen thousand years ago. Together they suggest that by the end of the Last Glacial Maximum, large dogs with noses shorter and broader than most wolves were common companions of the hunters on the steppe. In that sense, Germonpré and his colleagues have restored large dogs to the list of potential earliest dogs, which for some years had been limited to small dogs.[3]

At the least, the Goyet Cave dogwolf represents a previously unknown canid and raises again questions about the relationship between early humans and wolves. It has also refocused attention on the early dates for the origins of the dog derived from genetic analyses, which have themselves become more sophisticated and accurate since the dog genome was sequenced and more researchers have contributed sequences of dogs and wolves to public data banks. I can think of few experts who seriously argue that the Goyet canid is the first dog or that

Belgium is the site of dog domestication. A more likely scenario would have the animal traveling through the area, scouting or trading, with an anatomically modern human.

Using special computer software that allows them to survey the entire genome of individuals, geneticists can examine in detail the genetic relationships between people, populations, species, and any other groups they wish to compare. The new studies have revealed the limitations of earlier genetic studies of species' evolutionary histories, in particular studies of mitochondrial DNA, which have produced dates with margins of error measured in increments of tens of thousands of years. In geological terms, tens of thousands of years are next to nothing, but in biological terms, they are so large that they are useless except as relative values. In human terms, ten thousand years dates back to the Neolithic Age, the beginning of agriculture.

To use an optical analogy, the resolution of genetic surveys becomes sharper and provides more detail as the amount of the genome scanned —the magnification—increases. The discrepancies in results from the different approaches became graphically apparent in studies by the labs of two of the world's top experts in canid evolution. In October 2009, after analyzing the full mitochondrial genome of several hundred dogs and forty wolves, evolutionary biologist Pier Savolainen and colleagues declared without qualification that the dog originated in southeastern China, south of the Yangtze River within the past 16,300 years. Virtually all dogs alive today descend from that original population, they said.[4]

Not six months later, Robert K. Wayne's evolutionary biology laboratory at the University of California at Los Angeles, after the most comprehensive scan to date of nuclear DNA, mitochondrial DNA, and the Y chromosome from 921 dogs representing 85 breeds and 225 gray wolves, concluded that Middle Eastern wolves are the "wild source of most of the diversity in the dog"—or, to use a plant analogy, serve as root stock for the dog.

Rare, their territories and populations fragmented, the wolves of the Middle East are little understood behaviorally or genetically. Even less is known about those living in the region fifty thousand years ago. It is likely, for example, that the Western population of *Canis lupus pallipes,* known as the Iranian or Persian wolf, mixed freely with its cousins in the Levant, *C.s l. arabs,* or the Arabian wolf, and possibly lineages of Mediterranean wolves that became fragmented long ago.

Looking at modern breeds and a cluster of ancient and spitz breeds, the UCLA researchers found that Eurasian wolves (*C. l. lupus*) were important and, in some cases, dominant contributors to a number of mastiff and terrier breeds. When not primary, Chinese wolves (*C. l. chanco*) were significant progenitors of most Asian dogs. Genetically virtually all breeds represented an admixture of Arabian, European, and Chinese wolves. Reflecting the high level of mobility of wolves and humans, the new survey, while identifying relative genetic contributions from different subspecies of wolf, did not point strongly to any particular geographic locations for the dog to emerge, according to Bridgett von Holdt, primary author of the Wayne group's paper in March 2010.[5]

There were doubtless other mixing zones, since backcrosses were common in the early days of the dog—where there were wolves. Because backcrossing could not occur where no wolves existed, dogs moving into Africa, Southeast Asia, Australia, and Oceania either inbred or found dogs who had arrived with other groups. Dogs moving with the first people into South America had an initial period of mixing with wolves in Siberia and North America before reaching their new wolf-free home. The situation shifted dramatically at different times in different places, when newcomers arrived with their dogs.

Cumulatively, the apparently contradictory genetic and paleontological evidence confirms that the transformation of wolf to dog was both a biological and a cultural process involving two highly mobile species that occurred in many places at different times. Dogs were neither invented nor created *ex machina,* in a particular place and time and then sent forth to colonize the world. Rather, the evidence suggests that while today's dogs have their genetic foundations in the Middle Eastern wolf, they received considerable genetic contributions from other wolves. Where that mixing occurred is more difficult to say, although there are indications that much of it took place in an area like the one south of the Caucasus, where bands moving out of the Persian Gulf Oasis through the Levant paused among other travelers and their dogwolves or socialized wolves. Interbreeding occurred there and then people went on with their mix of animals, including some small dogs.

Wandering with and between their human groups, the dogwolves picked up mutations affecting their morphologies in ways that distinguished them from wolves. Such events could have been common without producing many animals, but those they did produce could have had a characteristic—smallness, for example, or a black coat, or a curled tail,or a brachycephalic nose, a combination of traits that made them particularly valuable. Smallness has multiple virtues. The dog not only is easily transportable but also is well positioned to pursue rodents and to harass and distract every manner of game. In fact, geneticists have found a "smallness" gene in dogs that they believe dates to their origins and is probably derived from Middle Eastern wolves.[6]

Geneticists have also identified a genetic mutation believed responsible for black coats in dogs and wolves that serves both in their milieus. Long tradition holds that black dogs are more frightening to people than light-colored dogs and thus better guardians of the home, and that dark-colored wolves are better concealed in deep shadow when hunting. Believed to have originated around forty-six thousand years ago in Old World wolves or dogwolves, the mutation was ultimately carried by dogs to the New World and passed on to wolves and coyotes.[7]

A few evolutionary biologists have speculated that black coats gave an adaptive advantage to wolves engaging predominately in ambush hunting in wooded areas because it concealed them in the shadows. While I am sure they have studied the question, I think it necessary to observe, as I did when interviewing the scientists for an article on their research, that wolves do not as a rule hunt by ambush. Big cats, most of them multicolored in natural camouflage for the dappled, filtered light in forests, are ambush hunters. Even woodland wolves appear to prefer hunting in forest meadows or clearings, where they can run.

In my experience walking dogs of various hues and colors at all hours, a black dog can be easier to see in natural darkness than a white one, I think because the black dog imposes itself as a vague but substantive perturbation of the darkness, while the white one is absorbed into the night. On the other hand, black dogs were favored by humans as house guards because it was believed that leaping from shadows or out of the night, barking and snarling, they would frighten off most intruders. That said, the significance of this work, lies in the demonstration that gene flow from wolf to dogwolf ran both ways in different parts of the world for perhaps thousands of years in hunting societies, where the connection among wolves, dogs, and humans was closest. The work also sheds new light on the origins of the dog and the people who first settled the Americas, since small dogs and black dogs traveled with them across the Bering Land Bridge.

Between forty and fifty thousand years ago, as nearly as anyone can tell, bands of humans began moving from the Levant into the Balkans, with some backtracking along the Danube River across the Pannonian Plain into Western Europe and others following it to the Black Sea and eastward. Another migration route went from the Levant to the Anatolian Plateau south of the Black Sea to the Caucasus, and yet another tracked east across the Iranian Plain to the Caspian Sea and into southwest Asia. Some of these groups moved on to the Mammoth Steppe running through central Eurasia and Siberia in the wind shadow of Europe's glaciers and into central Asia, from the Altai Mountains to the Amur River, the northeast Asian steppe, and the rest of eastern Asia. Yet another route passed along the northern coast of the Mediterranean, encountering the last pockets of Neanderthal as it left southwestern France.[8]

All of these routes traversed the Levant, but these humans did not arrive there by first crossing the Sinai Peninsula from Egypt. Their ancestors were forced from the Levant around seventy-five thousand years ago by Neanderthals seeking refuge from the second of the three great Würm glaciations that culminated with the Last Glacial Maximum. With the Neanderthal invasion, overmatched humans fled down the Arabian Peninsula, probably to the Persian Gulf Oasis, hunting gazelles in the mountains, moving between watering holes. Based on my theory that humans and wolves—specific humans and wolves— began traveling together as soon as they met, it is logical to believe that these Paleolithic refugees had more than a few socialized wolves or dog- wolves living with or near them who became fellow travelers. If they did not have any animals at the time, they at least had knowledge of how to obtain them. In any event, they encountered, as they had in the Levant, the little Arabian wolf, as well as the slightly larger Iranian wolf, and they continued a process of partnership they had begun there of so- cializing wolf puppies and accepting offers of friendship from adult wolves who occasionally became fascinated with them.

In that arid country, oases or mountain streams were major gath- ering spots for all creatures. In such tight quarters, boundaries could be tight with little buffer between zones. The socialized wolf colonized that niche, allowing itself to move freely between realities—there is no other way to put it—sometime during the sojourn in the desert.

When people went on the move again between forty and fifty thousand years ago, their dogwolves went with them. More significant, they went with the expectation that the wolf would be their friend, should it choose, and the knowledge of how to deal with it.

Paleoarchaeologists believe that these migrants shared language, customs, and social structure, with the traditional forager family unit of up to ten people, expanding into a band of perhaps twenty-five to thirty individuals related largely through blood or marriage. In turn, bands could come together in larger groups. They were interested in technology, art, experimenting with new materials and tactics, food preparation, preservation, and storage. They invented grinding and pounding stones for processing nuts and grains, and they made tools and weapons out of bones and horn as well as stone, using a new method that allowed them to make longer blades and microliths. Coming out of the Last Glacial Maximum, they invented, in relatively short order, the atlatl—the spear thrower—which let them achieve accuracy, distance, and speed with their spears; the boomerang, which found its most appreciative users in Australia; the harpoon; and the bow and arrows—the ultimate weapon for the time. They tailored points to match their new spears, harpoons, and arrows. They fashioned stronger and more flexible nets for catching and carrying. They created sculptures and paintings, body ornamentation, cloth of woven flax, leather harnesses and belts. They also established and maintained long- distance trade routes. Those routes followed paths worn into rocks and earth over tens of thousands of years by animals on the move and would remain the basis for Silk Roads and Steppes Roads that were the heart and soul of transcontinental trade twenty-five thousand years later—so enduring were they.[9]

The migration of these humans triggered the Upper Paleolithic Revolution, a perceptible shift from a world of hominins, as alien to us as the name we have given them, to the world of humans, of beings who seem familiar, whom we think we could understand. While the Upper Paleolithic Revolution had regional variations, determined by the technique they used to produce their stone blades and tools—the Ahmarian and Emerian in the Levant, and the Aurignacian in Europe, for example—it was widespread and coordinated, save for a time lag in Southeast Asia where the new culture did not take hold until about thirty thousand years ago.

In addition to a new stone-tool technology, the Aurignacian saw the advent of weaving and of representational art. Figurines of a mammoth, lion man, and horse carved from ivory, plucked from Vogelherd Cave in southern Germany, and paintings that brought life to caves in southwestern Europe, beginning with Chauvet Cave, bespeak a sophisticated visual and aesthetic sensibility. An obese Venus with exaggerated breasts, hips, and buttocks has long been considered some kind of universal statement on love and fecundity, the precise meaning of which is unavailable to us all of these millennia later.

Humans carried their Aurignacian technologies into Western Europe at the end of a brief period of intense cold that had followed the eruption of Campanian Ignimbrite in southern Italy around forty thousand years ago. The Aurignacian flourished until the beginning of the Last Glacial Maximum around thirty thousand years ago, the same time that the Neanderthal vanished. The period was one of extreme fluctuations in global weather patterns, with pulses of glacial expansion alternating with moderating temperatures—meteorological assaults and retreats—culminating in the final Würm glaciation, the surge of ice that covered much of northern Europe, down to the Alps and almost the entirety of northern North America, as well as most of the Andes along the west coast of South America, and whipsawed ecosystems and their occupants. The influence of the ice was inescapable, creating cold, dry, inhospitable conditions in much of the world, even in refuges where people and animals congregated in an effort to find food and shelter.

Some paleontologists believe that social and cultural changes during the Upper Paleolithic Revolution were of such a kind that they had to be the products of some sort of change in consciousness or brain structure or wiring. Transferring allegiance from immediate family to a larger entity requires an ability to accept "the other," the one who is not me, as a being equal to myself—or possibly superior to, but that involves other issues as well—and a concomitant weakening of the fear response to the new and unusual. Both of those affect social behavior—a large part of which is learning to modulate and moderate one's appetites, how to manage anger and aggression, when to be assertive, and when to show some restraint, to name a few. As an ethologist friend likes to say, "That is not primate behavior." It is wolf behavior, and its apparent adoption by humans is one of the reasons some evolutionary biologists argue that dogs and humans are joined in a dance of coevolution. I count high among the other reasons in favor of coevolution a shared love of being in motion—a need to be on the move to somewhere.[10]

Among its other benefits, long-distance travel by foot or watercraft was safer and more pleasant with a companion, especially one capable not only of hunting and carrying its weight in meat or in goods but also of scaring off people and other animals with bad intentions. Some dogs have a seemingly uncanny ability to judge people quickly or, as I say, to take an immediate universal dislike to someone they encounter on the street and judge of dubious merit or to someone who has just come to their house for dinner with their people. They also seem unfailingly to pick from a crowd a person in need of their special attention—an alienated party guest who is enticed into a game of catch, for example, or the one person in the room who is afraid of dogs.

Dogs can be wrong, of course, with unpleasant consequences if they have chosen to act on their own judgment. But in a remote cabin or yurt or tent, a biter generally has found itself welcome, at least sometimes. The Bedouin had a rule that a dog could bite anyone who came uninvited within fifty yards of its tent and be considered to be acting in proper defense of its home, but if it bit the person more than fifty yards away or an invited guest, it was considered the aggressor and compensation had to be made. Woe unto those travelers who had to leave the tent in the middle of the night, one early-twentieth-century visitor commented; the dogs would be on him in an instant. The guard dog has always been universal.[11]

Dissenters observe that several major developments in human social organization attributed to the human makers of the Aurignacian have turned out to be the work of more ancient hominins. *Homo erectus* divided its living quarters into sectors devoted to tool manufacturer, food preparation, and cooking well before anatomically modern humans, long assumed the only species capable of such a feat. Neanderthals expressed their aesthetic sensibilities through body paint and ornaments and have, as if from the grave, convinced all but their most hardcore detractors that they possessed the power of speech.

Still the evidence suggests that *Homo sapiens* was differently wired mentally, with a greater capacity for abstract and associative thinking, for making mental and physical connections where they had not existed before or had been poorly formed, and for imaginative leaps of faith that brought depth to symbols and talismans. That is deduced from what *H. sapiens* has done over the course of its existence, and while it might be technically incorrect to say that it alone has the capacity for these feats, it is fair to say that neither *H. erectus* nor Neanderthal came close to matching them in considerably more time.

NINE
Further Along the Road to Dog

*Socialized wolves join the revolution but it
takes a deep freeze to bring enough players
together to make a game. Pockets of plenty along
the trails. Did the hunters hunt together?*

I think it's safe to say that among the changes in the brains of wolves
and humans that the Upper Paleolithic Revolution triggered or was
triggered by were several that expanded their ability to recognize
and accept "the other" as a unique and independent being, while at the
same time showing fealty—even occasionally fawning devotion—to him
or her. I am reluctant to talk about the brain, except provisionally,
because my own experience with Parkinson's disease has taught me that
whatever we think we know to be true about the brain will doubtless be
proved wrong sooner rather than later. But I think the changes occurring
in the brains of humans and wolves in the Upper Paleolithic, although
substantive in their result, were more likely of degree than kind. I say
that despite a recent rash of reports about how the brain has been repo-
sitioned in the skulls of extremely brachycephalic dogs, like the pug.[1]

As dogs have been drawn into the house as pets in increasing numbers over the past one hundred and fifty years, breeders have attempted to make the smaller breeds more humanlike, or at least doll-like. In the pug they have created a little dog, with its nose pushed as close to flush against its face as possible and a concomitant flattening of the back of the skull. In order to retain its size, and presumably its functionality, and to fit the available space, the brain turned over in the skull. A fair assumption would be that the turning has affected the pug in some fundamental way, but that is not necessarily the case, and until additional studies are done, no one will know definitively what effect the upside-down brain has. No additional study is needed to confirm the popular little pug as a monument to some of the worst practices of modern breeding. The dogs have significant breathing problems because of the distortion of their noses, as well as spinal and central nervous system pathologies. The pug is a reminder that many of the distortions in morphology, like attempts to alter behaviors and behavioral patterns, are creations of the Fancy, the purebred-dog breeders who participate in dog shows.

Nor are "ancient" breeds or randomly bred village dogs necessarily better models of early days since their circumstances, like those of their people, are not analogous to those of Paleolithic dogs. It is difficult to avoid historical fallacies when talking or writing about ancient dogs, especially since so many of the fundamental uses for the dog remain the same, but it is important to try.

Total brain size decreased from Neanderthal to *Homo sapiens* and wolf to dog by 10 to 30 percent, depending on the expert. Body size decreased as well, and at least for humans it is unclear that size of the brain proportional to the body declined at all. Even with a slightly lower total size, the basal neocortex, believed involved in ethical and social behavior and personality formation, is larger, and other parts of the frontal cortex involved in advanced planning and language acquisition are turbocharged.

The cerebral cortex in all canids is enlarged, with some researchers suggesting it serves to inhibit certain predatory behaviors—another unproven claim. Dingoes show no predatory inhibition, nor do feral dogs elsewhere in the world. If they do not hunt successfully, they do not eat. In dogs, in general, the muzzle became shorter and broader, the head more domed, and the eyes more forward facing—in effect they became short-faced wolves more nearly resembling zoo wolves than free wolves from that period or the present. Both wolves and dogs at the time were highly variable in appearance. In addition to that variability, it is well documented that dietary change from strict carnivory to omnivory can have biological consequences, altering jaw muscles and the bones themselves.

The wolves who ultimately became dogs had a unique bond with humans that had to do in part with the social structure of family and pack, the culture of learning, and the emphasis on cooperative action to achieve a larger end than could one acting alone. Paradoxically, becoming dog also allowed wolf to break free from some of the strictures and responsibilities of pack life having to do with reproduction and rearing the young because they were provided, if only indirectly, by human society. More profoundly, and mysteriously, human and wolf both recognized at some primal level that they belonged together. The merger born of that recognition produced ultimately the dog, a creation of nomadic hunters.

It is possible that wolves and humans hunted in parallel from their own inviolate bubbles, not to meet until the wolf voluntarily became a sniveling midden maven, a foul-tempered, slinking, village offal eater—"diaper cleaner" is the usual euphemism. But they are too similar in their pack-hunting behavior alone to ignore each other for long. Plus, the wolf quickly noted that this newcomer to the Guild of Carnivores was, like itself, and more than the other bipeds, an opportunistic and at times profligate hunter, often killing far more than it needed. These bipeds, like wolves, could be both hospitable toward strangers and fiercely defensive of their tribe—including the animals. In those and other ways, including basic social structure, human and wolf recognized each other as kindred spirits; they learned from each other in what was from the start a mutual relationship—both benefitted; both desired it.

A cross-cultural example might substitute for the lack of direct prehistorical material: In 1789, Alexander Mackenzie, a fur trader in Canada looking for the Northwest Passage, encountered several bands of Athabascan Indians between Great Slave Lake and Great Bear Lake, along the river that has come to bear his name, and traveled with them for several days. When they stopped to make camp one afternoon, he killed a dog who was picking through his luggage. The woman who owned the dog fell into immediate lamentation and was inconsolable. She said, Mackenzie recounts, that "she had lost 5 children last winter for whom she was not so sorry as for the Dog."[2]

Fast forward 220 years from the eighteenth-century Athabascans just exiting the Stone Age to a young Korean woman I know who, preparing to emigrate to Canada, announced by e-mail that she had lost her beloved Marus, one of seven dogs, two children, and numerous cats in her household, and she did not know whether she would ever get over his death.

Then skip into Dreamtime and thus reach back perhaps five thousand years to Australia's Aborigines, who believe, "The dingo is what we would be if we were not what we are." They also say, "Dingo makes us human," in large measure because, according to their belief, the dingo gave up the opportunity for immortality in order to stay behind and help the furless biped survive. In nearly every culture, the dog's companionship, guardianship, and guiding ability are valued as noble and unwavering. Indeed, the weak link in the dog/human relationship is most often the human.[3]

Is it fair, or even accurate, to speak of "desire" when examining the origins and evolution of the dog or, for that matter, its relationships with other animals. Individuals can desire each other's company and form partnerships. But species cannot make conscious decisions—as far as we know—because they have no independent memory.

But cultural memory exists and, for all anyone knows, deep genomic resonances can occur—usually between individuals, to be sure, although there are exceptions that prove the rule. Dogs and humans were an experiment in interspecies coevolution waiting to happen, and that is another reason for suspecting that although *Canis lupus* could have been tamed individually by several human precursors, it never connected fully with them. The wolf was present and primed, but its human had not yet appeared.

Socialized wolves did not necessarily form a self-reproducing population within, or even adjacent to, human society. Often raised from the time they were puppies so that the only pack they knew was the human one, they were different from other wolves. Unless their human had taken them hunting and encouraged them to hunt, or unless they were able to learn on their own or from another older socialized wolf, their hunting prowess would at best be underdeveloped. That could change quickly if they dispersed and mated with a skilled hunter. Being wolves, some of them likely kept walking until they reached territory they wanted to claim and defend. Others among them made the moving human village their territory for a period of time, maybe life.

Following wolf custom, their offspring dispersed, except when other forces intervened, when, for example, two or three puppies were given very young as gifts or in payment for a bride or food or a prime wolf pelt. The young might decide on their own not to leave, especially if the *alpha* male or female died. These dogwolves remained quasi-independent, sometimes taking food from the humans or scrounging in their middens, but also securing their own food by hunting. At the resolution available to contemporary paleontologists and archaeologists, socialized wolves cannot be distinguished from natural populations, except they were always around human-occupied areas. But the genetic

record shows some shifts, and so geneticists at least believe they are observing a transformation.

For Charles Darwin natural or artificial selection operating on individuals by sex and by death drove evolution. They lay behind the ac-
cumulation of genetic and behavioral changes across a self-reproducing
population that led to the creation or the demise of a species or, in the
case of domestic animals, breeds. Under artificial selection, humans
consciously and unconsciously perpetuate certain traits, by controlling
reproduction and by culling unwanted animals. The precise mecha-
nisms for moving from genes to a new species remain mysterious
although evolutionary geneticist have done more in some cases than
simply glimpse the bare outlines of an answer.

The most powerful tool geneticists currently have for probing evolutionary relationships is the single nucleotide polymorphism, or SNP.
The four bases of DNA are A [adenine], T [thymine], G [guanine], and
C [cytosine], which always form pairs—A-T, T-A, G-C, C-G—on
double-stranded DNA. Because the bases form the same pairs, geneticists generally sequence only one strand of DNA and from it infer the
other strand. If all people or dogs were identical, they would have the
same sequence bases, but fortunately we are not identical; in fact, some
of us are more distantly related than others. These differences are
reflected in the genome in SNPs, which appear periodically in long
strands of repetitive bases as slip or glitch in transcription so that
ATTAATGGCC becomes ATTAATTGGCC, a single nucleotide polymorphism, in this case, G-C to T-A. Thousands of SNPs are found in
every genome.

A common operating assumption among geneticists is that these
SNPs can lead to dramatic changes in appearance and fitness if they
occur in coding regions, or gene loci, as the stretches of DNA that con-
tain genes are now known. They are important for studying evolutionary
relationships and histories because once they occur, they tend to remain
unchanged and thereby provide points of comparison among individu-

als, breeds, populations, groups, and species. Robert K. Wayne and his group employed a SNP chip in their recent examination of dog breeds and the dog's origins. Among their more overlooked results was a technical observation that using more SNPs to provide a denser, more complete view of each animal's genome often produced different measurements of the relative contribution of different wolf subspecies to particular breeds or types of dog.[4]

Geneticists have also found that "canine-specific short interspersed nuclear elements" (SINEC-Cf, in the acronym-laced parlance of biology), small elements of genetic material that comprise 7 percent of the dog genome and throughout it are either inserted or deleted from alleles, or gene variants. These elements have been associated with narcolepsy and merle coat color, but their function is still not well understood, as the pace of discovery often outpaces that of understanding a system that has consistently proven itself more complicated than the geneticists themselves supposed.[5]

Deep patterns of inheritance woven by whole chromosomes or combinations of chromosomes and variations in the number of copies of genetic material called copy number variations might ultimately prove central in determining how the genetic material in the loci those SNP surveys identify is expressed in the individual organism. DNA division and replication being inherently imprecise in many regards, individuals of any species might have received two copies of certain stretches of genome, including genes and their variants from one parent and one or none or three from the other. Or genes might be arranged differently on different chromosomes from one or both parents. The meanings of these variations are not yet clear, but they are believed to be involved with inheritable traits and propensity for disease, among other things. I suspect those kinds of analysis, which are just now being given serious examination, will alter somewhat our view of the socialized dogwolf.

Another popular assumption is that natural selection operates predominately on wild or natural populations, and artificial selection on domestic animals. The environment in which an organism is born, what it consumes, and how it is raised and lives can influence, dramatically in some cases, how its genes are expressed, as well as the individual's development and behavior. Essentially genes code for proteins, which are the structural base of biology—producing enzymes, hormones, and the like. Environmental insult can alter those genes, causing them to produce aberrant proteins that can cause pathology. On the other hand, some activities, like handling a wolf or dog puppy from an early age, influence its brain development in ways that will affect its mental and physical health, as well as its behavior. Studies have shown that predator control programs that smash the packs of dingoes and wolves leave the survivors bereft of the social structures that made them successful hunters and educated their young in the ways of the dingo. It takes generations to rebuild those social structures, if they can be rebuilt. Other studies have shown that human predation, which usually selectively targets reproducing adults, and habitat destruction can affect the evolution of wild populations more profoundly than natural forces by severely reducing their numbers, destroying their social structures, and undermining their genetic viability.[6]

The urge to form packs, to belong to an entity larger than the self seems to drive and shape the behavior of wolves, dogs, and humans. Judging from their behavior and adaptability, all three have flexible definitions of "pack" in terms of size and membership. A lone wolf, in this view, is simply a wolf looking to start or join a pack. Landing on Australia's shores some fifty-five hundred years ago as a dog without apparent knowledge of wolf-pack structure—it arrived by way of wolf-free southeast Asia—the dingo went walkabout with the Aborigine, living in more or less close affiliation with them. With the only model available to them being Aboriginal family groups, they created stable packs headed, like wolf packs, by the breeding male and female. Among the signal differences is the dingo's habit of infanticide against the offspring of any younger, subordinate females. It is interesting but doubtless only coincidental that some Aborigine also practiced selective infanticide.

Following wolves regularly, learning their habits and ways in order to hunt better does not inevitably lead to forming a lasting bond with them, but it establishes a minimal comfort zone on which both species can build. It is well documented that adult wolves can adapt to living in close proximity to humans even to the point of acting tame in their presence. Wolf puppies taken into the human home and intensively socialized through handling, especially during their early socialization period of three to eight weeks, can become devoted lifetime companions, if they are continuously socialized and if they don't decide at a certain point to rejoin their wild kin—if that option is available. Even adult wolves will become socialized to humans, but only on their terms, as University of Chicago experimental psychologists Benson Ginsburg and Jerome H. Woolpy found when they socialized adult wolves, as well as wolf pups. "Wolves are highly social in nature as well as under conditions of confinement when in groups. Once socialized," they reported in the journal *American Zoologist,* in 1967, "they are extremely gregarious to humans and exhibit all of the attitudes and mannerisms of a very friendly dog as well as some of them seen in most wolves but not usually seen in dogs."[7]

Indeed, whereas wolves socialized as puppies required constant reinforcement to remain socialized, socialized adults treated all humans they met in a friendly fashion—as long as the people treated them properly. The researchers found none of the "one-mannishness" common to some dogs in their socialized adult wolves.

Woolpy and Ginsburg knew that adult wolves must make the offer of friendship or trust, and can do so only if their curiosity overcomes their fear or wariness. At some point in our lives, most of us have to overcome a deeply ingrained fear in order to function. Indeed, some experimenters in the mid-twentieth century failed in their efforts to socialize wolves of any age and, following human custom, blamed the animals. Close examination revealed that the experimenters failed because they tried to establish physical dominance over the animals. Wolves will not tolerate abusive, punishment-based training, nor will a number of dogs of my acquaintance, and that refusal is not a fault.

Since the second half of the nineteenth century with the rising popularity of purebred sporting and gun dogs among the growing urban upper middle class, an emphasis among breeders has been on producing biddable or trainable dogs. Those are animals who would face and focus on their trainer or handler and obey instruction without hesitation. But they also had to be dogs who could withstand training that was more often brutal than not. Some trainers believed the dog should be periodically disciplined as a way of maintaining authority over it. Contemporary professional trainers who use shock collars say that those devices have created demand for dogs—be they field trial Labrador retrievers or police and military K-9s, who have abundant energy and high resistance to pain. Many trainers speak of putting "pressure" on the dogs to obey promptly and precisely and say that "hard" dogs are needed to withstand that abuse. In psychological language, that kind of training might be called conditioning with aversive stimuli. It has nothing to do with teaching and long-term learning.

At the same time, shock-collar trainers say that wolves cannot be trained in that fashion. No Pleistocene wolf would have tolerated such abuse, nor do many native dogs in Asia, Africa, India, and South America. Western shock-collar trainers deem the dogs unbiddable because they respond poorly to punishment and pressure. The unspoken truth is that many Western dogs are the same way. That hardly equates with being untrainable or uneducable, but it is usually easier to blame the pupil than the teacher or the method of instruction—in this case, shock collars and other punitive devices. I might add that in my experience with wild animals, ranging from birds to lung fish, the human must be patient and let the animal decide when and how to approach, rather than make bold intrusions into its space. Indeed, the same advice can be applied to approaching unknown domestic animals—and people.

Little noticed now, Woolpy and Ginsburg were among a small number of researchers in the United States, Europe, and Japan in the 1960s, 1970s, and into the 1980s interested in socializing wolves. Without much difficulty they largely succeeded in doing so. In describing his socialized timber wolf in *American Zoologist,* John Fentress at the University of Rochester went to the heart of the question of the dog's origins when he observed, "Dogs did not derive from wolves that exist today, but it appears likely that primitive man would be able to take a common ancestor and produce the highly socialized dog." The questions then and now involved the identity of that common wolf ancestor and how its descendants became dogs. Beyond that lies the entire history, much of it unrecorded, of why some dogs caught on and spread while other lineages and types perished—have continued to perish into our own time—and to understand that fully, we must look at what people were doing.[8]

Studying wolves, poodles, and poodle/wolf crosses he called *puwos,* the German ethologist Erik Zimen in the 1960s developed two scales that seemed to cover many of a puppy's behavioral responses to humans—"sociable to indifferent" and "timid to confident." At its best, the dog is sociable and confident, but in practice, puppies can slide in opposite directions along the parallel scales until they reach indifferent and timid. In the past, dogs in or near that category might have been removed from the gene pool or ignored; now they often come out of pet stores and puppy mills, victims not of genes so much as deprivation of stimulation and human contact.

Like his colleagues elsewhere, Zimen also found that wolves could be socialized to humans, if it were done early and constantly. But he admitted that he was surprised when his American counterparts reported success even with adult wolves, saying that comparing his data to theirs almost made him think he was looking at two different species of wolf. Ironically, he might have been, given that at least one of the wolves in question was identified as an Eastern (North American) timber wolf, *Canis rufus,* believed by some researchers to be a separate species from the Eurasian wolf, *C. lupus,* of Zimen's acquaintance. In a double irony, they may have been descended from the same wolf, *C. mosbachensis.*[9]

TEN
A Preexisting Bond?

*They met at the trail head and have been together
ever since—hunting, running, walking,
hanging out. Is there a tie that binds?*

Peering through the fog of times past, I can almost see deep into the shadows of a cave a person heading for the open air and light. Then I feel a perturbation in the darkness before I see coming toward me a wolf, impatiently looking back at the man, as if to say, *Time to go.*

Call him Lupe. When the old man and the boy who had raised him, with the help of the woman who had nursed him, failed to return one day, he felt the need to go looking for his own life. He split one evening when the moon was waning, got up and left because there was no one to wait for. On his journey he picked up the scent of a group of furless bipeds and since he was crossing territories thick with wolf packs, one of which had killed his parents and siblings two years before, he decided to shadow them. He knew from the smell that they were horse hunters, like the people he just left. He stole no food, but slept within the zone of their encampment—their territory.

As they traveled, Lupe became aware of eyes watching—those of the shaman, a raven spirit; those of a boy learning from the old man, his uncle; and those of a wolf on the far flank of the humans. The boy was a wolf spirit, but the band had no wolves at the moment.

That night he lay in the deep moon shadows watching the boy watching him and the man watching the boy and the flanking eyes the humans seemed not to see watching them all. The man said something and the boy cocked his arm and threw a ball of grizzled meat. Lupe in-haled it and crept closer, watching as the boy let fly again, only this time he sprang up and caught the ball almost as soon as it left his hand, then trotted past the boy and man to the watching eyes and spit it out as an offering. Call her Lupa.

They followed, and when the humans took up residence in a cave system overlooking a valley where reindeer, auroch, and horses grazed, where red deer and fallow deer browsed the riverine forest, they exca-vated a den in the rocks above. Obeying his uncle to learn the way of the wolf, the boy nearly lived with them, especially once the pups were born, when nearly all the children from the camp swarmed around. When the people moved on, the wolves stayed to hunt ibex and deer, and the boy and his cousin who wished to be a great hunter stayed as well, learning to hunt and eat the animals his own people tended to avoid except when hunger driven.

The next year the cousins left with two pups when the rest of their family did. Lupa and Lupe expanded their territory and kept their pack together until the young man had become an old man and his daughter was learning the way of the wolf from the last great-granddaughter of Lupe and Lupa. Call her Lupina.

She was watching another wolf who arrived with a tall, thin man with eyes so pale blue they were nearly white, big dots of white in a face covered with hair, dirt, and grease so that he smelled smoke-cured him-self. The wolf had those same eyes in a white face shaded toward yellow. The man told of the good hunting and bone-cracking cold on the endless *steppe he and his wolf had just left. He said he was the last of his family, because he was sitting in the entrance when their cave collapsed behind him, burying them, his knives, scrapers, and all but one spear and a sling. The first night, a bear would have killed him had his Laika not attacked it from the rear, giving him time to grab a firebrand and drive it off.*

He told of a starving time until, with Laika, he found a marmot colony and they managed to dig some out, fat for the coming cold. Having no place to go, he stayed with the old man and his daughter and with them followed horses in the shadow of mountains freeing themselves from ice. By then Lupina was with Laika, and they and their pups lived with the wolf-adept ice-eyed man and woman, who had become joined.

By the commencement of the Last Glacial Maximum around thirty thousand years ago, Neanderthal was nearly extinct, and animal and human populations declined precipitously in some areas, including southeastern China, while expanding in the Mammoth Steppe and other areas where big game concentrated when glaciers advanced. These people were following the same large grazing animals that wolves and other predators, including other hominins, had followed, but, as we have seen repeatedly, humans and wolves took to each other because they are in many ways so similar. Perhaps because of their family structure and sociability, wolves and humans are vocal species with a surprising ability, given some study, to understand each other, or at least minimize misunderstanding enough to work together. To varying degrees they did work together, and in the process some of them realized that collaboration paid off with more dead prey, making a surfeit of food for all, and less theft. Collaborator wolves learned that a little woof would bring the furless biped to a functional level of alertness to fend off danger. They were omnivorous carnivores together ruling the Guild of Carnivores.

These dogwolves were not house pets, but they weren't wild either. They probably hung around camp, scavenging, stealing, guarding the place, playing, moving more or less in unison with it, and hunting sometimes for themselves and sometimes with the humans. I would like to say that they whelped outside the camp, but I cannot say that because they might have whelped in or quite close for protection and food. These dogwolves could have been widespread without being numerous. This scenario accommodates the views of people who argue that the dog came from an intermediate population between the wolf and itself. That population, I suggest, was these dogwolves where they existed. And the more they bred to each other, the more the force of natural selection, with an assist from humans who might drive off or kill unsocial animals or animals they did not like the look of, worked to produce animals with longer socialization periods and delayed and reduced fear responses to the new, strange, and novel.

I anticipate that the amygdala and mirror neurons, which are involved in managing fear and social interactions and in development of empathy, are among the important parts of the brains of wolves and humans involved in making the shift. Long thought to be involved primarily in learning fear and responses to it, the amygdala is increasingly seen as perhaps the major information- and response-processing hub in the brain with a role in mediating emotional responses to the whole range, positive and negative, of social situations a person, or presumably a dog, encounters. It is involved in socialization, including calibrating the physical and emotional distance people and animals demand for themselves in relation to people known and unknown. That is an ever shifting calculation. More recent research has suggested that the amygdala and the hippocampus are involved in anxiety disorders.[1]

The transformation of wolf to dog looks and sounds simple so far, yet for all its straightforward simplicity, it was not universal or even all that common. This attraction of wolf to humans is not unlike the notion popular among some wildlife biologists that predators like the dingo or wolf can have prey images for a specific animal, like red kangaroos, so fixed in their minds that if the kangaroo population collapses and they are presented with fields of sheep, many of them will not even attempt to kill the sheep. Although it is hard to grant that the image of a particular animal can be passed on genetically, a propensity to fixate on an object or a person or another animal is arguably a common dog, not to mention human, characteristic. A dog weaned on red kangaroo, taught to hunt red kangaroo because it is abundant and easy, and never taught to hunt any other animal could well be rendered clueless and hungry if the red kangaroos abruptly disappeared.

Cast another way, it is well documented that dogs raised with sheep from birth bond to those sheep more strongly than to other dogs or humans. Many of them—not all—spend their lives with the sheep, guarding them and moving them along. So powerful is this bonding that Americans unaccustomed to the culture of big sheep-guarding dogs and shepherds common in the Mediterranean, Eastern Europe, and much of sheep-raising Asia believed, when they first started trying to use the dogs for predator control, that the dogs were genetically preprogrammed to live with and guard sheep. More accurately, dogs and wolves have the capacity to form such bonds and to develop deep affection—and animosity—for other creatures throughout their lives. The younger they start, the better, especially wolves, who should be caught and started well before the age of six weeks, when their first socialization period begins to close in. Sometimes, they even develop animosity toward animals in their charge for reasons probably they alone know.[2]

Some years ago, a rancher friend reported to me that a great Pyrenees guard dog for his wife's mixed flock of sheep and goats had one night killed all the sheep after systematically separating them from the goats. The great Pyrenees, one of the big white European livestock guard dogs the United States Department of Agriculture promotes as protection against coyote predation, had kept watch over the sheep and goats for five years, along with a little prick-eared dog of the sort the

Navajo use to guard their sheep and goats, without showing any aggression toward them. The only difference the night of the crime was that the rancher's wife had told him earlier in the evening that she intended to sell all the sheep because the falling price of wool had rendered them too expensive to keep. But that hardly explains why the great Pyrenees turned on its charges.

The Navajo herders understand that even among dogs raised the proper way, not all choose to "be with the sheep." In addition to "sheepdogs," there are "sometime sheepdogs," who split their time between herders and flock, and there are "no-good sheepdogs." Generally the sheepdogs drive those dogs into exile because they play too much and too rough with the sheep and goats or commit some other infraction against the proper order, which the guardians neither forget nor forgive.[3]

Navajo sheepdogs vie for a piece of cantaloupe
thrown by their shepherd, Navajo Reservation

Our Australian kelpie, Katie, a dog of outstanding physical and mental talent who will believe to the end of her days that people are incompetent, developed early in her life an intense animosity toward Rottweilers after two different pairs in one week had stalked and attempted to attack her while she was playing tennis ball, a game of her own devise that required pinpoint accuracy on the part of the thrower and obedience to her rules. The thirty-five-pound Katie ran the hundred-pound Rottweilers dizzy around the park until their clueless owners reined them in. But the attempted attacks left Kate distressed on three counts: The Rottweilers disrupted her game of tennis ball, which she took seriously; they failed to understand simple dog-speak when she told them with repeated bluff charges to quit and get lost; and they wanted to hurt her. The simple point is that animals know things quite well. To deny that is to deny them life.

In her old age, with spondylosis wrecking her back and necessitating that she be carried up and down stairs, Katie, the once glorious leaper, has developed an entirely new vocabulary of yips and half barks to tell us what she needs—to be carried up or down stairs; to be put on the bed; to be rubbed; for the bipeds to make the thunder stop; and the list goes on. Variable-speed tail thumping serves as punctuation.

The Kate, as she came to be known because of her imperious attitude when choreographing tennis ball, comes from a line of working kelpies, several of whom distinguished themselves as cattle dogs. Most ranchers who use dogs to work cattle will, if asked, admit that cattle dogs are a self-selected, self-sorting lot of volunteers with a suite of talents no one has consistently captured by breeding. Those talents start with a willingness to tangle with a thousand-pound steer who has spent three years in the back country without human contact and has no interest in joining a herd, and end with the combination of brains, physical stamina, fearlessness, agility, speed, strength, and will needed to move it. With good reason the French natural scientist Buffon and other observers of dogs and wolves believed that herding dogs were closest to the progenitor wolf in their behavior and mentality.

The socialized wolf or dogwolf willing to carry or drag its own weight was of special worth to people on the move. Despite a contemporary aversion against them on the part of competitive mushers, who want consistency and dedication on their teams that they find only in dogs, wolves and wolf-dog hybrids have a long tradition of sled pulling among the native people of the North American Arctic and people interested in training wolves, a challenge for dog handlers and trainers in the United States and Europe. Training wolves and then showing how well they performed was popular in the 1920s and 1930s, unfortunately fueled by the Nazi fascination with wolves and wolf-dogs. A Viennese police officer, Rudolf Knapp, trained a female wolf he had raised after shooting her parents in Bosnia. He especially enjoyed demonstrating how much better she was at police work than police dogs. In 1939, a female timber wolf was entered in the Westminster Kennel Club Show's sled-dog competition, an exhibition featuring four teams.[4]

Unraveling the ways in which human and dogwolf interacted is nigh impossible, not least because it probably varied from place to place. But clearly, neither animal in this match was a mere scavenger. Hominins, including the most recent one, like other members of the Guild of Carnivores, would have availed themselves of downed mammoths or beached whales, technically scavenging. But judging by the evidence from the caves where they processed bones for their marrow and dressed and carved and probably smoke-cured their prey, they placed themselves above the rest—if they even viewed themselves in the same class. While it appears that wolves were not above gnawing picked-over bones, hyenas were the scroungers of the Pleistocene. The guiding assumption among paleontologists and archaeologists excavating those ancient sites and examining the collections of bones, attempting to read the past—much the way soothsayers endeavor to see the future in the bones they throw—seems to be that wolves gnawed the bones after the hunters had left for the season, but at least some of them must have been socialized wolves taking their turns on the last bits of the spoils of the hunt.

No matter how they have constructed the study, academic researchers have consistently shown that people who hunt with dogs, independent of any other weapon they use, bring more meat to the table than those who don't—a lot more—and the amount increases with the size of the pack. A study of San Bushmen in the 1960s showed that those who hunted with dogs brought in 70 percent of the animal protein their band consumed. That truth is often obscured by objections to hunting in general or, at least, a particular style of hunting. It is also often obscured by the objections of non-hunters that the hunter is wastefully expending energy to feed the hounds who are supposed to be feeding him—a common complaint against settlers on the American frontier who often lived miles from any neighbor and relied heavily on their dogs to bring in the food they needed to survive.[5]

On the other hand, using dogs to track a single wounded animal and dispatch it, unless it clearly was mortally wounded, would in many instances prove a waste of energy and resources—unless it was a big bear or a young rhino or some other large, solo wanderer. Humans at the time hunted social ungulates who traveled in herds. Unless the herd had scattered so far to the winds that they could not easily reach any small cluster—unlikely on several counts—they were better off trying again with an unwounded animal. That situation changed with the growth of settled agricultural societies and scarcity of game, especially free-ranging ungulates, many of which went extinct or fled deeper into refuges at the extreme ends of their ranges.

Human hunters could have learned to look to the wolves by watching hominins do so, but I think it more likely they established their own relationships in various ways in different places. In Australia, tens of thousands of years after the earliest time we are looking at, Walbiri hunters searched the earth near their camps for fresh dingo tracks. Seeing them, they trotted off in dedicated pursuit until with luck and good running they arrived at the kill site in time to step in and deliver the coup de grâce on a large kangaroo with their woomera, spear throwers, before the dingoes could complete their task. The Walbiri hunters then field dressed their prize and carried it home after sometimes leaving some of its innards or other scraps for the dingoes. It is a simple technique that relies on imitative behavior and a certain level of interspecies cooperation. If the hunters failed to reach the site in time, they were liable to miss out because dingoes, like their wolfish forebear, bolt or "wolf down" their victims, often ripping them open before they are dead. Nor are they necessarily easy to drive from their kill.[6]

The Aborigines effectively discovered hunting with a pack of dogs or wolves through observation, the way Paleolithic hunters did. While the basic form has changed little, the means of maintaining contact with the hounds has varied according to local needs and conditions. The pygmy tie large bells around their hunting dogs, their basenjis, so they can follow them through the jungle. Later, Eurasian hunters employed horses and dogs that would sound off when they hit trail and then when they bayed up their prey, communicating the way wolves do, only using different vocalizations. Ancient Egyptian hieroglyphs show hunting hounds whose chondrodysplastic (dwarfed) legs forced them to trail game at a pace that was easy for humans on foot to follow. Egyptian hunters also had sight hounds with the swiftness, tenacity, and power to overtake gazelles or wolves and kill them without human assistance.

I can also imagine human hunters following wolves following herds of reindeer or horses or bison across the steppe, watching the sky for the vultures and ravens who marked the path of wolves on the hunt. Once there, the hunters donned their own wolf skins, hoping they could stay concealed until close enough to launch their spears or shoot their arrows.

There are also some indications that, like wolves, Neanderthal might opportunistically have taken advantage of a shallow lake or bluff to stampede entire herds to their death. But anatomically modern humans mastered the mass kill. After starting a stampede, human hunters would attempt to steer the frightened animals with flames, noise, their physical presence, or makeshift fences over a bluff or precipice, into a bog or lake, or through apparent weak spots in the fence into hand-dug depressions. They would die in the fall or become easy targets for hunters with spears. Those landscape traps were intended to kill large numbers of animals, and they usually succeeded in producing excess that doubtless found its way into the mouths of wolves and assorted other creatures, great and small.

Spectacular though they must have been, mass killings by geology were apparently rare. Like hominin hunters before them, including Neanderthals, human hunters focused largely on adult horses, reindeer, gazelles, ibex, and the like, presumably because they had more meat on and marrow in their bones. I can imagine situations in which wolves attacked their intended prey—a young gazelle, for example—and its protector, preoccupied with staving them off, never noticed the alert human hunters who took its life. They left the young animal for the wolves.[7]

Other studies have shown humans turning to ibex, an animal at home in uplands long hunted by wolves, when extreme cold began to reach into their warmer refuges, causing declines in available prey species and in their own numbers. It is doubtless coincidental, but certainly curious, that goats, near relatives of ibex, and sheep were the first ungulates humans domesticated. That process began when humans in the Zagros Mountains overlooking the Tigris and Euphrates rivers started gathering and holding wild sheep and goats in mountain meadows as a way to insure a more steady food supply. Adopting a wolf hunting tactic, humans also dropped their habit of hunting adults of both sexes in favor of selectively harvesting young males and past-reproductive-age females, seeking thereby to ensure that breeding females would produce more offspring. I imagine human herders employed their dogs in this process, but that is running ahead of the story somewhat. For now, it is fair to say that the days of the herd-dogging hunter were far from over; indeed, as the ice broke, humans and their dogs headed to new hunting grounds.

Hunters and gatherers relied heavily on their dogwolves primarily for comfort and companionship; for protection; for finding, and sometimes attacking, prey; and for keeping the camp clean of food scraps and vermin, which had the benefit of making it less appealing to other scavengers. Dogwolves also served as food in some places.

People would have encouraged and sought barkers, I believe, both as a warning of impending danger and as an auditory beacon for travelers or hunters out at night. The Bedouin ask, "How does a Bedouin find his way to camp in the desert at night? He listens for the dogs barking."

ELEVEN
Breaking Out;
Breaking Free

Did the dog emerge in Europe, the Near East,
central Asia, southwest Asia, southeast Asia, or
northeast Asia in several different refuges?
In all? In one? Outcrossed and sometimes
crossed out, distinctive types take shape.

As a biological and cultural construct of itself and humans, the dog has always adapted, with varying degrees of human assistance, to the society in which it finds itself. I say that because the niche the dog fills, when left to its own devices and not confined by walls or fences, is the same as that colonized by the socialized wolf—the interstitial space between the human zone of influence around the camp, village, or field and the rest of the world. That is still the dog's realm, occupied by dogs affiliated with people on enterprises that include protecting the flocks and herds from marauders and reporting on the appearance of strangers. They also have moved into cities, so that their niche runs from the heart of the city to fringes of agricultural fields and beyond. If persecution of wolves would stop, they would soon be coming fast from the other way, like coyotes, only since they are more sociable and more easily tamed than coyotes, they would probably soon be making friends with people and even some dogs. According to a number of anecdotal accounts, they already are. The dog's innate ability to adapt to new social and ecological conditions may be the same as it ever was, but in many parts of the world, concerted attempts are under way to curb its freedom to do so and to make it a full dependent rather than an ally, assistant, companion. In many ways the history of the dog's evolution is also the history of its domestication—still a work in progress that is tied to our own evolution and development.

In generalizing about dogs and humans and all the good they have done each other, it is easy to brush past or ignore the abuse of dogs by people, including that meted out by those seeking total control. From ancient times people have attempted to change permanently some dogs' behavior by physically altering them. People have castrated their dogs, broken off or knocked out their teeth to keep them from chewing through leashes or harnesses, and poured hot seal fat down their throats to destroy their vocal cords, so they would not betray the presence of a hunter over a seal hole. Dogs are frequently neglected or physically abused in the name of discipline. Especially in developed countries where purebred dogs are popular, the trend over the last two hundred years has turned away from the mutualism on which the human-dog relationship was built toward total human dominance and control of the animal's freedom of movement, reproduction, and ultimately its death. Were we to learn to control ourselves first, we might not have the need to hold dominion over others.

Fortunately for humans and dogs there are strong countercurrents that involve people exercising their dogs' minds and bodies either in work or sport, as well as taking time to educate and not simply train or condition them. Dog archaeologist Darcy Morey believes this special relationship is manifest in dog burials, the earliest of which dates from fourteen thousand years ago in Bonn-Oberkassel, Germany. This dog was buried with two people. More commonly they are interred with one person or with other dogs, the most spectacular example being the dog cemetery at Ashkelon, Israel, where seven hundred to one thousand dogs were buried in what could have been an exercise in mass mourning for all dogs in the village, except they do not appear to have all died at once.[1]

When all the utility is removed, the fundamental delight in the existence of the other must underlie the relationship of human and dog. Often that delight finds expression through simple games.

If I sit and close my eyes, I can almost hear cicadas singing in the late afternoon heat and see through a haze of dust a man sitting on a log. His name is Judt, I think, pronounced in a rush and with a guttural so it sounds like "Jud" punctuated with an "ut" at the end. He seems to have caught a fair number of rats he is throwing one by one to a smallish short-faced wolf who catches and dispatches them on the fly or, failing that, spears them with his front feet after an exaggerated pounce. He brings the dispatched rats to Judt, who tosses them toward a pack of dogwolves nearby who know not to interfere. As the game goes on, more people gather, bringing, I soon realize, not gifts but rats and more rats, as if the village were put up on a rat city. The people are amused at the spectacle but also in awe of the wolf and of Judt—all but the children, who push ever closer to the game until one young boy with perfect timing snatches a rat out of the air, nearly out of the wolf's mouth, and runs through the waiting pack, the other children in hot pursuit. . . .

The scene fades and shifts over untold thousands of years through worlds I don't recognize, although they are of this one, until finally I see a blur—

She is the Kate, springing upward, stretching as she ascends, twisting for more altitude until at the moment of full extension, she realizes she has gone too high. She jackknives, plucks the ball from the air, and then partly rights herself for a vertical reentry. Bobbing to the surface, she swims toward the pool steps with all the calm and grace of a retriever, three small children attached to her tail. She's been at this game since she arrived at the party, by special invitation, an hour ago.

Tennis ball is her passion. She invented this particular game of toss and catch after realizing that one wall of the pool was higher than the other, and therefore, if she could persuade M to pitch the ball right down the middle line, she could make a daring leap and catch it before hitting water. At this pool there is no high wall and the diving board is an unpredictable launching pad. She improvises. After the first hour, with food being served and her audience dwindling, the Kate climbs out of the pool, looks around to make sure the right people are watching, and trots up to a young man sporting a geometric Maori tattoo from the late Anglo-American Era on the left side of his face, and a new, heavily waxed purple mohawk. He has talked to no one, simply sat watching the Kate without affect. She places the ball on his plastic chair in such a way that it touches his leg and is guaranteed to succumb to gravity at the slightest perturbation in its space. It falls, and the Kate snaps it up after one bounce, then positions it in precisely the same way. She turns and sprints for her spot by the pool. The boy understands the game. He stands and throws it, turns back for his chair. The Kate brings him the ball. He hesitates. She barks at him once, twice. . . .

The boy's mother comments that he's never done anything like that before. "Like never played with a dog before?" M asks. She shrugs.

Leaving, the boy tells his mother, "I want a dog like that kelpie, that wolf." The Kate looks for all the world like a small wolf or dingo.

His mother looks at him as if he were an alien being. The Kate has turned her attentions to an older man, another guest's dyspeptic father. It is a wonderful party—for her.

That was the deal, and it did not take long to reach. The socialized wolf who remained close to humans got attention, which it craved, sexual freedom, a steady food supply, and considerable reduction in time spent raising the young and hunting. Even if the gruel was thin, it was better in lean times than what the wild wolf might get. The human got a guard against things that went "Boo!" in the night; hunting partner; camp cleaner; companion; bed warmer; guide in this world and the next; and emergency entrée, for those people who would not rather go hungry than eat dog. That, too, is the same as it ever was.

The appearance of the dog has changed and changed again, but for the most part, the majority of the world's one-billion dogs continue to do what dogs have always done, which is roam where they please and breed freely. They live on leftovers and scraps put out for them or dump grub supplemented with rodents, reptiles, birds, livestock carcasses, and occasionally a purloined lamb or kid. The wolves of the Abruzzo region of Italy and the Negev Desert in Israel have the same diet as the local free-ranging dogs, except they are wild and the dog is domestic, and that designation largely defines how they are treated.

The cleaving of dog and wolf occurred psychologically, perceptually, culturally, even genetically before the Last Glacial Maximum had begun to melt away. But it was when livestock began to replace wild stock on the grasslands and in the pot that dog and wolf found themselves facing each other across a lethal divide. Then there was no longer any way for human, dog, or wolf to turn away and change the course of their evolution.

But even while we appear finally to have captured the dogwolf on its way to assuming the mantle of dog, like its counterpart in Chauvet Cave, it wavers in and out of focus, a dog one moment, a socialized wolf another. Boy and dogwolf were in that cave near the height of the Last Glacial Maximum around 26,500 years ago, a period of intense cold when the glaciers altered virtually all the earth's ecosystems. Tundras and deserts spread as rain diminished; entire plant communities changed, forcing all manner of vertebrates and invertebrates to adjust, move, or die. And die they did. And move they did.[2]

When the deep cold blew in between thirty-three thousand and twenty-eight years ago, people began congregating in warm refuges with their dogwolves, if they had them, the way desert people gathered at an oasis or along a mountain stream, and the North American Plains Indians pitched their winter camps along the Yellowstone River, forming a multicultural community with all the animals who sought shelter in or near the riverine forest. By all indications the most important of these areas was the ancient Near East, expanded for this purpose into the Caucasus-Levant-Gulf-Oasis superhub, a mixing zone that incorporated the once and future crossroads of continents and of history, the cradle of civilization, the area where agriculture and animal husbandry began, the birthplace of at least four of the world's great religions, the repository of much of the petroleum that holds the world in thrall, and home to the dogwolves at the root of today's dogs. The Caucasus formed a natural barrier between the cold and arid Mammoth Steppe to the north and, to the south, a warmer, wetter climate people and animals sought. The ranges of the Chinese, Eurasian, and Middle Eastern wolves who figure most prominently in the contemporary dog overlapped there. Southwestern France was also of importance, less for dogs than for its people who were exploiting—in addition to their usual horse or ibex or aurochs or red deer—fish, birds, and smaller prey, much of it seasonally, as they stopped migrating after the herds and became largely sedentary—without agriculture. Their dogwolves were present, but it is not clear that any of their lineages have endured. Other areas of refuge were Italy south of the Alps as well as, it appears, central Asia and after an attack of cold, southeastern China.

The admixing of wolves that has shaped dogs is often attributed to backcrosses to wolves after an initial domestication event, but for that to have happened, people on the move with their domesticated Middle Eastern wolves would have had to pass through areas with sizable populations of European and Chinese wolves. It possibly could have happened where central Asia met the Mammoth Steppe, but it is more plausible, I think, to look for the admixture at one or more genetic crossroads. A major refuge during the Last Glacial Maximum had people and socialized wolves from many regions at least passing through, and their dogwolves were mating because they were more available and closer to each other—ecologically, temperamentally, and behaviorally—than to wild wolves even of their own type.

We do not know all the variations and subpopulations of the three gray wolf subspecies involved, but most available evidence indicates that Pleistocene wolves were highly variable and widespread. Shortface wolves were fairly abundant, and their presence in the canid stew could resolve a lot of the mystery surrounding the final slide from dogwolf to dog, with its congenitally shortened nose—relative to the longerfaced moderns.[3]

Socialized wolves and even dogwolves were animals in flux, straddling the human world and the natural world until circumstances, which I suspect were related to the abrupt movement of their people, reduced the breeding opportunities of at least several populations. This period of mating not with wild wolves but other dogwolves, and consolidation of a self-reproducing population that nonetheless could accept backcrosses to the parent stock, is what passes in hindsight, aided by the lens of modern genetics, for a domestication event. After they began to inbreed a few peculiar animals began to appear, and some of those oddities became valuable to the people as amusements, spirit animals, hunters, and companions. An extended socialization period and delayed onset of fright response became fixed in the new dog during this period. The dogwolves lost a scant 4 percent of the genetic diversity of their wolf cousins during the hard times, but they emerged as dog. On the move with their people, they began to spread, mating with local wolves and wolfdogs, passing dog genes on to them while increasing their own diversity. Inbreeding and admixture, or mongrelization, are responsible for the dog, most of it occurring within a human context but largely free of human intervention.

Around twenty thousand years ago, temperatures took a dive and radically altered the southern refuges, leaving people and dogs no more places to hide. Sea levels stood an estimated 394 feet lower than today. That translates into a huge number of archaeological sites, given the fondness of the furless biped for water and the fruit of the sea, including evidence, no doubt, that humans and probably earlier hominins knew how to trap fish.

Then, as if they could face no more, temperatures began to rise. Many animals, including humans, downsized and became less robust as the weather warmed, and many that could not downsize or adjust to the new temperatures and vegetative changes perished, perhaps with an assist from the smaller big-brained biped.

Springing out of their refuges, if they had not fled already, were humans, armed with their spear throwers and new stone points, their boomerangs and adornments, in the company of their dogs. Those dogs reflected the deepest and oldest divide in dogdom—that between big dogs and small dogs. The initial and traditional divide between big dogs and little dogs in America is around twenty pounds, with a fudge factor up to thirty pounds, a large feist dog. The fudge factor allows for the occasional big little dog and coming the other way the thirty-one to forty or forty-five-pound little big dog. They bore other distinctive features considered unique to dogs, like a curled tail—a sure way for humans to separate dog from wolf at a glance. I have seen a thirty-pound black Labrador retriever competing in a hunting trial beside her long and lean ninety-pound black Labrador half sibling. Neither was registered with the American Kennel Club, nor could they have met the Labrador standard, but both were outstanding retrievers.[4]

It appears that pulses of consolidation and expansion mark the early history of dog as surely as patterns of inbreeding and outcrossing attend the emergence of modern breeds, many of which show signs of multiple morphologies, especially in terms of size, leg length and shape, and degree of brachycephally. For example, the basenji, looking so much like the common ancestor of the Bedouin/Canaan-type pariah and of the classic sight hound, found its way up the Nile to its source and then into deep jungle where it appears to have been preserved in its ancient form. Wayne's and Ostrander's research teams have grouped the dingo with the Chinese Chow Chow and the Japanese Akita, both said to be ancient breeds. I suspect that more study will show that grouping to result from admixture between the dingo and the common ancestor of those two breeds, which are at least several thousand years old. Other genetic assays have suggested that the Bali dog, which has been on the island for twelve thousand years, is also related to the Chow Chow and the Akita, and it is easy to imagine dingoes mating with them either on their way to Australia or once there. Aboriginal artists are believed to have recorded the arrival of the dingo in rock paintings, but that does not preclude the presence of other dogs on the island continent. It is also possible that the common ancestor of dingoes, Chow Chows, Akitas, and Bali dogs was one of the early dogs coming out of the original mixing zone in the Middle East.[5]

Moving back to the sociocultural world, I think the importance of the expanded Middle East in the evolution of dogs is manifest in the strength of the habit of dogs among the people. It has withstood, albeit not easily, the dog prohibitions of Islam, which, as a matter of faith, believes that dogs are filthy and that Allah will not bless a house that has been befouled by the presence of such a beast. Islam does make allowances for working dogs—the pampered sight hounds devoted to the chase and other refined activities; police and military dogs; and flock-guarding dogs, of which there seems to be a variety in every tribal region from India to Turkey and beyond. Indeed, the tradition of the dog is so strong that the traditional sight hound of the desert, the Sloughi, or Saluki (depending on the sources), was traditionally given complete freedom in the Bedouin's tent. The Bedouin took every precaution to prevent unwanted mating between their hounds and their guard dogs—hobbling their female hounds so if another dog tried to mount her, she was forced to sit down. Unfortunately, in Saudi Arabia today the native dogs are not well kept, as the old traditions—good and bad—die out.[6]

Geneticists love the often inbred, multigenerational pedigrees of purebred dogs for studying complex patterns of inheritance of disease and behavior and increasingly parsing out intricate histories under domestication. But they sometimes forget to remember that they are dealing with a small percentage of the world's dogs, whose evolutionary trajectory since the time their breeds were established has been largely controlled by humans, whereas the majority of dogs still have at least one paw in the natural world, subject to its constraints and demands. In recent decades, purebred-dog associations have moved to boost their registrations, and income, by recognizing more and more of the estimated four hundred dog breeds extant in the world today.

These include landraces or, more frequently, autochthonous breeds refined from regional types of dogs—various feists and curs from the American South, the Kintamani dog from the Bali dog, the earlier, successful consolidation of the Canaan Dog from the Bedouin dog, the Carolina dog from free-ranging dogs in South Carolina, as well as Sioux and Navajo Indian dogs from undifferentiated, randomly breeding reservation dogs. Breeders of the New Guinea Singing Dog have a longstanding campaign to have it recognized as a separate species of *Canis* or, failing that, a subspecies of the gray wolf. It is closely related to Australia's dingo, but unlike the dingo, it appears always to have had a social and working relationship with the native highland people of Papua New Guinea.

Useful as studies involving modern dogs have been, a growing number of geneticists interested in the evolution of the dog and history of breeds recognize that it is necessary to compare DNA from ancient dogs and ancient wolves—as much as possible. Such DNA is difficult to obtain, because it breaks down under natural conditions and is prone to corruption. But evidence abounds that maternal lineages, as expressed through mitochondrial DNA, have changed over at least once since the dog raced out of the Last Glacial Maximum. That is why I think it's fair to talk about basic types that resulted from fundamental mutations or combinations of characteristics. These changes in appearance, with behavioral adaptations, collectively define the domestication event that led to the dog.

→ landrace - local variety of a domesticated animal

TWELVE
Why a Dog
Is Not a Wolf

So close together, yet so far apart. The human element
cannot be overlooked. People define dog—and wolf.

A signal problem in re-creating the evolution of the dog predates the advent of modern genetics: What physical changes clearly say this animal is a dog? Implicit in that question is the conviction that without physical changes there is no dog, only a socialized wolf. The debate over these matters might seem arcane to some, but it is ultimately about the processes of evolution and domestication, and about the history and essence of a unique interspecies friendship, that remain largely shrouded in mystery, myth, and received wisdom.

Over the years, archaeologists have worked out a suite of characteristics, many of which are said to be common by-products of domestication: these include an overall reduction in size and robustness so that the dog is always slighter than the equivalent-size wolf, from toes to brain; an overall broadening of the snout and shortening of the jaw, causing crowding of the teeth until they, too, shrink. In many breeds, the dog's head is more domed and the eyes more forward looking—

more binocular and human-looking. The tympanic bulla, the bone behind the middle ear that is reduced in size and flattened in dogs, is reportedly the most foolproof distinguishing feature.

Dogs' bites are less powerful than those of wolves except when selective breeding has made them more powerful—the pit bull, for example, generates biting force greater on average than a wolf. This reduction in bite force is often said to be due to malnutrition at the time of domestication. When the half-starved dogwolf finally obtained food, it was composed of more vegetative matter and meat scraps, which in a culture that used every part of the animal must not have amounted to much. That period of too little of the wrong kind of food caused a weakening of the masticatory muscles largely responsible for determining the shape of the jaw and skull. Malnourishment is said to have stunted the growth not only of the starved animal but of her descendants as well. It is not clear whether this projected dietary decline coincided with the hard times that hit humans and animals in the Levant and other refuges at around eighteen thousand years ago, or at some other event, or even whether malnutrition has such long-lasting effects. A more parsimonious explanation might lie in a change to more human-derived food that did not require the powerful jaw muscles needed to tear flesh from still living animals or crush bones and brought a relaxation of the selective pressure to maintain them. The same diet change affects zoo wolves in similar fashion so that their jaws often resemble those of early dogs. Once the heavy musculature is reduced from lack of use, the shape of the jaw changes and the teeth undergo a reduction in size.[1]

The wolf's supracaudal gland above its tail, used for scent marking and identification, is absent from the dog. Dogs are believed to show more white in mixed pelage, more solid red and tawny yellow coats than wolves. A curved tail and lop ears distinguish many dogs from wolves. The dog's footsteps look like the animal making them lists from side to side; the wolf goes where its toes point. Coats that obscure the eyes, and tails that are too short or too curled obstruct the dog's ability to communicate.

Dogs mature earlier sexually than wolves and, free of the seasonal constraints that govern the timing of reproduction in wild canids, come into estrus twice yearly rather than once. How much of that is genetic rather than social and environmental is difficult to determine, especially since the current trend in science is to blame genes for everything. Yet among wolves, social controls within the pack and environmental conditions, especially the availability of food and absence of stressors, like prolonged abnormal weather, disease, or human persecution, regulate breeding of subordinate—young—females. If the breeding alpha female dies, a young female can come into heat, and subordinate females sometimes breed in packs that have access to abundant prey. The combination of early sexual maturation and delayed growth or development of other organs and limbs is called paedomorphosis and is believed by many archaeologists and biologists to be the reason dogs are slighter than their opposites among wolves. Early sexual maturity and accelerated growth, hypermorphosis, produce dogs larger than wolves, although it must be said that some very large dogs appear to be slow to mature physically, even if they mature early sexually.

Slowing the rate of development enough is said to lead to the retention of juvenile traits into adulthood, a phenomenon called neoteny. The paleontologist Stephen Jay Gould resurrected this nineteenth-century notion of neoteny in a popular book, *Ontogeny and Phylogeny* and with an article in the May 1979 issue of *Natural History* magazine, titled "Mickey Mouse Meets Konrad Lorenz." He drew the bulk of his examples from the world of popular culture—the juvenilization of many rough and rustic folk figures like St. Nicholas, or of popular cartoon characters like Walt Disney's proletarian rat, Steamboat Willie, who became the denatured Mickey Mouse. Gould did not recognize that this softening and juvenilization were part of a cultural trend begun in the mid-nineteenth century to "civilize" and fully domesticate man and beast. Just as cultural figures were changed, so were dogs, as breeders strove to make them more cuddly and human, with rounded skulls, eyes forward, their demeanor forever puppylike. The Pomeranian is an early example of this trend. A medium-sized German working dog of the spitz type, as manifest in its tightly curled tail, was reduced to Lilliputian proportions in the late nineteenth century because Queen Victoria had some small Pomeranians of which she reportedly was inordinately fond.[2]

Applying the cultural concept of neoteny to dogs, evolutionary biologist Raymond Coppinger developed an elaborate chart showing the degree to which various types of dogs were physically and behaviorally juvenilized, playing their lives away. His prime example of a neotenic dog was the Saint Bernard, whose head, he said, resulted from the dog's development being stuck at a very young stage, rather than from the work of breeders. Coppinger is also a leading proponent of the idea that wolves first tamed themselves by feeding on midden heaps of Mesolithic villages at a time when people were becoming sedentary. Eventually, people noticed the dump divers and turned the tamest among them into dogs.[3]

Researchers who believe the dog is a neotenic wolf invariably cite Dimtry Belyaev's Siberian farm fox experiment in which animals bred over multiple generations for tameness toward humans alone ultimately produced juvenilized, doglike foxes. But none of their arguments supporting the theory that domestication proceeds by neoteny brought on by selection for tameness pertain to the already socialized wolf. Those arguments might not hold anywhere since the phenotypic changes in the tame foxes also occurred in a population of the same silver foxes bred to no purpose at all, albeit at a lower frequency. Over the years, more than one observer has reported seeing in captive-bred wolves and other zoo animals the kinds of phenotypic changes usually associated with domestication.

There certainly is no evidence that wolves were selected by early humans for tameness the way the farm foxes were, since selection in that experiment was also made "against aggression." In many cultures, from its origins, the dog has been valued as a loud and, when necessary, aggressive guardian of people, their homes, possessions, and livestock. The vast majority of the world's dogs breed without direct human interference, and many of those landraces are known as intractable and unwelcoming, if not actively hostile toward strangers.

It is helpful to remember, in this regard, that most of the concern with tameness or trainability dates to the nineteenth century, when "civilized" dogs became the rage, "civilized" in this case meaning they knew their place and paid attention to the human. But it also meant looking more human, even doll-like. Unrefined dogs, pariahs, are undesirable precisely because they have not been subjected to proper breeding. Until they are, by definition, they can never be "civilized." Nearly everything is wrong, but it persists for reasons have more to do with people than dogs.[4]

Even Raymond Coppinger's poster dog for neoteny might not be what it seems. A 2007 study by Abby Drake and Christian Peter Klingenberg at Manchester University showed how breeders in America have dramatically and drastically altered the appearance of the Saint Bernard over the past 120 years in order to make their dog conform to an ever changing breed standard. Their emphasis has been on producing dogs with broader, higher skulls, with larger, more binocular eye sockets at acute angles from a shortened, broadened snout. They have succeeded in making a giant doll.[5]

To reiterate an important point, there is no evidence that the dog originated from self-taming, submissive, neotenic wolves. That theory is based in part on the mistaken belief that dogs originated during the Mesolithic Age, when people were settling into permanent settlements complete with garbage dumps. All the evidence, archaeological, genetic, and cultural, places the first dogs in the camps of hunters and gatherers. In Italy, Israel, and other parts of the world, wolves have fed on human garbage dumps for decades without becoming tame or manifesting the morphology of the fox-model domesticates. The food in those dumps is

doubtless higher quality than what they would have found in a Meso-
lilthic midden or a Paleolithic boneyard, but it has clearly not been good
enough to persuade them to become dogs.

It is not even clear when in the dog's history semiannual estrus
became the rule. Basenjis have an annual cycle, as do dingoes, Thai
pariahs, Indian pariahs, and Russian Laikas, to name a few dogs who
never seem to have made the adjustment.

Most paleoanthropologists and paleontologists readily admit that
differentiating between early dogs and wolves is a difficult task made
worse by the poor conditions of the samples. Usually they fall back on
context—if it was buried with a person, for example, then it probably is
a dog, except when it is a wolf. Many of the measurements are made
against modern wolves or genders are confused or samples are dismissed for comparison purposes because they do not reflect anticipated
differences in size.

Late in the nineteenth century, workers building the trans-Siberian
railroad found hundreds of Neolithic graves at the confluence of the
Irkutsk and Angara rivers on their approach to the southwestern end of
Lake Baikal. Dubbed Lokomotiv in honor of workers who uncovered it,
the area was a cemetery that had been used over a long stretch of time
and included single, double, and triple burials of men, women, and children, most likely northern Mongolian in origin. In 1995, archaeologists
found and excavated the seventy-three-hundred-year-old grave of a
large tundra wolf, *Canis lupus albas*. His head was raised as if looking
outward and onward, paws placed against his body, a human skull
tucked between his elbows and knees. Partial remains of at least two
other people were also found in the grave. Because this region is home
to the Chinese or Mongolian wolf, researchers concluded that this tundra wolf traveled into the area as a socialized wolf, probably in the company of a shaman. Dogs were widespread by the time, but clearly in the

north, where the wolf remained sacred to warriors and hunters, they coexisted within a community that included wild and socialized wolves.[6]

Absent such contextual help, those archaeologists who tend to view genetics like an unruly child at a symphony doggedly insist that morphological change associated with neoteny is the sole determinant of domestication. Yet clear evidence, not only from wolves and dogs but also from goats and sheep and a number of other animal domesticates, indicates they are wrong. Goats were brought under human management in the Zagros Mountains five hundred to one thousand years before any morphological change that could be attributed to domestication occurred, and even those changes may have been secondary to selection for other attributes, evolutionary biologists Melinda Zeder and Brian Hesse wrote in the March 24, 2000, issue of the journal *Science*. Reductions in size occurring before then were probably due to environmental factors. Presumably, the changes could also have been of a nature that appealed to humans, who did not cull them and may even have encouraged their propagation, especially in the case of a freakish twist in the goat's horns or an odd color. Other studies have indicated that habitat fragmentation resulting from human activities and captive breeding inevitably alter the phenotype of the animals involved.[7]

In fact, determining when these changes occurred is as important as understanding the reasons for them. There is a strong tradition among the scientists who have studied this question for years to look for a regulatory gene or RNA sequence or some other genetic switch that, when thrown, will set off the proper sequence of events to create the dog as a paedomorphic wolf. Despite intense efforts, no one has yet found the gene or genes or any other chemical or enzyme or hormone responsible for paedomorphosis, much less neoteny.

In recent years, paleoanthropologists who study humans—their traditional subject matter—have produced material that casts an interesting light on the transition from dogwolf to dog in terms of the latter being a more gracile, less robust, smaller brain cavity animal. Those terms fit almost precisely a transformation that occurred in the human population that emerged from the Last Glacial Maximum. In the *2008 Yearbook of Physical Anthropology,* Brigitte Holt and Vincenzo Formicola describe how human legs were less robust, overall body proportions and stature were reduced, and craniofacial dimensions were altered. A general gracilization occurred. Asymmetry was the order for development.

That sounds surprisingly like the neotenic dog, except that in the case of people the explanations are grounded in the physical. Holt and Formicola observe that studies have repeatedly linked mobility and physical activity to the robustness of human leg bones, and that during the crunching cold of the Last Glacial Maximum, their mobility was restricted and constrained by the increased density of human settlement and decreased amount of territory available for hunting and hauling. The decline in stature and proportion appeared related to technological advances—the atlatl and bow and arrow—that made hunting easier, meaning it required less energy to kill the smaller prey, like deer, then most commonly available in the refuges, as well as to a long-term switch from a diet composed exclusively of land mammals to the incorporation of marine life, including seals. Moreover, many animals were experiencing a change in body size—a general downsizing with a "mosaic" of shifting body proportions associated with the changing climate.[8]

Geneticists probing the dog genome have found gene variants or alleles associated with changes in different parts of the cytoskeleton or even the whole organism. The expression of these genes with the relaxation of natural selective pressure, which tends to reject extreme changes that do not help the organism survive and reproduce, and the subsequent capture by humans of those features in the captive or domestic population, appear to account for the phenotypic changes attributable to domestication. Many of them are the sort of "hopeful monsters" Darwin said were regularly thrown into the evolutionary brew—freaks that most commonly die on their own because they are maladapted or are killed by their own kin who find their outlandishness unacceptable.[9]

That is especially true of the extreme size reduction of many dogs, as well as the oversizing of heads in many brachycephalic breeds to such a degree that the dogs can no longer give birth except by Cesarean section. Breeds with elongated, or hypercephalic, snouts, like the fox and Scottish terriers, suffer the same fate. The animals survive birth only through human intervention.

The discoveries of genes responsible for this dazzling display continue to pile up. In 2010, a team of dog geneticists announced that they had associated 51 gene loci on the dog genome with 57 breed-specific physical characteristics using a detailed new canine SNP map, called CANMAP. Surveying 60,986 SNPs across the genomes of 915 dogs from 80 breeds, 83 wild canids, and 10 randomly breeding African village dogs, they found that, in most cases, differences in three or fewer loci accounted for the large phenotypic differences between breeds. They include overall body size and external dimensions; head, tooth, and long-bone shape and size; coat characteristics; floppy ears; and snout length. These findings appear to support the argument that breeders selecting for specific traits, especially freakish ones, are responsible for the dogs we have, not some mysterious biological process of juvenilization. They should spur the search for the genes involved and how this entire puzzle fits together, a puzzle that seems at once simpler and infinitely more complicated than anyone had imagined.[10]

Geneticists have found a variation in fibroblast growth factor-4 in breeds with disproportionately short and bowed limbs, a form of dwarfism called chondrodysplasia in dachshunds, basset hounds, corgis, Scottish terriers, and similar breeds. Scientists have also shown that changes in the forequarters, hindquarters, and jaws of animals are interrelated in such a way that selective breeding for strong, straight, heavy leg bones forces a shortening and broadening of the muzzle, enlargement of the cranium, and strengthening of the jaw muscles in the head. The result is a mastiff-type animal. Long, straight, light legs mandate a longer, thinner head to produce the greyhound/sight hound type. Aware of itself physically, as all dogs consummately are, the mastiff makes its way through the world with power and explosiveness, rather than speed, the way the sight hound does. Other work has shown that the dog's skull in morphological terms is comprised of modules that can be manipulated separately to create the vast spread of heads apparent today. These findings follow those showing that the masticatory muscle is responsible for much of the size and shape of the dog's jaw, so that if the animal's diet changes in such a way that it doesn't have to crush bones and break through cartilage regularly, the muscles will weaken and, over time, the jaw and muscles change to reflect that. Tooth size and shape change, as does the morphology of the skull itself.[11]

Perhaps the earliest—and most obvious—morphological change in the transformation of dogwolves into dogs was reduction in size—creation of small dogs and, with it, as I noted earlier, the fundamental divide in dogdom between big dogs and little dogs. That was because the small dog was "new" under the sun and associated with human, not wolf society. The appearance of that mutation and its propagation through early dogwolves led to the emergence of an animal that did not exist in the natural wolf population. Its rarity made it even more desirable. It is possible that other quirks appeared earlier among dogwolves—brachycephaly or curled tails for example—but those mutations were not rare enough to be category changers.[12]

These alleles seem to make for simple explanations that fail to address the behavioral issue of juvenilization in the transition of wolf to dog, manifest in part, the argument goes, by the failure of the male dog on going walkabout to track, stalk, hunt, kill, and dissect its food. Even in the most wolflike of dogs, the ultimate act in the hunting cycle—

killing the prey—is interrupted. For mastiffs, the situation is even worse, since their level of neoteny dictates that they cannot engage in any predatory activity, that instead they thwart predator attacks by attempting to play with the attacker, thereby confusing it to such a degree that it stops and retreats—laughing, I hope.[13]

Historically, mastiffs have been prized for their ferocity and tenacity against predators and humans. The sheep-guarding dogs, working in conjunction with shepherds, killed predators in defense of their flocks. They also reportedly could spot at a glance any sheep who didn't belong and gently escort it home. What appears genetic can often be something else, especially among highly social animals. The desire to hunt is innate, I expect, but desire without education leads to floundering experimentation as I have noted. Wolves born and raised in captivity without exposure to wild wolves are fundamentally clueless about hunting, killing, and consuming prey not because they've undergone a genetic mutation but because no one has taught them how to do it. Recent studies have shown that free-ranging dogs will kill profligately without eating, not necessarily because they do not know how or because they are inhibited but because they are being fed regularly by humans or otherwise are obtaining human food.

Feral animals present conceptual problems for scientists and environmentalists because they are category benders. If domestication involves juvenilization of the parent wild stock, in terms of appearance and behavior, how can the resulting animal revert behaviorally without also resuming the wild form? The problem is especially acute in dogs, where conventional wisdom holds that the dog is so enfeebled, it cannot establish itself in reproducing packs or groups independent of human food—even if only garbage.

Male feral dogs, it is said, unlike wolves, seem not to contribute to the rearing of their young, except when—like Indian dogs and dingoes and feral dogs in Alaska and anywhere else they live free of human society—they do, and how they came to do that is an excellent unasked question. Part of the reason for this apparent contradiction is the habit among some observers of erroneously grouping free-ranging dogs with feral dogs, as if they were the same. They are different: Free-ranging dogs are simply roamers who usually are associated with a person or family from whom they receive food. They are dependent on that food, even though they may also scavenge and hunt. Feral animals, on the other hand, are domesticated animals or their offspring who live free of human society.[14]

Sometimes, scientists simply redefine, or put into a different category, the animal who seems an exception to the rule rather than address directly the reasons it is different and possibly modify their basic definitions and categories. The dingo, for example, is a feral dog who is so wolflike, save for its curled tail and a tendency toward a ginger coat, that taxonomists and wildlife biologists insist on classifying it as a separate subspecies of wolf from other dogs. Many scientists include in their papers statements that the dingo is a primitive dog or a "semi-domesticated dog," which allows them to judge it separately from dogs in general.

By most measures, the dingo arrived in Australia fifty-five hundred years ago, close to fifty-five thousand years after the Aboriginal people. There were probably just a few of them who arrived by dugout, and, I like to think, escaped their cages, knowing they were being carried for food because they had already watched two of their siblings die. They went walkabout and never looked back. By comparison, the Bali dog is said to have arrived there close to twelve thousand years ago, as a fully domesticated dog, which it has remained. The Aborigine embraced the dingo, the dog, after their own fashion, forming with it in some places, especially the Outback through which they roamed, a loose confederation that involved taking and raising dingo puppies until, grown, they dispersed back to dingo society, following them on the hunt, and dealing with them day and night in the Dreaming. In coastal villages, which tended to be permanent to take advantage of the abundance of the sea, the Aborigines kept them on as dogs. Throughout Australia, Aborigines accorded the dingo an honored place in Dreamtime, their cosmogony, and their superreality.[15]

The dingo, of course, had the good fortune to land on an island without what we might call a terminal, or apex, predator, the larger, putatively more powerful marsupial thylacine wolf notwithstanding. A dog among other dogs before arriving in Australia, the dingo managed on its own to re-create wolfish pack society, albeit with a few twists that were probably useful adaptations to local conditions. The only model the dingo had to guide it in that endeavor was the society of its Aboriginal friends, which is why I have suggested that the infanticide committed by the alpha female against the puppies of any other breeding female in the pack might be an adaptation of the infanticide practiced among the Aborigine. It is also interesting to note here that the first early socialization or sensitive period in dingoes appears to stretch to about eight weeks, compared with fourteen in modern dogs and five to six in wolves. Whether the dingo's socialization period is significantly shorter due to the pressure of life in the wild and more than a century of human persecution, or the modern dog has been stretched beyond its ancient forebears, is difficult to say. That is another way of suggesting that the initial extension was short and remained that way in the early dog well into the Neolithic.

Demands for purity of blood and category create interesting problems. Persecuted in the name of predator control since the arrival of Anglo-Europeans in the nineteenth century, the dingo, with its lands invaded and its packs shattered by death, has, not surprisingly, hybridized with imported dogs—sometimes with the active encouragement of humans, according to reports, to improve herding dogs on far-flung outback stations. But while the wild dingo is believed to help the domestic dog, the domestic dog is considered the ruination of the wild dingo. The domesticated herder is celebrated for its toughness, independence, and intelligence; the wild hybrid is one of the most reviled creatures on the planet, more despised than the dingo itself. The contemporary dingo-dog hybrids are accused not only of befouling the unique dingo genome but also of being more relentless killers of livestock.

A major genetic bottleneck occurred with modern breed formation when the loss of diversity was nearly nine times greater than with the origination event—35 percent compared with 4 percent. The late eighteenth century, when modern breed formation began, to the present is arguably the time frame in which the dog can be said to come close to domestication. Now, with the takeover in breeding and the removal from the streets of free-ranging dogs in many industrialized countries, it appears that humans are finally on their way to completing domestication and commodification of the dog itself, with certain freaks among them maintained as Thorstein Veblen's "objects of conspicuous consumption," created and maintained for human possessiveness. Among some social groups, the dog is little more than a biological doll.[16]

These changes make it difficult to determine how much the contemporary dog differs from its forebears, yet the little visual and written descriptive data we have indicate that the changes physiologically, at least, are serious, be they the downsizing of the Pomeranian into a Lilliputian lap dog or selectively breeding dogs like Labradors, golden retrievers, spaniels, Newfoundlands, and a raft of others for more domed heads and pronounced binocular vision; or breeding old English bulldogs and Boston bull terriers with heads so big the females cannot whelp naturally. Veterinary behaviorists and trainers have told me in interviews that they believe the temperament of many dogs has been changed to emphasize the close handler-dog attentiveness and coordination necessary to win competitions, instead of the sort of independence of thought and action required of true working dogs. Today, as I pointed out, people in developing nations often eschew their native dogs in favor of Western purebred dogs both for their genealogies, which are believed to guarantee quality and purity, and their perceived obedience. Demand keeps growing while native dogs languish, accused of every form of impropriety, sloth, and ignorance.

Native dogs from anywhere south of Europe are classed with pariahs and curs—creatures of no breeding fit only for shepherds and poachers and other low-class people. In at least one major dog encyclopedia, the Canaan dog is correctly said to date from Antiquity and to have served the Bedouin as "a herder and guard dog." Those are fair and accurate statements; in fact, as I said at the beginning, I think it highly probable that this desert dog figures in at least some of the European and Australian herding dogs. But the rest of the text says that the Canaan dog was a scavenging pariah until the 1930s, when Dr. Rudophina Menzel took some and trained them first for mine detection and then as guide dogs. She consolidated her dogs into a breed, the Canaan dog, who, following the tradition of breed formation, became endowed with all the positive virtues and attributes of the original. Also in keeping with the tradition of breed formation, the native dog was stripped of all its virtues and coated with all its vices.[17]

Inherently, the free-ranging village dog in India is every bit as domesticated as the pampered Papillion, and both are behaviorally and perceptually different from wolves. Those statements are based on the widely accepted assumption that domestication involves inheritable changes in the demeanor and behavior of the animal. With the exception of the extended socialization period and delayed fear response, as well as specialized behaviors, like pointing, found in specific breeds or types of dog, those changes are not easily identified. Scientists studying communicative ability have found that some dogs are incapable of reproducing the full suite of wolf vocalizations and body language because of long hair that conceals their eyes, floppy ears, truncated tails, and other features that humans value. A number of scientists have recently reported that dogs have a capacity to focus on and follow human social cues that is close to that of children but absent from wolves.

Those are compelling results that seem to point to a fundamental difference in cognitive abilities between dogs and wolves. But other researchers have demonstrated that the results are heavily influenced by the context in which the animals are tested. The standard protocol for those experiments tests dogs in a laboratory and wolves in an outdoor pen. When wolves are tested in the lab and dogs in the pen, the wolves perform with the same or greater focus on the human than the dogs had, while the dogs do worse. I have always found that while these sorts of comparisons make interesting headlines, they ultimately say little about dogs, wolves, or children. Studies that do so are rare but necessary.[18]

Throughout the history of dogs and humans, individuals who have done best with dogs have been those with the ability "to get inside the minds of their dogs," to understand what they are thinking and feeling collectively and individually. These human adepts made the original meeting of species work and have kept it flourishing since. The successes they have had on the hunt or in making a safe journey have encouraged other people to try a dog, to take into and trust their lives to an animal capable of mauling and even killing them.[19]

How dogs are treated depends on the human culture in which they live, and therein for me lies another mystery. I have assumed that some furless bipeds were as fascinated by wolves as wolves were by them, but while mutual fascination can lead to alliances on the trail, it does not translate automatically into a fifty-thousand-year coevolutionary journey. I have seen no reports that humans must become socialized as infants to dogs in order for them to become bonded, but like other animals, humans do pass through periods of increased fear of strange animals, people, and situations that, if not addressed, can lead to the all-too-familiar, reflexive human bias toward different individuals or groups. That is why I think humans, no less than wolves, experienced some subtle alterations in the amygdala and elsewhere that allowed them to accept the dogwolf into their lives.

On the eve of the third millennium, it was still popular, despite mounting evidence to the contrary, to argue the opposite position—that children with pets were not properly socialized to other people. Since then, evidence to the contrary has become overwhelming. A study of Japanese men published in 2010 indicated that benefits of dog owner-ship early in life were long lasting. Elderly Japanese men who had owned dogs in childhood were more sociable than those who had not, and the earlier the exposure, the better. That conforms with studies showing that animals help make children more social, and it suggests that the effects are long lived. People with dogs in America tend to have lower blood pressure and be generally healthier and less isolated than their peers who do not have dogs. It is difficult to imagine how these positive effects of association with dogs are new to the relationship; rather, they must go back to the beginning.[20]

PART IV
Running with the Dogs

The dog, bearer of the secret, who runs with ease over the abysses of time, because for him there is no difference between the fifteenth and the twentieth centuries, knows many things more accurately than we do. His left (domesticated) eye is attentively fixed on us; the right (wild) one has a little less light, strikes us as averted and alien. And yet we sense it is the over shadowed eye that sees us[1]

—W. G. Sebald

Clio

THIRTEEN
Ice Breaks;
Frees Dog

Dogs and humans settling in for the long terms.
Dogs and humans on the move. Dog is
everywhere, it seems, no longer hiding
in wolf clothes. The small dog reigns.

A t its mind-numbing maximum, when the pine and scrub forests of the Levant had turned to dry steppe, cold and forbidding, and elsewhere even the cold-loving plants and animals were maximally stressed, the ice cracked, broke of its own frozen weight. Some of the adepts and their dogwolves detected a hint of warmth, the scent of dampness blowing off the sea. The big grazers were preparing to move. It was just a hint, but the cold forced people to move on. When they went, they did not proceed in lockstep with one approach or one answer, with the result that attempts by people who study ancient prehistory to apply the same names to this period in different regions create a welter of confusing dates that are constantly being refined and re-sorted. For different reasons, genetics also suffers from a multiplicity of names for various structures and pieces of the genome and disputes over how to interpret what is observed. Straightening out the nomen-clature would doubtless resolve more than a few conflicts among archaeologists, paleoanthropologists, and geneticists.

For now, as a rough guide, the time frame for this section is from the peak cold of the Last Glacial Maximum, eighteen to twenty thou-sand years ago, to the first sign of agriculture, around twelve thousand years ago (10,000 BC) in the Fertile Crescent, Anatolian Plateau, China, and possibly India. To show how some aspects of the story of humans and dogs stretch out over thousands of years with little change except in material conditions, I will follow major events, like colonization of the New World, well beyond this time frame. That kind of time surfing is possible because the suite of tasks that underlie the human-socialized wolf/dog relationship are so fundamental that they persist despite dra-matic, even revolutionary, sociocultural transformations.

The great cold forced people everywhere to adapt or perish. In refuges like southwestern France and the Levant some groups began to exploit an expanding array of local plants and animals rather than wan-der after the horses, reindeer, and bison that had sustained them since before memory but were no longer moving in their former large herds. Some people erected stone hovels or huts and stayed longer near river mouths and estuaries where they could catch and trap fish, hunt seals and other marine and freshwater mammals, and harvest shellfish, in ad-dition to hunting game, including boar, that was easier to bring down with the help of dogwolves. They also developed new microlithic points to increase the killing power of their arrows, spears, and harpoons.

When the cold began to relent around eighteen thousand years ago, people, animals, and plants had to adapt to a climate that was turn-ing warmer and wetter. In areas like southeastern China, hunters along the Yangtze River began to exploit a wider range of game the size of deer, and even smaller, as they became more sedentary, like their counterparts in Europe, except they appear to have had no dogs.

Groups living that way in the Levant ushered in a new cultural phase, the Epipaleolithic, a last hurrah for the hunters and gatherers who would take their sedentism to the next level. Just as omnivory had replaced carnivory, the Epipaleolithic gave way to the Mesolithic, the Middle Stone Age, a transitional period between the Paleolithic and Neolithic, that in the Levant ended in the Natufian around 12,500 years ago, when the first seeds of agriculture sprouted. In China and India, as well, agriculture came early while groups in Europe pursued their hunting and foraging ways until Neolithic farmers arrived around 10,000 years ago. By that time, the dog was well established in much of the world, as befits a creature born traveling.

The consensus model of dog domestication has dated the dog's emergence to 15,000 years ago, squarely within this period of rapid global changes in climate, ecosystems, and human society. Specifically, the dog is seen as a creation of the increasing sedentism of the Mesolithic people and their middens, except that it is not. Selection of that date has long been dictated by insistence, largely on the part of archaeologists, on proof of dog on the basis of morphological changes, even if the result contravenes the mounting genetic, physical, and cultural evidence that the dog is older even than the 31,500-year-old Goyet Cave dog.

That is a bold statement given that between the Goyet dogwolf and next oldest dog remains from the Czech Republic stand around four thousand years. The dogs from the Mammoth steppe hunting camp at Eliseevichi I appear eleven thousand years later. Yet in all cases, the animals were large hunters and consumers of horse and reindeer. Along with other slightly younger but equally large dogs from hunting camps on the Mammoth steppe, these finds suggest that the dog was a common companion of the paleohunters on the steppe by the end of the Last Glacial Maximum. From an early date, big dogs were creatures of the hunting camps, doubtless as prized in that milieu as the first small dogs to be buried with their people were in theirs.[1,2]

I believe that the first dog will not be found in a burial site because they were born on the move to people of the desert and steppe where bodies have been left to scavengers and the weather for tens of millennia. Also, socialized wolves, dogwolves, and even dogs appeared in different times and places and may have flourished for long periods before their lineages faded out. The Middle Eastern contributor to today's dogs apparently developed some unique genetic quirks perhaps as early as forty-five to fifty thousand years ago, but that does not make the Middle East the center of dog domestication any more than an actual body or two would. It does suggest that early burials are best viewed as potentially significant indicators of the value people placed on themselves and a particular type of dog.

Strong circumstantial evidence suggests that the dog was already widely traveled by sixteen thousand years ago when it was preparing with its people to take the Americas, the dog-specific mutations that would manifest themselves in both the Old and New Worlds already locked in its genome. To be in that position, dogs would have to have been in place at least through the end of the Last Glacial Maximum or once warming began, moved quickly the length of a continent, picking up and exchanging dogs as they went. It is possible that the mutations responsible for certain physical characteristics, like smallness, chondrodysplasia, brachycephaly, and coat color, occurred independently among their dogs in the New World or were introduced later by other dogs coming out of Siberia, but it seems unlikely.

Even while in the aftermath of the great cold some groups continued to become more rooted in their place, others took advantage of changing conditions to move into previously unwelcoming lands. Universally, they had dogs or soon acquired them, showing that the animals enjoyed considerable status. No matter how lupine some of them appeared, these animals were clearly dogs firmly anchored in human society, looking out from the camp, whereas the wolves who remained on the outside were staring in—to redeploy a spatial metaphor. They were dogs, too, in that they bore the morphologies of dog that had risen and been captured by accident and design of their limited mate choices. The small dog was the clearest example of this. Unique and rare, it was traded, presented as a gift, and, we might safely assume, stolen.

Small dogs, I suspect, ultimately went into the mix-and-match that became the quick and mobile herding dogs. They certainly had a hand in the terriers that appeared in England. Frederick Zeuner in his influential 1963 study, *A History of Domesticated Animals,* says that the herding type was firmly established in England and Europe by fifty-five hundred years ago, coincident with the arrival of animal husbandry and agriculture in those areas. Dozens of varieties of this rough type existed, all bred for local conditions.[3]

In our time, researchers have fixated on size reduction as a prerequisite for dog; small canids appearing in human settlements after twelve thousand years ago were thus dogs almost by definition. Large wolflike canids at the same sites were almost always classified as wolves. Zooarchaeologist Juliet Clutton-Brock has suggested that the ubiquity of small dogs in prehistoric sites means that "a small population of [small] dogs diffused from a founder group. . . ." I am confident that small dogs were initially a prized addition to the bestiary and that their repeated appearance in human burials bespeaks both their value in that culture and their ability to move inside and outside the home, whereas the large dog, with notable exceptions, like prized sight hounds, was an outdoor animal. Clutton-Brock believes these globetrotting small dogs were quite inbred, which accounts for their similarity in size and shape at different European sites.[4]

Clutton-Brock is probably right. Desired as an oddity, an extravagance, small dogs were largely obtained by trade from a lineage founded by the paleohunter forebears of the New World's colonizers who first isolated a mutation for smallness in the population of already small Middle Eastern dogwolves that traveled with them on their way from the region of the Fertile Crescent and Arabian Peninsula through the Levant to central Asia.

This isolation could have occurred long before changes in human culture opened the door for small dogs.[5]

Well before herding dogs appeared, paleohunters on the Eurasian steppes and in central Asia and the Middle East had massive dogs. As I plot their distribution on the map of Eurasia, I see that they, like other dogs, probably originated in that great mixing zone south of the Caucasus and north of the Levant from short-nosed and long-nosed European wolves from the Carpathians and Dinaric Alps, Chinese wolves from central Asia and southwestern Asia, and Middle Eastern wolves in addition to the dogwolves of the adepts. Dogs moved freely and quickly in all directions along established corridors.[6]

A huge Caucasus mountain dog, the ancestor of present-day mountain dogs and mastiffs, traveled north and east with the adepts and their dogs from the Levant, until they came to the territory defined by the Altai Mountains and Amur River in central Asia, where they decided to take shelter from the cold, such as they could. Their large dog headed back south and west as the Asiatic mastiff, contributing to the Tibetan mastiff (believed by some to be the founder of all mastiffs) before crossing southwestern Asian to slip between the Caucasus and the Caspian Sea where it mixed with the Caucasus mountain dogs. With Neolithic farmers, it pushed through Turkey into the Balkans. In Turkey, this yellow dog with a massive head and a classic black muzzle became the Kangal dog. In the Balkans it appears to have made some contribution to the Molossus and other southern European sheep-guarding dogs. Its cousin the white Akbash dog ties Siberian dogs genetically through Turkey to North Africa, which it crossed on its way to Spain to contribute to the sheep-guarding mountain dogs, and then into England and the Continent where it was a progenitor of mastiffs.

The bold, large-scale migration straight out of Siberia and across the Bering Land Bridge, Beringia, into the New World suggests a plan had been put into effect to seek out a new land, perhaps one not so cold or one richer with game. In all likelihood, wanderers had already been there and reported back.

There are many theories as to who these people were, whence they came, and how many waves of them crossed over. According to the most recent genetic analysis, New World Indians descended from the group of hunters and foragers who moved into central Asia about forty thousand years ago and established themselves between the Altai Mountains and the headwaters of the Amur River. They had apparently started that journey ten thousand years earlier from the Persian Gulf Oasis, a rich alluvial plain dotted with oasis, fed by rivers and springs. Now inundated by the Persian Gulf, it was at the time a major mixing zone for plants and animals bordered by the Tigris and Euphrates flood plains, the Zagros Mountains, and the Arabian Peninsula. It was here that early humans formed a partnership with wolves from the Arabian and Iranian sides, who went with them when they set off on their collective, great migration.[7]

Their exact route is unknown, but on their way to the Caucasus and beyond, their dogwolves mixed with wolves and dogwolves from all directions. Its genomes destabilized by the cross-breeding, this miscegenated population is, I believe, the pool from which virtually all Native American dogs and many, if not all, types of dogs extant today are derived.

Other groups had their own dogwolves, to be sure, but few were as adept with wolves and dogs as these central Asians, possible forebears of the Turco-Mongol people who would repeatedly come off the steppes to change the world's history, of the Jomon of Japan, and of the proto-Koreans. According to myths prevalent in the Altaic region of central Asia and through much of North America, many of these groups believed so strongly that they were born of the union of a woman and a dog-man that their myths had the quality of revealed truth. Like the Dreamtime stories of Australia's Aborigines, they can provide a window deep into the past to confirm that central Asia was

the distributive hub, if not the birthplace, of the dog. These were hunting, and later pastoral, societies, farming only to supplement the meat
that they ate with their dogs.[9]

Another group leaving its refuge could have come out of the western Balkans or southeastern France, heading north into Europe. Southwestern France could have sent dogs into the Iberian Peninsula, which
also would have been receiving them from the Middle East by way of
North Africa, and north along the Atlantic coast to England and Denmark, when it opened. I am fairly confident that dogs resembling desert
pariahs traveled around the coast of India into Southeast Asia, specifically Thailand, and thence to Australia and north into China. But the
dogs could also have come southeast through China from central Asia,
the way Japanese dogs had come along the Amur River valley. A group
of dogs certainly could have come out of a Mediterranean or central
European refuge, perhaps even by incorporating the alleles for smallness, picked up from visitors or some of their own traders. And they
would have continued to come to trading posts off the steppe with
their dogs.

The Jomon people arrived in Japan from China around fourteen
thousand years ago with a small dog the size of a Shiba Inu and held
sway there for nearly twelve thousand years, during which time they
created what might be the oldest ceramic pottery in the world. Hunters
of pinnipeds and accomplished fishermen, the Jomon were dog lovers
who buried their favorites.

The Yayoi people entered northern Japan from China around
300 BC and quickly replaced the Jomon through war or epidemic or
both. Indeed, that seems their sole purpose, since they were gone by
AD 300. But in that time they not only deposed the Jomon but inverted

their value system and introduced agriculture as well. Unlike the hunting, dog-loving Jomon, the Yayoi favored their dogs in the pot. Yuichi Tanabe, the leading Japanese canine scholar, has said that the Yayoi were aberrant, that neither the Jomon nor modern Japanese would tolerate eating dogs. The Yayoi did contribute to Japanese dogs, however, by bringing dogs from Korea and perhaps the mainland, that mixed with local dogs to form geographically localized types. Only in the twentieth century were those types consolidated into breeds as a way to protect them from crossbreeding with Western dogs.[9]

Nearly all the genetic surveys, and the Chinese themselves, point to China as a center of wolf—not to mention human—domestication, and multiple mitochondrial studies place it first, especially the area below the Yangtze River, which the dog geneticists call Southeast Asia or China but which more correctly is part of southern China. That region covers the Yangtze's drainage from south of the Yellow River to Southeast Asia. There is evidence of dogs in some parts of the region from eight thousand years ago, but for a center of wolf domestication, the area seems deficient in wolves, dogs, and interacting dogs and people. It is true that people in the western part of the region continued to obtain most of their animal protein from wild game well into the Neolithic Age. They hunted deer, birds, pigs, and marmots, and they caught freshwater turtles and fish while harvesting shellfish. People living along the river were also among the earliest to domesticate rice. But the evidence for them having dogs much earlier than eight to ten thousand years ago is slim, and the dog was already old by then.

I suspect that early Asian dogs dispersed from the central Asian pool into northern China and Japan where the legends of wolves, men, and dogs were strongest. But others, like the dingo, would have come the southern route around India. Big Mongolian mastiffs from the east and terrier-size dogs from the west probably helped colonize the high

Tibetan Plateau around twelve thousand years ago. Big dogs are still used there to guard the flocks. In nearly all cases, except perhaps those from the steppes still following the carnivore route, these dogs and their people would, like other survivors emerging on the warm side of the Last Glacial Maximum, including wolves, have been generally smaller, less robust, and more gracile physically than their forebears on the cold side had been. The newcomers would in all likelihood have had the broadened, shortened nose of a dog.[10]

It was a downsizing born of many factors, including hardship and changing eating habits that removed selective evolutionary pressure on the nose and jaws of human and beast. But those changes could also have been amplified from crossbreeding with short-nosed wolves, which were not uncommon, as well as crosses between quite differently sized wolves. The exaggerations came later.

Warming weather speeded the pace of dispersal for people and dogs. It also seems to have brought cultural changes to the people who stayed in their refuges, more focused on building than on moving. Among those were social stratifications based on wealth and family. The new social order brought a change in funereal practice in some groups who renounced the habit of leaving their dead exposed to animals and elements in favor of burying them with their favorite objects, the symbols of their wealth and standing, among them small dogs.

Buried because of its rarity and value, the small dog became the most visible and sought-after marker for distinguishing dog from wolf—at least among modern archaeologists.

However it showed up, the small dog had an immediate and devoted following who guaranteed it would survive, whereas the high probability was that it would not have made it in the wild where freakishness is unwelcome. Thus, the first agreed-upon dog from the Middle East is a small dog, interred about 12,500 years ago with a person whose arm is resting over it at Mallaha, one of the earliest mud hut villages. It is believed an early sign of the increased sedentism of people in the Natufian and, as such, invoked as proof of the theories of dog origin based on sedentism and garbage dumps. When Mallaha was the oldest dog in the world, that theory made sense, and although with the discoveries of older, large dogs in hunting camps in western Europe, central Europe, Siberia, and even the Levant it no longer does, there are still people who insist that the first dog was "small."[11]

Other canid fossils found in the Middle East, their species not yet agreed upon but close enough to the dog to warrant more study, date from fourteen thousand to twenty-four thousand years ago in Krebara Cave, near the Mediterranean; twenty-five to thirty thousand years ago in another Krebara Cave level; and fifty-four thousand years ago in Tabun Cave, Mount Carmel, a site that could have coincided with human dispersal from the Middle East and subsequent spread into central Asia and then the New World. The small dog might be the first clearly identifiable dog—the dog from the Oberkassel double burial was small, too—but it is the first dog as a matter not of biology but of semantics and sociocultural context, which is to say, in a dead person's arms.

Small to smallish dogs abound around ten thousand years ago, showing up at Kongemore on Denmark's Atlantic coast; at Star Carr and Seamer Carr near Yorkshire on England's Atlantic coast—England was still part of the Continent at the time—and in the wetlands at Bedburg-Koningshoven, Germany. Other Mesolithic dogs have shown up from around seven thousand to seventy-six hundred years ago at Padina, on the upper part of the Danube Gorges in the north central Balkans. The Seamer, Kongemore, and Padina dogs fed on marine life, a habit I would bet their ancestors had acquired along with their humans measureless years before, and it had served their heirs well as they hopscotched up a coast that seemed to vanish in their wake as sea levels rose in the glacial meltdown. The Star Carr dog was apparently a deer and bird eater, a landlubber, with a large canid beside him, dubbed a wolf by many researchers, yet it is not clear that the animal has ever been tested to see what genetically it is. More likely, given the diversity of shapes and sizes of dogs from the beginning, one or more small-dog types spread over the land even while people continued their relationship with wolves and dogs that looked more like wolves than not.[12]

It is important to remember in dealing with the prehistoric socialized wolf and dogwolf that no one has ironclad proof for his or her favorite theory, but nearly everyone shares the fundamental human ability to express his or her own opinions as if they were revealed truth. They are not. No one knows with certainty what happened. But an array of different types of evidence points to the main event in the ancient Near East, today known as the wider Middle East, where an allele for smallness took hold in a cluster of dogwolves already derived from wolves that could be as small as twenty-five pounds and with the expanding human population following the last glacial meltdown quickly spread in five or six directions.

Looking at small dogs today, I would say that any type can be and probably has been, at one time or another, downsized. Because some remixing might be required to get there, the genetic profiles of the small dogs might sometimes look unfocused and confused in terms of ancestry. But they are the manifestation of a change from dogwolf to dog that otherwise might have gone unremarked until other mutations arose that, when captured, denoted a new animal who had been hiding in plain view.

FOURTEEN
What the New World Knew
That the Old One Did Not

*Did paleohunters and their dogs cause a
mass extinction? Small and large dogs
are everywhere in America where dogs are
the only "domesticated" animal for thousands
of years. They did just about everything else.
A young naturalist on the prowl.*

y sixteen thousand years ago, before the glacial retreat was
complete, the dog-born paleohunters from central Asia had
reached the New World, a land where humans of any vintage
had not gone before—or if they had, not impossibly, they left no
trace that has yet been found. The New World had every kind of
animal the paleo-hunters had pursued in Eurasia, plus a few new
ones, so they must have felt like they had fallen into happy hunting
grounds. They hunted so efficiently and ruthlessly that they wiped
out entire groups of related species, or genera, in one of the great
mass extinctions on record, according to paleogeologist Paul S. Martin—thirty-three of forty-five genera of mammals weighing more
than one hundred pounds in North America and forty-six of fifty-
eight in South America. Martin believes that the paleohunter invasion of the New World amounted to a hunting blitzkrieg that was

completed over several centuries from the Arctic down to Tierra del Fuego.[1,2]

Mammoths, mastodons, *Bison antiquus* and *B. occidentalis*, giant rhinos, cave bears, giant ground sloths, camels, flightless rheas, tortoise-shelled glyptodonts, the indigenous horse—all fell to the arrows and spears of paleohunters. When they went down, the carnivores who fed on them could only follow. Those were familiar too: saber-toothed cats, giant lions, and dire wolves and other bone-crushing canids. Their demise spelled the end of entire ecosystems. Since Martin's thesis first came out in the 1960s, he has defended and expanded it, along with other researchers who have now applied the blitzkrieg theory of Pleistocene extinctions, as it is known, to the extirpations of the moas and other large, flightless birds on New Zealand, as well as to an earlier mass extinction on Australia that has been dated to the arrival of anatomically modern humans around fifty-five to sixty-five thousand years ago.

A more logical and accurate explanation holds that rapidly warming—melting—temperatures, rising humidity, and transformed biomes were taking a severe toll on the large, cold-adapted animals. They could not get the food they wanted because the vegetation had changed, or, if they could, it was insufficient to their needs. They were built to retain heat, not to dissipate it, but they could not turn their metabolisms around. In a warming world, they were slow-cooking themselves to extinction.

That does not deny the evidence periodically found at a stampede-hunting site or mammoth kill site of profligate mayhem. In Wyoming, hunters, perhaps with dogs, sent more than one hundred of the huge *Bison antiquus* over a bluff to their deaths from the fall or subsequently from hunters. Similar hunts had occurred in Spain and France and on the Mammoth Steppe, usually for bison or reindeer, but there, too, their frequency is unknown. Fierce storms, fire, and wolves could cause fatal stampedes, as well, so that even if frequency were known, the cause might not be human at all. Evidence that paleohunters shifted away from their preference for reindeer and horse once they arrived in the New World and discovered they could kill mammoths is also far from conclusive. Nor is it clear why they could not have killed mammoths on the steppe. On the order of six to eight sites of human mammoth kills have been identified, hardly enough to cause an extinction. Even in the New World, it seems, the furless biped preferred more manageable game.

The blitzkrieg theory is dependent on a number of assumptions, among them that the group or groups who became known as the Clovis people, after the site in New Mexico where their distinctive stone points were first identified and dated to 13,500 years ago, were the first people to enter the New World; and that they pushed the megafauna of the Americas to extinction with their aggressive, wasteful hunting. Completely naïve about the new biped and its capabilities, many of the animals were easy marks.

The new date of sixteen thousand years ago, for when the first Americans crossed the thousand-mile-long, fifty-five-mile-wide Bering Land Bridge, has begun to gain some acceptance and offers an alternative to the blitzkrieg model. What we have now are one or more groups of various size from that first central Asian migration reaching land's end in Tierra del Fuego thirteen to fourteen thousand years ago, most assuredly with dogs moving along beside them, and little idea where they had got to or why.

Thousands of years later in calendar years, but perhaps not so far when measured against the daily rhythm of life of the people, who followed the old ways of their ancestors back to their beginnings, without change and challenge, the young naturalist aboard H.M.S. *Beagle*, Charles Darwin, had an open window into Neolithic traditions and dogs. He watched the Yahgan people of Tierra del Fuego, South America, use terrier-size, web-footed dogs they carried from island to island in their dugouts to hunt down wounded otters—the mainstays of their existence. Up the coast in Patagonia, the Chono people used a similar dog to herd fish into traps and nets.[3]

Other people and their dogs went on to fill two continents. Around six thousand years ago in a separate migration, the Inuit and Aleut island-hopped in skin-clad canoes and kayaks across the Bering Strait to take up residence along the far northern shore from Alaska, for the Aleuts, to Greenland, for the Inuit.

In the Americas, the central Asians drifted apart and banded together by choice and by force, following their own historical and evolutionary path, so that the first domesticated animal in the Western Hemisphere was in many regards the last, with exceptions and qualifiers. In South America, llamas and vicunas were domesticated, as were guinea pigs and turkeys in Central America, along with certain plants, including cacao, coca, tobacco, maize, and tomato.

On the Great Plains, Indian dogs and wolves intermingled and interbred freely well into the nineteenth century, when all three were attacked with savagery by Anglo-Americans. The Indians and wolves survived, after a fashion. Indian dogs by all accounts did not, save for the Chihuahua, the smallest and one of the most aggressive of them all, a dog used variously for chow and for companionship. The Chihuahua, I suspect, is a ringer, either a cross between the German hunting terrier and a native dog or a nineteenth-century Chinese import.

Along the Atlantic coast, early settlers also reported that the wolf they encountered, commonly believed to be *Canis rufus*, looked very much like the Indian dog and often was mistaken for it. I suspect that around some Eastern tribes, dogs so intermingled with wolves that they were indistinguishable, like they were on the Plains. Conditions were different in South America, where *C. lupus* had no hold and the local canids had no connection to the dog or the sudden extinctions, unless they served as vectors for disease and parasites brought to the New World by dogs and people. The mass extinction in South America was more severe than in the North, and some of that might have been due to human hunting, but it is more likely that the large South American animals were victims of a changing world to which they could not adapt faster than they died.

Attempts to tie dogs and hunters to the disappearance of seven out of twenty-three genera of Eurasian animals over one hundred pounds—including bison, cave bears, cave lions, scimitar cats, and saber-toothed cats—have largely failed, as well, with the jury still out on the demise of Neanderthal, which would rank as the most spectacular, and ghastly, human-caused extinction of all.

Thanks to the naturalists who traveled among America's Indian tribes before they were militarily beaten and culturally smashed, there is some record of the way they used dogs that might be applicable, to a degree, to wandering and gathering people of Europe, disregarding significant differences in weaponry. Small dogs offered enormous benefits not only as companions but as hunters capable of flushing everything from a badger to a bear or an elk, as well as killing rats in the village. The Tlingit and Tahltan people of Western Canada kept small black-and-white dogs they carried in baskets until their big hunting dogs had bayed a bear. Then they let loose the little black-and-white dogs to harass and distract the bear while the hunters moved in for the kill. The Clatsop tribe at the mouth of the Columbia River used a smallish dog with prick ears and a long, thin nose to bay elk.

Various small, but not dwarfed, dogs were found throughout the Americas and often prized for their hunting and fishing abilities. In Patagonia, people hunted guanacos, a variety of wild camel, and the flightless rhea, now gone, with small, wire-haired wolflike dogs. In the high Andes, paleo-Indians hunted alpaca and llamas until around six thousand years ago when they began to corral and herd them with the help of dogs. They had a small collie or sheltie-type hunting and herding dog; a tall, long-haired mastiff-type dog who guarded children, herds, and villages; and a pug-nosed dog from the Andes highlands.

The people of coastal Peru were active participants in trade involving the most bizarre dog in the Americas—the hairless dog isolated by the Colima Indians of Mexico about AD 250. Hairlessness in dogs is caused by a lethal dominant allele or mutation, which makes offspring with one copy hairless, and with two copies dead, spontaneously aborted. It is often associated with bizarre dentition. Always a hairless dog must be mated with a normal dog, producing a mixed litter. *Xoloitzcuintli,* as they are known still in Mexico, came in three sizes— medium, small, and smaller—and were valued as bed warmers and cure-alls for various ailments who could also be sacrificed to break drought or eaten for medicinal purposes.

Anthropologist Alana Cordy-Collins found that the dogs were traded down the coast to Peru, into other parts of South America and the Caribbean. In fact, Peru had its own variant, the Inca Orchid. Demand for the nude dogs outstripped supply, so breeders—or suppliers—rubbed turpentine on puppies, causing them to lose their hair.[4]

Many American Indian tribes ate dog—generally small dogs or puppies—at least on ceremonial occasions or as part of religious rites, and some of them consumed it regularly. Dogs were sacrificed and eaten to seal alliances between tribes; to welcome special guests; at weddings, deaths, and other special occasions; to promote healing; and to purify warriors and hunters. In the third century BC, in Florida, Timucuans of central Florida ate their small dogs and hunted with their large ones. The Taino of the Caribbean had small dogs, *aons*, they pampered and used for hunting *hutia*, a large rodent, and iguanas. Some they castrated, fattened like piglets, and grilled. The maize-cultivating Huron of the Northeast raised dogs for consumption on special feast days, including those decreed by the shaman to hasten healing of the sick and to mark the New Year. The Mayans of Guatemala from 1000 to 600 BC fed corn to the dogs before they killed them for ceremonial purposes, supposedly to make them more succulent. Feeding grain to dogs was a worldwide practice after the advent of agriculture, a dietary shift that played out in their phenotypes.[5]

Dog eating seems largely a matter of taste, of cultural tradition. Some tribes in the Americas eschewed the practice, with those like the Inca in Peru and the Shoshone on the Great Plains viewing dog eaters with contempt. Athabascan people from Alaska to the Southwest ate no dog. It has been common to interpret the rituals that often accompanied the practice as proof of the overall importance of the dog to Native American societies. In truth, we today, even avowed dog lovers, can barely glimpse what it would be like to be so reliant on a single animal—or perhaps we can picture it all too well, and it disturbs us. Many Plains Indian tribes organized themselves by societies—fraternal groups of warriors who lived under a totem animal, usually. Among the Cheyenne and several other tribes, the fiercest, strongest warriors belonged to the Crazy Dog Society.

Little wonder that many tribes sacrificed a dog or more on the death of its person. Meriwether Lewis came upon a scaffold holding the corpse of a woman and two harnessed dogs. A third large dog lay at the foot of the scaffold, killed, he surmised, when her body was laid to rest as its "reward" for dragging her to her final resting place.[6]

Dogs' importance as companions and guides is manifest in burials from around the world, not least in North America where they are interred with their people or near them, to help them find their way to the next life. A number of groups followed the ways of their forebears in the Altai Mountains in considering themselves part dog, including many Athabascan people, and the Tlingit of the Northwest coast.

The year was 1769. Samuel Hearne, a young officer for the Hudson's Bay Company sent to search for the mythic Northwest Passage, spent time with the Chipewyans, an Athabascan people of the Canadian plains, and learned their myths, including the account of their creation. The first person on earth was a woman, they told him. She had been alone for some time when one day, while out picking berries, she encountered a dog who followed her back to her cave. That night and for many nights to come, the dog transformed himself into a handsome young man, only to turn back into a dog, so that the woman believed that what happened at night was hallucination or delusion, but it was not. She became pregnant, and immediately a man whose head reached the clouds appeared, and with his walking stick leveled the roughly formed earth and created lakes, rivers, and ponds. He then seized the dog and tore it to pieces, throwing its entrails into the water to become fish, scattering its flesh to become animals, and tossing its skin into the air to become birds. His work done, he vanished, but not before telling the woman that she and her offspring by Dog-man would have the power to kill and eat all that he had created for them.[7]

Native American dogs received their first and last full review and analysis from Harvard University zoologist Glover M. Allen in 1920, by which time, he admitted, a pure representative was not to be found. The only known exceptions to Allen's pronouncement among American dogs, according to Heidi Parker's genetic assessments, are the diminutive Chihuahua, the wolflike Alaskan Malamute, and the Siberian husky, a more recent immigrant included because the northern sled dogs are considered transarctic in their range. Those recent findings have spurred searches for more relict indigenous dogs, especially on reservations and in South and Central America, through mountain valleys and jungles.[8]

Allen divided Native American dogs into three classes on the basis of location, relative size, and overall appearance: wolflike Eskimo dogs; wolflike Indian dogs; and small Indian dogs found in the Southwest, Caribbean, southern Mexico, and South America. He subdivided his three main groups into seventeen types, without paying much heed to the dynamic movement of populations and subsequent mixing of dogs, which gave some types wide distribution. He believed, for example that the wolflike Eskimo dogs had become larger since Anglo-Europeans had begun using them as draft animals. More difficult to define were the wolflike Indian dogs, who ranged in size from small to large and in territory from interior Alaska through Canada and the Great Plains to Florida and down the West Coast into Mexico, with some types appearing in the Andes and Patagonia. This group included the large Sioux Indian dog who mingled freely with wolves and was often indistinguishable from them; the medium-sized Plains Indian dog who came in some shade of tawny or black and gray; and the large, common Indian dog who was black and white or all black. They could easily have been variations of the same basic dog or wolf.

Paleoanthropologist George Frison, who exposed the description of paleohunters swarming and killing a mammoth in a bog as sheer imagination because mammoths were at home in bogs and would only be trapped there if already old and infirm, examined remains of prehistoric dogs in Wyoming and concluded that crosses to wolves were common and resulted in a very wolflike dog in need of perpetual retaming and redomestication. His conclusion seems largely a matter of conviction since the bones say little about the animal's level of domestication, and visiting nineteenth-century naturalists usually reported the opposite. For example, Maximilian, Prince of Wied, a world traveler and naturalist, who visited the northern Plains tribes in the early 1830s, observed that the dogs appearing most wolflike behaved like all the other dogs in their tribal pack.[9,10] The observation matches ethologist Erik Zimen's comment more than a century later that among his cross-bred poodles and wolves often the most wolflike in behavior was the most doglike in appearance.

In his classifications of North American dogs, Allen attempted to recognize as many unique types as he could; indeed, the proliferation of different types of dogs from what must have been a limited initial assortment that accompanied an equally undifferentiated collection of humans into Alaska is astounding in its own right. Dog hair was used for clothes and blankets. Dogs were sacrificed to the gods in thanks or contrition. Dogs were medicine and food. They were also herders, hunters, companions, and haulers.

The women of the Clallam tribe kept isolated on its own Puget Sound island a dog whose wooly black and white hair they used for weaving clothes and blankets—until the Hudson's Bay Company blanket rendered the dogs obsolete in the nineteenth century. By the end of that century many of the native dogs of the Americas had met the same fate.

In many ways, the story of the dogs of the Apache encapsulates the history of the dog in America, from its crossing of Beringia through the struggle of its people against colonialism and genocide. Around AD 500, ancestral pueblo people, as the group that preceded the builders of the pueblos in New Mexico and Arizona are known, buried a long-haired, large white dog with a coyote-like small dog and a person—one assumes their person—in what became known as White Dog Cave. They are called "Basketmaker dogs," for the human cultural tradition current at the time in that corridor. Like the Clallam, these people wove dog hair into clothing.

About the time the Basketmaker dogs were being buried, several bands of Athabascans tied packs on those among their large wolflike dogs—perhaps a thousand or more animals—who would tolerate them, and headed south from their interior Alaska homes down the spine of the Rockies. Finally they reached the Southwest, where they found something that made them stay. They became the Apache and Navajo, and ultimately adopted sheep husbandry using dogs and methods for raising them learned from the Catholic priests at the missions that had invaded their country—not that they had much choice.

The Apache achieved fame for the dedication of their sheepdogs, who were raised from birth with sheep in the Spanish tradition so that they would bond to them. The Spanish had brought their big white sheep-guarding mastiffs with them to the New World, in the sixteenth century, along with their sheep and goats. Some of those appear to have mixed with Apache dogs who tended to have distinctive copper spots above their eyes and white paws—thought by the Apache to represent the sun and morning light and taken to mean that they would protect their people as long as they lived.

By the end of the nineteenth century, the Apache were the smaller of the two tribes, numbering perhaps six thousand split among small bands and persecuted on both sides of the Mexican-American border. Bands of Apaches seeking to escape pursuing troops repeatedly had to slit their dogs' throats to keep their howls and barks at night from betraying their position—thereby depriving themselves of their helpmate and protector.

The Americans wantonly killed the Apache dogs, too. Charles Fletcher Lummis, an editor for the *Los Angeles Daily Times,* described what happened at Fort Bowie on April 7, 1886, when the wife of Goyahtlay, a Bedonkohe medicine man known to the Americans as Geronimo, came in with their children and others of their band, their horses, and their dogs. The Apache were quickly locked in train cars and sent on their way to Fort Apache from where they would be sent to exile in

Florida. Already stressed by the initial separation, their dogs followed the train, yelping and howling their distress. A single runner kept pace with the locomotive before dropping back in exhaustion. After the train was gone, the locals shot dogs and horses for sport, pleasure, and vengeance.

Geronimo was captured not long after, and soon all the free Apache were languishing and dying in prison in Florida. Although he ultimately became a celebrity of sorts, Geronimo was never allowed to return to Arizona, so much fear did he arouse in people even as a disarmed old man. But some of his people did return early in the last century, and they still struggle to get by.

The more numerous and sedentary Navajo fought their own battles to preserve their independence and ended up with a dry, high desert reservation in New Mexico and Arizona, remarkable for its stark sandstone formations, its light, colors, and uranium deposits where the grandmothers and daughters tend to care for the sheep and goats, aided by small dogs that look like the little Basketmaker dog. These are the dogs people trap and steal in their efforts to reconstruct Native American dogs.[11]

In Scandinavia, another two groups of hunters, at least one with roots to the Pleistocene—by culture if not genetics—and their dogs present an interesting parallel that reinforces how close to wolf these early dogs were, until people began actively manipulating the phenotype. In May 2010, Peter Savolainen, who has consistently said that China below the Yangtze River is the center of dog domestication, introduced a partial exception. He and a group of Finnish and Swedish researchers proposed that the Finnish Lapphund, Lapponian herder, and Swedish Lapphund—all reindeer-herding dogs of the indigenous Sami people—and several varieties of Norwegian and Swedish elkhounds originated in northern Scandinavia 480 to 3,000 years ago from crossbreedings of local dogs with wolves. Looking like short-nosed wolves with curly, spitz-like tails, these are sturdy, stolid dogs who sleep outside in the coldest weather, curled up on themselves, heads covered with their tails. Some years ago in Finland, I was reminded forcefully of the timeless transportability of the dog, when I watched a Lapponian herder jump on the back of a little dirt back and speed off with a Sami reindeer herder in traditional dress to round up some reindeer for a tourist show-and-tell.[12]

Lapponian herder, Arctic Circle, Finland

FIFTEEN
Call Me Shepherd;
Call Me Dog

*Agriculture arrives to stay as plants show the
evolutionary way to domestication. Transhumance
replaces following the herds. Dogwolf makes a
choice and ever after bears the marks.*

In the northern Iraqi foothills of the Zagros Mountains, west of
Kirkuk on the border with Iran, some fourteen thousand years
ago, a band of people archaeologists have called Zarzi came upon
a cave they decided to call home. History has known the site since
1950 as Palegawra Cave, a dry spot in a warming world, with pista-
chios and almonds growing outside and wild horses grazing on the
steppe vegetation. Horse hunters like their forebears from before
time, the Zarzi apparently came with dogs: A sediment layer dated
to twelve thousand years ago held a piece of a dog that, reconstructed, looked for all the world like a dingo, according to the
archaeologists who studied it carefully to make sure it was no wolf.
The dingo type is represented in this region by the Bedouin/Canaan
dog, and the Palegawra dog appears to confirm a connection

between those tent guards and the frequent subject of Aboriginal Dreamtime.[1]

Palegawra represented a way of life that was already fading from the Middle East. People had moving from their dark, dank caves, into dwellings they constructed from unbaked clay or wood and hides or stone. The dawning Neolithic Revolution marked a fundamental change in the people's relationship to food, not only in terms of what they ate but how they got it. They went from taking—bringing down prey and gathering what Nature produced—to handling eventually all stages of the production of their food—planting, nurturing, harvesting, preparing, and preserving it from other animals while planning to do the same in the next season. They also had to learn the ways now not only of carnivores and big grazers but of birds and other creatures, from squirrels to bears, who watched and waited for the moment of ripening to strip a tree bare of fruit or denude a berry patch overnight. Stopping them became a large issue.

Changing diets meant morphological changes for people and their dogs, as we have seen. They also produced changes in the landscape around the villages or camps. Seeds sprouted in midden heaps or where birds and animals, including people, had spread them, leading to greater concentrations that in turn made the site a more attractive place to settle. Villagers began to collect and plant their own seeds in sites of their choosing—not all of which proved good choices. Plant cultivation did not proceed smoothly, as every frustrated gardener knows. But people relatively quickly began to cultivate grapes, figs, dates, barley, einkorn and emmer wheat.

They turned their backs on their traditional hunting practice of taking only mature adults and, borrowing several pages from the wolf book of practical predation, they began driving goats and sheep into pens and selectively slaughtering the young and females who were past their reproductive prime. They left the young females and mature males to produce more offspring. In due course, these animals became more tractable for humans and dogs.

That might sound like a dodge, but livestock that goes back to the wild side and living independently has to be trained all over again to obey dogs and humans. This reversion happens in large measure because in evolutionary terms, the organisms that adapt to changing circumstances and contexts are those with the best chance of survival—and an important key to that is avoiding predators, including dogs.

In the ranch country of central Florida, the tradition of working cows with curdogs goes back at least 150 years, when cow hunters started rousting feral Spanish cattle out of the scrub on the Palmetto Prairie and driving it to ports on the Gulf of Mexico for sale to Cuba. The landrace of small Spanish cattle is nearly gone, replaced by various-

Catahoula leopard dogs working cattle, Louisiana

blooded stock, but the tradition remains like an old, familiar habit largely because there is no better way to collect the herds and because the people doing it like dogs. Some families have bred their own lines for multiple human generations. I know one rancher who had on his large ranch more feral cattle than he could count. They were there when his father bought the place and they had been there for his twenty-five years. Then he turned to dogs.

My dad used to round up a few head every year with trucks and sell them. They'd pound on the roof of the truck chasing 'em one at time into the corral. I tell you that was cruelty to animals. He'd never used dogs. They were banned for the screw worms when he brought the place because if they bit the cow, you know, they'd lay their eggs in the wound and the larva would just eat 'em up. Anyway, he wasn't into cows much and didn't really know what was there. So I asked him when I came home if I could have the cattle, and he said sure. I knew there was ranch families that had never gave up their dogs, so I talked to some of 'em and decided to bring in some dogs to hunt my cows out of the swamp and thickets and redomesticate them. These cows had been born and died out there for generations without people or dogs in their way. They were wild. I knew I needed some "rank and raily" dogs to hunt 'em. And so I hired a guy who was a cow hunter and he had these dogs near as wild as the cows. Those dogs just charged into scrub and swamp and drove them cows out to an open field. Then they'd "windmill" 'em, run circles around 'em to make 'em bunch up like they do with the calves inside and their horns pointing out. Once we got 'em bunched, we called the dogs back till the cows settled down and then we pushed 'em toward the corral. It took some years, I'll tell you, to get 'em all and get 'em used to the dogs, and those that wouldn't get used to the dogs, I turned to hamburger. I got my own dogs now. They're easier on the cows because you don't need those wild curdogs once you got the cows tame. But it always helps to have one or two of 'em around for when you need 'em.

People relied on dogs to herd and guard, not hunt and kill, their livestock, and so they began actively favoring those who did that best while killing or ignoring those who could not master the new rules. They also needed hunters, since they still brought game to the table, as well as guards for the village and the granaries. They used their small dogs for the latter, and another carnivore, a little wild cat from the Fertile Crescent who started patrolling on its own accord.

Some nine thousand years ago, a group of about 150 men, women, and children, with nearly as many dogs—the remains of 103 were excavated in the 1940s—built a village known to us as Jormo, not far from Palegawra Cave. It is one of the first agricultural villages found in the world from an area often called the Fertile Crescent, the birthplace of civilization—a bit extreme, but the flood plains of the Tigris and Euphrates rivers are certainly among civilization's birthplaces. The Jormo farmers grew lentils, wheat, barley, dates, and flowers. They raised sheep and goats, and added pigs and cattle along with their dogs. The livestock was under their control. The dogs were a more individualistic matter, but if they were good, they were hoarded.

The Neolithic Revolution rolled over the world, altering the species involved, the way and places people lived, what they ate, what they looked like, how their brains were wired; their social, economic, and political structures; and their relationship with other people and animals. Before they were done, humans would with their new tools and draft animals alter ecosystems and ultimately whole landscapes more profoundly than the glaciers, because few places would escape agriculture's transformative power. The days of the small band of ten to twenty-five hunters and gatherers were numbered, except for a few who managed to linger in places time seems to have bypassed—with an emphasis on "seems" because the question has never been whether but when change would come to them, even if it took thousands of years.

In Europe the changes came swiftly, as farmers began moving from the Fertile Crescent and Anatolia through the Balkans seventy-five hundred years ago and into Eastern Europe and then west to the Paris Basin within five hundred years, accompanied always by their distinctive pottery styles, and burning to open new fields as they went. They doubtless brought dogs with them that mixed in with the dog-wolves that still dominated northern Europe and the Eurasian steppes. But how far west the migrating farmers went is subject to debate. Some genetic evidence suggests that paleohunters adopted their agricultural practices while blocking their advance.[2]

In southern China, the area from the Huang He (Yellow) River to Southeast Asia and including the Yangtze River, proposed home of the dog, the transition from the Paleolithic to Neolithic ran from sixteen to ten thousand years ago, almost longer than the Neolithic itself. During that transitional period, people in the region began to make pottery, harpoons, shell knives, and bows and arrows. Over the next eight thousand years, different areas in the middle and lower Yangtze alluvial plain, the southern Nanling Mountains, and the Youngai Plateau to the south served as centers of activity, and then fell into decline and were abandoned.[3]

By eight thousand years ago, people along the Yangtze had dogs and pigs, both used for food. Some experts argue that large mastiff-type guard dogs were also present, but that is difficult to confirm. Dogs were not the priority for the people of the Yangtze River basin the way they were in places like northwestern China where they were becoming increasingly common and important hunting companions. By six thousand years ago, all parts of China had small, medium, and large dogs, with brachycephalic dogs in each group. From five thousand to thirty-five hundred years ago, people on the upper Yangtze were still living as hunters and foragers, while lower on the river pigs became increasingly important in the local food economy. About that same time, people appear finally to have domesticated rice, a feat also accomplished by Indian farmers.

If the wolf came into human orbit largely through the forces of natural selection, so did plants. The late anthropologist David Rindos in his seminal study, *The Origins of Agriculture,* theorized that plants were domesticated as a result of people harvesting wild plants and throwing the seeds in the midden heap or on the ground of the camp-sites they occupied seasonally. The plants took root and over time built up their numbers, making the site more attractive to the roam-ing hunters looking for food supplements. They would return to the same site, and over time the concentration of favorable food and plants would become greater, to the point in some places of becoming a sacred grove. This process reinforced the growing sedentism of the people and led eventually to an agricultural settlement where people tried to avoid future disasters and shortages by laying in stores of plants and seeds.[4]

Animal domestication proceeded along with plants. Like it had been with dogs, the process was cultural and biological, and in recent years, archaeologists and geneticists have repeatedly documented mul-tiple origins for many domesticated species. An exception may be the horse, and that would be an odd one, given the fondness of paleo-hunters for horse meat, only surpassed, if at all, by their desire for rein-deer. Although consensus has yet to emerge, current thinking seems to center horse domestication—first for mare's milk—on the Botai culture of the Eurasian steppe in the area of Kazakhstan around fifty-five hun-dred years ago, followed by mixing with local wild stock as it spread and became transformed from an object solely of consumption to the main and favored mode of transportation for thousands of years to come. Not to be outdone, the African wild ass joined the ranks of domesticates about the same time as the horse—in Egypt.[5]

More animals followed in the parade of domestication, although the argument is frequently made that domestication is a rare and special event that only a few predisposed animals could have experienced. That may be, but I would propose that no one really knows how hard or easy it would be to domesticate a species until they have tried—the Siberian foxes were not that hard, once an effort was made. In fact, Neolithic farmers in short order domesticated their favorite mammal prey—horses, reindeer, aurochs, goats, sheep, asses and donkeys, cats, Asian elephants and African elephants of the subspecies Hannibal would later lead across the Alps to invade Rome, yaks, water buffalo, various Southeast Asian wild cattle, ducks, chickens, rabbits, rats, and mice. In the New World it was, turkeys, guinea pigs, llamas, alpacas, vicunas, and occasionally the bush dog and raccoon dog. More recently, humans have added catfish, trout, salmon, shrimp, and other marine organisms to the list.

The list is expansionist in that I have included species like the Asian elephant that reproduce in the wild but nonetheless are tamed and have been employed by humans for thousands of years in parts of Southeast Asia, India, and Sri Lanka; and wild cattle, like kouprey and *benteng,* which, following ancient patterns of domestication in the region, breed without human interference or direction. The dogs do that, too. I have also included reindeer who, despite increased fencing, continue to migrate across the Arctic, followed by the Sami people and their dogs.

Categories begin to fade and blur when captive-bred zoo animals and feral animals are added to the discussion. Most populations of zoo animals are today maintained by selective breeding for wildness as defined by humans. They are more carefully bred than any free-ranging or feral domestic animal, yet with the exception of the dingo, the feral animal remains a domesticated one, while the captive animal, which has never walked beyond its cage, continues to be called "wild."

No record exists of how Neolithic herders gathered their animals, but logic says their dogs were essential in a process that is similar to the wolf tactic of driving a herd or group of animals into a box canyon or bog from which there is little hope of escape. Dogs and men had to learn not to move in and start killing once they had the game corralled. They had to learn to defend their livestock against their own kin if necessary.

They still hunted, too, these early dogs, guarded camps, and by this point were used to carry or haul. Neolithic dogs were widespread and numerous, large, medium, and small, black, yellow, ginger, white and combinations thereof. And more than a few were wild or nearly so.

The form of early agriculture helped shape the postglacial landscape, while the people engaged in it physically and culturally refashioned human societies. They practiced swidden, or slash and burn, farming—cutting trees or scrub and torching the downed wood and undergrowth to ash, then sewing their seeds.

The herders traveled with their flocks or herds, often of sheep, goats, cattle, yaks, or whatever other grazing animals they had, and dogs to usually high pastures in the spring and to the warmer valleys in the fall. At some point in this process, they began burning the fields in the spring, in order to ensure the growth of new grass. Separating natural from set fires is often difficult, especially when the burning took place thousands of years ago, but fundamentally the human fires were intended to enhance the effect of or anticipate seasonal rains prior to the move into those pastures. *seasonal movement of people w livestock - sum wtr pastures.*

In one form or another transhumance was based on the migratory patterns of the herds humans hunted and probably was used, in fact, in the initial capture of those animals. The rhythm of the herds' migration served as the basis for the movements of herders and their livestock, with distances varying according to topography, climatic conditions, and pasturage, but once established locally, the routes persisted, albeit with modification, until the system itself vanished. In most areas of the world it persisted long enough for tradition to be codified into law but could not survive industrialized farming and ranching that sealed off traditional routes in order to protect their property.

The forms of this early agriculture helped reshape whole ecosystems, according to some paleoecologists. Deforestation was an obvious result of the spread of farms and repeated burnings. Grazing and burning of pasturage are said to have contributed significantly to the suppression of tree growth and maintenance of the grassland/scrub landscape that defines the Mediterranean ecosystem and keeps many mountainsides free of trees even below the tree line. Suppression of those traditional burns has led in many parts of the world to periodic catastrophic fires and degraded pasture.

Like the society of humans, the society of dogs was stratifying, beyond the divide of large and small. With populations expanding, people played favorites, choosing dogs with the intelligence or agility or sociability or skill at a particular useful task to accompany them, while leaving the rest to fend for themselves in the growing pool of dogs scavenging around the camp. In some parts of the world where hunting and gathering persisted, unwanted dogs were probably absorbed into the native wolf population. But where wolves were less numerous, that assembly of cast-off dogs became a genetic reservoir, with dogs moving from it fully into the human orbit or outward from that inner circle, based on their sociability, intelligence, and utility.

This process was at work at Dadiwan, a seasonal hunting camp in northwestern China, north of Tibet and of the Huang He River, where it is too cold for rice cultivation. There, around seventy-nine hundred years ago, hunters began intensively harvesting broomcorn millet for supplementing meat they and their dogs were getting from hunting several species of deer and apparently wild pigs. They drew their dogs from a larger pool of wild dogs, taking the most social, who were also most likely to help them on the hunt. If they worked, they were rewarded with food—the same food the humans ate—millet and meat from the hunt, plus whatever they could scavenge or kill on their own. A chief reason for these hunters to make a trip to the millet camp every year was to ensure they had sufficient provisions to feed themselves and their hunting dogs. The dogs who failed as hunters were eaten or ignored and allowed to rejoin the larger group of camp followers, so they could be eaten another day or produce a talented hunter. Those camp followers could have been either dogwolves or dogs, or more likely a mix of the two. Wild dogs lived on what they could forage or kill and received nothing from the hunters, reported Loukas Barton of the U.S. National Park Service and colleagues from the United States and China in 2009 in the *Proceedings of the National Academy of Sciences*. Such a change in diet can be a trigger for some of the morphological changes associated with domestication in humans, dogs, and grain, they wrote.[6]

Abandoned around seventy-two hundred years ago, Dadiwan was reoccupied seven hundred years later by people from the Yangshao Neolithic culture, who were full-time farmers raising pigs, dogs, and two kinds of millet—cultivating their own foxtail millet, as well as the local broomcorn millet. They fed millet to themselves, their hunting dogs, and pigs, thereby rewarding participants in what the zoologists call an "early integrated agricultural system" that met all their dietary needs. In this case, the heavy reliance on millet helped trigger changes in their morphologies, adding substance to the phrase "You are what you eat." Reflecting the difference between a hunting camp and early agricultural village, the camp-following wild dogs had vanished.[7]

Around 3500 BC, a population explosion in Southern China was accompanied by a rise in larger farming villages, separated by stretches of unused land—some of it perhaps played-out land from slash and burn. Farmers had adopted plows and begun to cultivate rice successfully and to push into southwestern China, formerly the land of hunters. By 2500 BC, pigs accounted for 70 percent of the terrestrial meat consumed in southern China, chicken a large portion of the rest. It seems that dogs were either in the pot or guarding it from people and other dogs in a society growing more rigid and hierarchical by the day.

Dogs appear in rock art in Bhimbetka, in central India, where the petroglyphs were painted over tens of thousands of years, as a visual history. Dating from eight to five thousand years ago, the beginning of the Indian Neolithic, several of the dogs are on leashes and apparently are hunting with their humans. The art is hardly refined, but it does indicate that the dog was probably all over India by then, and that it had a variety of uses. My guess is that they came into the subcontinent by way of the Iranian Plain, or from the northwest, and from various points along the coast all the way to Southeast Asia. They would have been of the dingo type. But India also appears to have free-ranging dogs of the Akita type, and so it would seem that the Indian dogs have several influences from the Middle East, Europe, and eastern Asia. Recent mitochondrial genetic work has suggested that the Indian wolf and Himalayan wolf are from lineages far more ancient than the gray wolf and thus played no role in the dog, something I believe needs more study.[8]

The numerous free-ranging dogs of India, like those elsewhere, have seldom been closely studied in terms of their behavior and relationship with humans. As a result, they are usually cast by Western "experts" as pariahs, ownerless dogs who live off the offal of the community, as direct evolutionary heirs of the self-domesticated Mesolithic dog. I raise the point again here because a recent study showed that in the country, at least, these dogs receive most of their calories from human-derived sources. Much of that is put out for them by their [non]owners, the households they watch over, according to a study of free-ranging dogs in a village abutting the Great Indian Bustard Sanctuary in central India, published in the *Journal of Mammalogy* in 2009.[9]

The study's authors, Abi Tamim Vanak and Matthew E. Gomper, divided the village dogs into three broad categories—herding dogs who accompany livestock beyond developed agricultural fields to natural grasslands by day; farm dogs who own the interface between plowed fields and natural grasslands and have a population density of 24 dogs per square kilometer, and village dogs at 113 animal per square kilometer who seldom venture into the plowed fields, much less the natural grasslands. Vanak and Gomper did not address a fourth zone—inside the house, where puppies and dogs are occasionally taken. The dogs' diets tended toward the vegetarian, with 40.7 percent put out by humans and composed primarily of millet bread and scraps; 25.8 percent of farm crops, like corn and millet, grapes, and other vegetation; 18.3 percent from scavenged large-mammal carcasses, wild and domestic; and 15 percent from small creatures hunted and killed, including birds and snakes. Calling these dogs dump-dependent pariahs represents a leap of imagination past the reality on the ground. In composition, their diet closely resembles that of American dogs who daily chow down on expensive dry dog foods, comprised of grains and cereals, meat by-products, and vegetables, supplemented by table scraps that can be anything from choice cuts of meat to wilted salad greens.[10]

Pigs and chickens, like dogs and other livestock, had become nearly universal, as the stone ages of humans began to yield to the ages of metallurgy, democracy, and empire, which forced changes upon dogs, especially around the Mediterranean. By one recent account, maternal lineages from Neolithic dogs in southwest France, Italy, and Sweden—

and, because of that geographic array, it is thought from most of Europe—were replaced completely in centuries to come by conquest and breeding. Wolf lineages changed as well, due primarily to persecution that would only intensify, as societies grew more rigid and wild became unacceptable to "civilized" life.

PART V
The Classics Rock

"The twenty-year-old hound, who had stubbornly willed himself to live for this day, thumped his tail in recognition, a motion to break the hardest heart, and died . . ."

from *The Odyssey*[1]

Diogenes with dog

SIXTEEN
The Wages of Empire

*Of hounds, mastiffs, pariahs, stockdogs,
and dinner. Stones give way to metal and control
increases, meaning subdivisions become palpable.
Any society that tolerates slaves and serfs will
have no problem with canine strays. Chains
and cages will keep the gentry free.*

Farming was no bargain in terms of hours of labor or individual freedom; rather it seemed to encourage formation of larger, more structured, and hierarchical villages with divisions of labor and inequalities in wealth and power based largely on kinship becoming more entrenched. The villages' food supplies and livestock brought with them fears of spoilage or theft by man or beast or crop failure—brought with them, that is to say, the need for control, organization, and vigilance. That meant plenty of work for humans and dogs—some humans and some dogs more than others.

All the animals and humans in close proximity meant that disease leaping from one species to another was a real danger. The most notorious instance of that came just six hundred years ago when *Yersinia pestis,* the Plague, the Black Death, decimated a third of the human population of Europe, perhaps more in Asia, and untold numbers of dogs. The plague did not kill dogs; rather, they were left to fend for themselves and failed.

Far more common was rabies, known for much of its history as hydrophobia, and in a classical example of faulty associational thinking believed to afflict dogs in summer. That was when overheated dogs, panting to dissipate heat or wildly slopping water while trying to drink, were judged to be hydrophobic and were killed. Periodically, animals were slaughtered in large numbers when rabies appeared, and they still are in some parts of the world, especially large urban areas in developing nations, due now less to ignorance than to a lack of vaccine or a way to deliver it to unfriendly village dogs.

Yet the dog was also valued for its therapeutic powers, most famously for keeping wounds clean and infection free by licking them, and for easing people's mental woes. Their value in that regard, and in working livestock and guarding the home and farm, was such that even religions or cultures that condemned them as filthy beasts made exceptions for working dogs. They also made allowances for well-bred hunting dogs, a concession that in most cases has less to do with theology than power politics, I suspect, since what is being protected is the sport of the ruling class. In other societies, like those of the North American Indians and Jomon of Japan, dogs were the only domesticated animals, sometimes for thousands of years.

In early farming communities and emergent societies, dogs' relationship to humans remained different from that of other domesticates because of their utility and emotional appeal. Among some groups particular types of dogs were cultivated to suit local conditions and desires, which usually means that they performed in certain ways. As I discussed earlier, it is difficult to determine what characteristics in addition to smallness and coat color were captured prior to the Neolithic Revolution. But using New World dogs as a measure, characteristics extant more than sixteen thousand years ago included various muzzle and nose shapes and sizes associated with brachycephaly; "corded" coats; and chondrodysplasia, or dwarfism, which affects large and small dogs; but not lop or floppy ears. The Molossian type has been identified in fossils from Peru, but the big mountain dogs and sight hounds do not seem to be represented among New World dogs, although that does not mean they did not exist before the Neolithic. They may have taken form in other refuges: Sight hounds were not in eastern Asia either. Herding dogs were creations of animal husbandry and thus came somewhat later than sight hounds and guard dogs.

Wherever its origins, the heavy-boned mastiff first shows up in a sculpture from Mesopotamia around 1500 BC, and then goes everywhere. Yet I have the feeling that its sudden appearance in art has less to do with its origins than with human needs for such a dog. In other words, the mastiff existed in some form long before humans turned it into a lumbering, feared, and fierce guard.

In fact, given the level of mixing of Eurasian wolf, Chinese wolf, and Middle Eastern wolf in virtually all early dogs, and the movements they make with their migrating people, it might be more beneficial to look for a founding dogwolf population than a particular geographic place of origin. It is interesting to note that the socialized wolf of Goyet Cave and the early dogs out of Siberia tended toward shorter, broader noses, pointing toward a more European than Asian origin for at least some of the Molossian mastiffs. Since the number of genetic mutations involved in defining these basic forms is probably relatively small, they might have been passed on quickly but in limited numbers, so that the people would have had to nurture their own version, if they could, or attempt to obtain more dogs from elsewhere. It could well be that a number of mastiff-Molossian type large dogs developed locally throughout their distribution long before the Mesopotamians put them to use.

The ancient Egyptians clearly enjoyed hunting with their lean, fast sight hounds, who show up in hieroglyphics from 3000 BC, along with chondrodysplastic, dwarf-legged, spotted basset-type hounds, or dachshunds. They also had mastiffs they apparently dispatched in battle to sow terror. Mastiffs and hounds were often portrayed with thick collars and leashes, denoting their direct connection to privilege. Royalty—or Deity—hunted but only with royal dogs, handled ultimately by slaves or servants. Allthough they predate the Mesopotamian mastiff, the Egyptian variants appear to lack its structural solidity. But that is probably a matter of human artistic style.

The Chinese *Book of Rites,* originally written in the third century BC, perhaps by Confucius, then burned as subversive by the decayed Zhang dynasty and reconstructed in 1 BC, mentions hunting dogs, watch dogs, and food dogs, often eaten with hemp seeds. It also mentions a "black wild dog" whose fur was valued for gloves. As is the case in nearly all cultures, no descriptions are given of these dogs.[1]

By the start of the Current Era, the Han dynasty watch dog was a mastiff. In ancient China and Japan, villages bred and maintained their own dogs, large and small. In China, people raising dogs for food would place an emphasis on high numbers of reproductive females, which, along with little or no selective breeding of their watch dogs, is manifest today in the high measures of mitochondrial diversity that geneticists detect in southeastern China dogs. A small, chondrodysplastic, brachycephalic, long-haired dog said to resemble a little lion spread apparently from Tibet through much of Asia in the first millennium while taking the form of the Tibetan spaniel, shih tzu, Japanese Chen, and Pekingese. According to lore, the Pekingese of the Dowager Empress Tzu Hsi in the waning years of the Manchu dynasty—in the early twentieth century—were assigned wet nurses and bodyguards. With breeding for extreme brachycephaly still an uncertain art, breeders would help nature along by starving the puppies to keep them small—royal wet nurses notwithstanding—breaking the cartilage in their noses and between their shoulders and corseting them in wire. Now the look is fixed by selective breeding.

In Japan the focus was on hunting and guarding dogs. Most distinctively, they varied widely in terms of size, with the small Shiba Inu and large Akita forming the end points for the majority of what are best described as medium-sized dogs. The differentiation that did exist was established early in the Jomon period and did not change dramatically for more than nine thousand years, except for the influx of some closely related Korean dogs around the beginning of the first millennium of the Current Era, which were quickly absorbed. Fearing that forced opening of their harbors by the United States would bring freely copulating Western dogs to their shores, Japanese dog lovers took steps to protect their canine heritage from what they considered ruinous crossbreeding.[2]

Around fifty-five hundred years ago, in 3500 BC, agricultural people moved from India into northwestern Thailand and created a series of villages, including one called Ban Chiang, where they farmed rice, raised among other animals pigs and cattle, and foraged, hunted, or fished for dozens of other species of plants and animals. Accomplished metallurgists, they also had dogs that resembled small dingoes, and whose direct descendants, nearly unchanged phenotypically, are the Thai village dogs. These dogs are interesting because although they are small, they have none of the tooth crowding long considered a sign of domestication in dogs. They also had to have arrived with those first agriculturalists, probably from India or someplace closer (although not China, since there is no evidence of interaction between the Thai rice farmers and those on the Yangtze in southeastern China). Whatever their origin, the people who settled in Thailand crossed with them, or adopted along the way, the habit of eating dogs still practiced in Thailand today.[3]

The relationship between these Thai dogs and Australian dingoes is also unclear. By around the same time the farmers settled in northeast

Thailand, the dingo arrived in Australia. Whatever their origin, the people who settled in Thailand carried with them, or adopted along the way, the habit of eating dogs still practiced in Thailand today. Their cousins might have carried the dogs who became dingoes to Australia, but to date that remains conjecture.[4]

Basic types aside, the dog changed little through the Neolithic and antiquity. People distinguished between dogs based on their habits and styles, which were tied in turn to their physical abilities and attributes. By the sixth century BC, the Greeks recognized four groups of dogs: strong Laconian, or Spartan, hunting dogs; slow, powerful Molossian guard dogs; Crete dogs, crosses of the Laconian and Molossian; and Melitan, a small, long-haired, short-legged dog. The Laconian hunting dog seems to have had two varieties—a baying scent hound who worked slowly so that hunters could follow on foot, and a faster-moving hound.

I can barely see old, blind Homer, but if I cock my head to one side, I can hear him reciting the Odyssey at times as if he were throat singing. Back then in Ithaca, but hardly home yet, Emmaus, the swineherd for Odysseus, tells a strange beggar the sad tale of Argos, the beloved hunting dog. Raised by Odysseus from the time he was born, Argos was devoted to him, and when with him, was relentless in his pursuit of game. No animal could escape him, but he fell upon hard times once his Odysseus left for war. The women ignored him, the servants did nothing at all. He was cast out of society onto the midden heap where, flea bitten, he lay until he recognized his master disguised, like himself, as a beggar. The twenty-year-old hound, who had stubbornly willed himself to live for this day, thumped his tail in recognition, a motion and sound to break the hardest heart, and died; Odysseus had to turn away to hide his tears, for fear they would betray him before he could exact vengeance.

—Adaptation from The Odyssey

While it is tempting to leap directly from Greece to Rome, a detour to the Levant and a Mediterranean port city, Ashkelon, is in order. The city was already several thousand years old when it came under control of the seafaring Phoenicians, operating as Persian proxies. The renowned sailors and traders of the Mediterranean had extended the reach of the Silk Roads from China across North Africa and southern Europe, and Ashkelon became one of the ports in their transcontinental chain. About 450 BC, the people of Ashkelon began burying dogs usually described as whippet-like—that is, standing about twenty-one inches tall and weighing thirty pounds—right on the margin of small, by some measures. Over the course of fifty years, the people of Ashkelon buried more than one thousand dogs, each lying on its side, its tail wrapped around its legs, for reasons unknown. With those numbers for the same type dog, I would have to say that they were breeding or trading dogs on a large scale, whether for internal use or export it is difficult to say, although there is no sign of trauma that would go along with ritual sacrifice or a program to kill.

As a port city, Ashkelon was a major mixing zone for cultures and people, some of whom worshipped dogs. For example, the dog was the sacred animal of the healing goddess of Mesopotamia, Gula Ninisina, and seems as well to have been associated with a Phoenician deity involved in healing, but that is speculation. The Ashkelon dogs apparently died of natural causes, perhaps an epidemic of some sort, and because they had inherent value, they were buried. That they had inherent value seems irrefutable; the rest for now is conjecture. The confusion over what type of dog they were underscores how similar and undifferentiated "types" were at a time when what the dog did was more important for most people than what it looked like.[5]

Expropriating what they considered the best of Greek civilization, the Romans recognized hunting dogs (*Canis venatici*), divided by sight and scent hounds; watch dogs (*C. villatici*), who could serve, according to their predilection, as draft, war, and guard dogs in times of need; sheepdogs (*C. pastorales*); and small companion dogs, which could be chondrodysplastic, like a dachshund, or a brachycephalic, like a Pekingese. A fifth type, rarely mentioned but found in the ruins of Pompeii, was *C. pugnaces*, a large, fierce brachycephalic dog of the mastiff type who made war in the Coliseum and also served as home guard. They were staked by day, so that they could rest and become restless enough, it was assumed, to patrol the grounds all night. By tradition hunting dogs were to have coat colors resembling wild animals or be black and tan; black, tan, and white; or yellow.[6]

Lucius Junius Moderatus Columella, an early student of agriculture, summarized the proper qualities of sheepdogs and farm dogs in *De Re Rustica* in the first century AD. He eschewed hunting dogs on the grounds that they kept farmers from their work, a lament echoed almost precisely eighteen hundred years later after a visit to the Ozarks in the United States by a young mineralogist, Henry Rowe Schoolcraft. Every settler along the frontier, he complained, had up to a dozen dogs with which he hunted, while neglecting the plow and leaving whatever livestock he had to forage freely in the forest. He had to hunt to feed himself and his dogs, which otherwise were worthless, Schoolcraft said. He seemed not to consider the advantages derived from hunting—food, clothing, and income from the pelts, for buying supplies. Neither he nor Columella centuries before knew of the hunters in northwestern China who cultivated millet to feed their hunting dogs.[7]

Assuming they had abandoned the hunt, farmers always needed at least two good dogs, Columella said in volume seven of his treatise. One was to be black, with a square head and a square physique, large chest, stout legs, broad shoulders, large feet and toes, a short tail, floppy ears, bright black or red eyes, and a deep, booming, terrifying bark to scare miscreants away. The dog was to be black so that by day it would frighten away brigands, and at night be unseen so it could surprise thieves. Since it patrolled near the house and granary, it could be slow. It should be rather even tempered but capable of attack if necessary.

That was not the case with the cattle dog, as Columella called it, making it presumably applicable to sheep as well. The cattle dog had to be robust, long and lean, swift enough to run down a thieving wolf, and fierce enough to kill it. It should be white, so the farmer could see it at night and in failing light. More significant, it was to come from good breeding and have been trained to follow cattle and sheep rather than to hunt. It wore a stud collar for protection and to damage any wolf who dared attack. The cattle dog, in short, was more akin to the Laconian dog than the Molossian, or perhaps a cross between Laconian and Molossian, or a lean and rangy Molossian. In many ways, the dog sounds like a houndy version of the modern Great Dane—long, lean, and overall big, a formidable animal. I found no support for the argument that white dogs were selected because they did not frighten the sheep.

The Molossian was a particular type of *cane villatici*—not even the only large, heavy-boned black dog to put teeth in the common mosaic at the entry to private Roman homes and certain shops, saying "*cave canem*," "beware the dog." But through common usage over the centuries, the Molossian has become the name of the mystical forebear of many different mastiffs and mountain dogs.

The tradition of the big white dog for guarding livestock in tandem with a human, and sometimes a canine herder, has also extended to the present, with many autochthonous breeds still extant or reconstructed. The Romans also had large Celtic sight hounds from the British Isles—one called Vertraga and resembling, it is sometimes said, a greyhound, but I suspect it was more in keeping with the Scottish deerhound. The other sounded like the Irish wolfhound, who vanished after the last wolf was killed on Ireland in 1720, following their extirpation from the British Isles in the seventeenth century. The modern Irish wolfhound

is   a
reconstruction from the late nineteenth century. The sight hound could
have entered Europe by crossing from North Africa to the Iberian
Peninsula and moved from there northward into the British Isles, or by
coming through central Europe with the first migrating Near Eastern
farmers. During the empire, Romans brought animals and people from
around the world for the spectacle of their games in the Coliseum—
not as audience but as participants—including Molossian and Celtic
dogs, who would fight lions and other carnivores, each other, or gladi-
ators. Sometimes they would be sent to pursue stags or deer. No one can
currently say how much any of these imports contributed to the pool of
Roman dogs and whether any of their genetic material was passed along
to the present.

Of such bits and pieces are the prehistory and ancient history of
dogs made, with increasingly strong, but still somewhat confusing,
data, from genetic analysis and archaeological sites. What they reveal
is that the dog, born in motion, never stopped moving. Wherever people went, the dog went. Because the subsequent mixing or outright
lineage replacement was greatest in trading hubs and other mixing
zones, the search for relicts or ancient breeds—like the dingoes of
Australia or Ban Chiang or the basenji—might best focus on places
that have drawn neither pilgrims nor colonizers nor occupying forces.
Left unresolved, for example, are questions of whether ancient breeds
are simply dogs that have escaped admixture with other types for a
long time, or whether they go back thousands of years. Even then, deciding how old they are is a difficult task because primarily what the
genetic surveys show is the degree of admixture of genetic material
from different types of dog. Scientists make the assumption, based on
assumed rates of mutation, that lack of admixture confers antiquity
on the dog. At the same time, those dogs are expected to show high
levels of genetic diversity because they have bred freely, unless they
have been isolated on an island or in deep jungle and forced to

inbreed, and then they will have low levels of diversity. To gain a different perspective on the origins and evolution of the dog, a group of geneticists from Stanford University began studying village dogs from around the world in the hope that their random breeding through thousands of years will have preserved important genetic markers. The researchers have already shown that village dogs represent a tremendous reservoir of genetic diversity.[8]

Dogs and Wild Boar

SEVENTEEN
Middlin' Dog to Guard, Hunt, Haul, Herd, Fight, and Preen

*The Middle Ages' midsize dog guards home and hearth,
and stands between dogs big and small. But big is about
the hunt and class and power. Small is companionship
and privilege, except when it is not. Dogs conquer
a New World. The masses strike back.*

As a rule, the world's great religions veer from a form of benign ambivalence to absolute denunciation and condemnation of the dog, with a few exceptions for dogs that are deemed useful. Among those are herding dogs, guard dogs, hunting dogs, and, for Christians, little companion dogs—all useful and fine exemplars of loyalty and fidelity except when they are not. But there are also the dirty village dogs, the excrement-, corpse-, and garbage-eating, livestock-killing, chicken-thieving, disease-bearing, flea- and tick-spreading, low-born, downwardly mobile dogs. Islam recognizes only working dogs and hunting dogs, than which no creature is more noble, and Judaism dispensed with the hunting dog but came to employ police and military dogs after its reestablishment the latter half of the twentieth century.

Hinduism sees dogs as links between the quick and the dead, and so has times when sacrifices are made to them. Their chief value to the living is as protectors of wealth, the home, and women and children—a significant assignment.

Chao-chou Ts'ung-shen, the ninth-century Zen master, answered a series of questions about the dog that seem to capture its essence as a noncompliant rule breaker from the start. When asked by a fellow Chinese monk, "Does a dog have Buddha-nature or not?" Chao-chou responded, "Wu," which translates, "It does not." In the exchange that follows, Chao-chou makes clear that the dog has "karmic consciousness," and that means the dog has no Buddha-nature because it *is* Buddha-nature. Since it is already one with "karmic consciousness," in order to exist physically in this world, it "knowingly commits a deliberate violation."[1]

The dog "is."

Christian attitudes toward dogs are the most contradictory and the most contingent on the status of the dogs and people. As a rule, through the Middle Ages, the dogs of the nobility were, like their masters, deemed special because of their station in life. Those secular hounds had their spiritual counterparts in the cynosure wearing *Domini canes,* "hounds of god," who held special status derived from their Lord, Jesus, the "hound of heaven." The Dominicans became the Grand Inquisitors of the thirteenth century, responsible for stamping out heresies, including the common practice among peasants of granting godhood, or at least great spiritual power, to animals, including dogs. When the dog in question was a greyhound more noble than the noble who owned him, the situation was judged beyond the pale.

That is the case with the tale of Guinefort, which dates from at least the thirteenth century, the south of France, where a young lord was living the fine, noble hunting life with his wife and newborn baby and his devoted greyhound, Guinefort. Following custom, he gave the hound the run of the house and trusted him to guard castle and child. Returning home one afternoon, the noble couple went to the nursery and were greeted by a blood-soaked Guinefort in a blood-stained room. The child's bed was overturned, the child nowhere to be seen. Leaping simultaneously to conclusion and action, the lord drew his sword and slew his beloved dog. By then his lady had discovered the child unharmed under the bed, and together lord and lady noticed the bits and pieces of bloody flesh scattered about the room. They reassembled them into a giant serpent—surely the devil's own agent. Guinefort had performed his task brilliantly. The guilt-ridden parents dumped the body of Guinefort down a well, sealed it, and planted an oak grove hoping both to conceal their perfidy and commemorate their dog.[2]

The peasants understood who the saint was and brought their children to the sacred oak grove in the hope that he would cure them. He worked well enough that the Church periodically complained but did nothing, until the Dominican inquisitor Stephen of Bourbon exhumed what he said were Guinefort's bones and scattered them to the wind. Then he cut down the oak grove and declared it a crime and mortal sin to go there seeking help from the devil. But people brought their children there for seven hundred more years, until antibiotics proved a more effective remedy.

The dogs of medieval European nobles followed roughly the Roman classifications, real and imagined, with specific types, usually geographically defined, increasingly improved upon in terms of special coat-color combinations, ear length, overall size, vocalizations, working styles, and other identifying characteristics. These may have amounted to little more than variations on an established type of local hound, but that was less important than the status owning them provided. As land became increasingly devoted to agriculture, forests and game grew in short supply, so nobles who could, set aside forest preserves to provide wood for themselves, but more precisely a place to hunt. "Laws of the forest" were promulgated to protect them and their wildlife from poachers, who, if caught, could be castrated, blinded, or wrapped in a deer skin and turned loose for the hounds' sport.

In England, the law of the forest, promulgated by Henry II early in the twelfth century, forbade peasants and laborers from keeping mastiffs or hunting hounds within or near royal forests. Freeholders and farmers could keep mastiffs—defined as being of the Molossian type and including "barking curs"—to protect their homes and farms. But if they were bigger than a certain size—measured by whether their front paw would pass through an iron stirrup—they had to be expeditated. The middle three nails on each forepaw were chopped off at the flesh with a blow from a mallet on a sharp chisel, reportedly so that the dog could not leap on a stag's back and kill it with a single bite, or even get traction for such a move. A person caught with an unexpeditated dog was fined three shillings, unless he had a royal patent to keep mastiffs and hounds.[3]

The English law and others like it effectively forced peasants and laborers near such restricted areas to keep medium to small dogs who were not high born or fancy-looking but who were often well trained and wise in the poaching arts. In some cases these were the same peasants and freedmen who ran the kennels for the nobility—or their relatives.

Many noble families had one or more representatives in the clergy or a religious order as a way to hedge their bets and keep Church power in check, and it was not unusual for them to bring their preoccupations with them when entering an order.

Naregdue

In the ninth century, the Belgian Benedictine monastery of Saint Hubert developed an eponymous line of tracking dogs that soon became famous for their ability to track humans and hold them in their teeth until the authorities came. These were slow trailing dogs with long, droopy ears and pendulous lips said to be descended from the ubiquitous Molossus. This desire for connection to the Molossus of Rome, and, more profoundly, Greece, smells strongly of the desire to wrap uncertain parentage or authority in the mantle of tradition—the way Augustus commissioned Virgil to pen the *Aeneid*, the epic of Rome's founding, to bestow on it an aura of historical inevitability and legitimacy. To track a dog's heritage to the near-mythical Molossus was to grant it standing in the world, which the Church did not like. But the people who supported the Church liked hunting with dogs; therein rose a problem.

The Saint Hubert hound existed into the nineteenth century, often paired and compared with Britain's entry in the field of slow trailers, the Talbot hound. They were legendary, and the legends represented a reality born of the person's desire. Thus, to say that ninth-century Benedictines knew of the Molossus—that any number of putatively not well educated medieval lords knew of the Molossus—is to say that knowledge of the classics was not fully lost in the Middle Ages, at least when it came to matters of dogs, birds, and hunting or heraldry.

If such knowledge had been lost, some of it was regained in the repeated invasions of the Holy Land during the Crusades in the twelfth and thirteenth centuries, when the Crusaders brought back whatever booty they could loot or steal—from dogs to illuminated manuscripts, doubtless dealing with the hunt and military arts. The thirteenth-century Mongol invasion brought new dogs into Eastern Europe from across central Asia.

Hunting hounds and war dogs were for men; little spaniels were for women, especially the hunters among them, and so were often freakish little sleeve dogs, barely bigger than a rat. The little dogs were just amusements, adornments for ladies who enjoyed rank and privileges above the servants who nursed them and cared for them. Despite local, regional, and continental differences in appearance and treatment, the broad divisions largely held where ruling classes kept dogs, often maintaining them in their own kennels. They might not look very refined in part because the emphasis was on what they did: the sight hound/greyhound deployed in open country to deliver the coup de grâce; scent hounds of various sizes and shapes and vocalizations, from leggy chase hounds, Chien courants to saddlebag-size beagles, with squared-off harriers and slower-going Saint Hubert or Talbot bloodhounds in between; the silent "finder hound," the lymer; and the brutish *alaunt*—the hunters' version of the brachy-cephalic mastiff or bowlegged bulldog—a catch dog for boar, bear, and badger, a foul-tempered bully. Conflation aside, the important point is that a divide between the dogs of people with power and wealth and those laborers, peasants, and everyone else that had to have formed with the earliest civilizations had deepened. Being a thug, the *alaunt* was allowed to look like one. Not infrequently a small terrier turned the role of the *alaunt* into that of a "baying-up dog," responsible for holding a much larger animal's attention while the hunters quietly took its life.[4]

Despite such fine distinctions, the greatest number of animals in medieval villages and towns from Scotland to Russia were medium-sized dogs. Built in the ninth century, Veliky Novgorod, the Great Novgorod, was the first capital of Russia and through the fourteenth century a major trading hub between the Baltic Sea, central Asia, and Byzantium, and thus a mixing zone for all manner of people and goods. Its dogs followed the medieval trinity—a few large and small dogs and abundant medium dogs supplemented during the town's first three centuries by husky-type dogs, according to Russian archaeologist Andrei Zinoviev, who cataloged a large collection of canid bones from the period of Novgorod's ascendancy. Calling the medium-sized dogs "scavenging curs," he speculated in 2010 in the *International Journal of Osteoarchaeology* that they were primarily barking alarms for town houses and farmsteads, the purpose being to alert the residents and frighten intruders, who would rather try another house than test the dog's willingness to back up its bark with a bite. The few large dogs were the size of the Caucasus mountain dogs, while the small dogs, at twenty-three pounds, matched the size of the Finnish spitz, a famous barker in its own right. Both types seemed to belong to wealthy people in the community.[5]

In other cities, relative proportions and size of the groups might have varied, but the dominance of the midsize dog in terms of sheer numbers did not change. Many scholars make a mistake in thinking that this population of medium dogs was comprised only of free-ranging, scavenging curs who did little but bark warnings if someone approached a house they considered their own largely because a resident fed them scraps.

Packs—more precisely, groups—of free-ranging and feral dogs periodically rampaged in various parts of Europe in the aftermath of battles that decimated the countryside and following local outbreaks of the plague or cholera or some other epidemic. None of those approached the continent-wide disaster that was the Black Death in the mid-fourteenth century, which obliterated nearly one-third of the population, with some cities, like Paris, losing 50 percent, and others, like Venice, plummeting by 80 percent. That left dogs on their own to scavenge corpses or any other food they could find, and unquestionably they did.

The greatest public health risk for dogs came from rabies, which, because it was so thoroughly misunderstood, annually brought on the death of many fine dogs.

To dodge legal prohibitions against owning large dogs, farmers and shepherds developed their stock dogs from a size that allowed them the combination of agility and power they needed to work everything from ducks to cattle. What species of livestock the dog worked was determined by the dog, and more than a few of them were capable of working cattle or sheep and pigs by morning and hunting by night. Whereas "the hunt" by nobility might be the daily reenactment of the quest for the Holy Grail or a sport with the serious result of putting food on the table or preparing for the next war or crusade, since they were constants of medieval life, the "poach" was a subversion necessary for physical and psychological survival.

Dogs pulled carts for people too poor for livestock. They turned wheels that powered machinery or drew water from wells. They stole food and purses. They fished and set nets. They dug animals out of their burrows. If a task needed doing, someone somewhere at sometime probably succeeded in training a dog to do it. The dog so trained was more likely than not from the ranks of those medium-sized dogs so common in medieval towns and villages.

Work for the butcher's dog was a blood sport, a violent spectacle repeated throughout the day. He grabbed the bull by its nose and held on while the butcher opened its veins and bled it to death.

Fine though these dogs were, in the eyes of the lords and ladies they were no better than people who were poorly bred. Medieval and Renaissance notions of noble breeding and blood purity reached their apotheosis of sorts in fifteenth-century Spain, where forces gathered to complete the expulsion of Jews and Moors and all their spawn, no matter how distant and no matter that they may have been Christian and Spanish for generations. *Limpieza de sangre,* "cleanliness of the blood" or "purity of the blood," was demanded of all Spaniards, and if they did not have it—and a wise nobleman or priest could tell at a glance—they were gone.

The Spaniards attempted to maintain that purity in breeding livestock, horses, and dogs in their monasteries, castles, and haciendas. The dogs were close to those in the rest of Europe in classification: *lebrel,* a greyhound a fast chase hound mix; *mastin,* dark for home protection and light for the flock; *sabueso,* a slow scent hound of the bloodhound sort; *alano,* a foul-tempered wolfhound; *perro de presa,* a catch dog, or short, powerful bulldog type; and *perro de ayudas,* an aid or assistance dog. Spanish troops deployed these dogs to devastating effect in *la Monteria Inferna,* "the infernal chase," which turned infidels and impure humans into prey to be hunted down and torn asunder. Developed in the Canary Islands, it was refined in the final campaign against what remained of the Moors at the time Columbus was making his first voyage to what proved to be the New World.

Starting with Columbus, Spanish conquistadors and adventurers deployed their dogs, especially the *lebrels, mastins, alanos,* and catch dogs, to such murderous effect that they destroyed millions of people. Millions more perished from combat and introduced disease, especially small pox. A Dominican priest, Bartolomé de Las Casas, began to protest the slaughter with thirteen other priests around 1516, winning some attention and concessions from the crown, concessions that were rolled back almost as soon as they were promulgated. Serious reform was not undertaken until promulgation of the New Laws in 1542 by Charles V restored some native rights.

By then the Conquest was nearly complete. African slaves were replacing the rebellious and increasingly dead native people on the newly formed plantations. But Las Casas refused to let go, and in 1552 he published a detailed and graphic account of the brutality, *Brevísima Relación de la Destrucción de Las Indias* (*A Brief Account of the Destruction of the Indians*). The encyclopaedic *Historia de Las Indias* was published in 1570, twenty years after his death. If any good could be said to have come from such slaughter, it was that the magnitude of the atrocity was so great that British, French, and Dutch colonists subsequently eschewed the use of war dogs in the New World—not always happily—and lost no time pillorying the Spanish for their brutality.

That was a major concession since dogs were a common weapon of war—usually aimed at opposing horsemen. No one quite matched the Greek fire helmets, which were dogs with pots of burning oil tied on their heads sent to panic enemy horsemen, or the Celtic catch dogs, who would grab the nose of enemy horses—no one without a firearm, that is. A gun neutralizes even a large dog very quickly, as do well-placed arrows.

Perhaps the first European compendium devoted purely to the dogs of a place was Johannes Caius's *De Canibus Britannicis,* published in 1570 in Latin, as befit a scholarly work prepared at the behest of the distinguished Swedish naturalist, Conrad Gessner. Abraham Fleming, a former student of Caius's, translated the book into *A Treatise of Englishe Dogges* in 1576. Dividing British dogs by function, Caius produced a comprehensive work that showed how much humans in just one part of the world had altered the dog since the fall of Rome. Following custom, hunting dogs dominated the field: the bloodhound and harrier for "smelling"; the gasehound for quickly locating game; the greyhound for "swiftness" and "quick spying"; the leuimer, or lyemmer, a cross between a harrier and greyhound known for its enthusiastic pursuit of game; the "tumbler," a "sly," "crafty," acrobatic dog who bunched game and then caught its prey by the nose, the way curs do, and ambushed rabbits; and the "theevish dog," the silent running, nighttime hunting poacher's cur, a sort of prick-eared downsized greyhound, whippetlike, renowned for its rabbit hunting. Caius also names as hunters the *terrare,* the fierce little terriers as willing to bay a bear as to dig a critter out of its den.[6]

Caius identified two groups of fowling dogs—upland bird-hunting spaniels, so named because of the belief that most of them originated in Spain, an otherwise unidentified blue merle French dog, recently arrived, and setters. He names water dogs, too, among them the "Fynder," a water spaniel, not unlike the French barbet. Also a fishing dog that hunted among the rocks for stranded fish. And the Spaniel Gentle or Comforter was identified with the Maltese and Cavalier King Charles spaniel by proponents of those breeds.

Hounds generally got top billing, but the "dogs of the coarser sort" were the stars, starting with the shepherd's dog, who responded to voice and whistle and would sometimes condition its flock to gather on hearing the whistle and begin moving toward the fold on its own, rather than face the dog. Caius also names the less refined mastiffs—large, short-faced, fighting, guarding, and hunting dogs; the "mooner," whose purpose in life was apparently to bark at the moon; the "water drawer"; the "messenger dog"; the "tinker's cur," erstwhile companion to the itinerant tinker who fixed pots and other metal goods; and the "defending dog," who never deserted his master. The big shepherd dog is absent, Caius said, because there were no wolves in the British Isles and so they were unneeded.

The tinker's cur carried all of the tinker's tools and also provided him protection on his travels, something the socialized wolf began for traders who always had to look out for thieves. They love their masters and despise strangers, Caius said,

> *whereupon it followeth that they are to their masters, in traveiling a singuler safgard, defending them forceably from the invasion of villons and theefes, preserving their lyfes from losse, and their health from hassard, theyr fleshe from hacking and hewing with such like desperate daungers. For which consideration they are meritoriously tearmed.*[7]

The most infamous of the mastiffs were the Bandogges, who guarded the Tower of London and were used in the "sports" of bull and bear baiting, and the butcher's dog. A Molossus was also present, but Caius has little to say on that score.

Those dogs bred to type, meaning they were identifiable as whatever they were supposed to be and thus were a higher class than the "rascals," the randomly bred and breeding mutts who were employed as "turnspits" for churning butter or turning spits of meat; "wappe," who barked outside a house it called home to announce to everyone, inside and out, that visitors were on the grounds; and the "dancers," who performed various tricks and acrobatics on the street to earn money for their masters. Dogs are as capable of being clowns as people are, without question, and that is one reason we get on so well with them.

On the eve of the eighteenth century, Richard Blome revised Caius's list in *The Gentleman's Recreation*, adding the lurcher, a medium-sized crossbred hound beloved of poachers; a shrunken harrier called a beagle; and a new terrier born of the crossing of a beagle and a mastiff that sounds like the forerunner of the Jack Russell terrier.

The French had multiples of hounds, pointers, mastiffs, mountain dogs, and herding dogs, including several types found around Paris alone. Indeed, most places had their own distinctive dog or dogs that may have changed over the years with changing fashion or war or disease. Not long before he became president, George Washington sought some French hounds—perhaps grand *bleu de gascogne*, considered the most regal of French hounds—to incorporate into his pack of foxhounds. His ally in war, virtually his adopted son, the Marquis de Lafayette, who obtained them for him, explained that the hounds were difficult to find because the king favored the faster, smaller English hounds, and the nobility went along with him. Nonetheless, he had secured three males and four females and dispatched them for America in the care of young John Quincy Adams, bound for Harvard University by way of New York after a summer in Europe.[8]

Washington also sought from Ireland one of the big, legendary wolfhounds, only to learn that they could no longer be found since extirpation of wolves from the island. He was offered a well-bred mastiff instead but turned it down for lack of mobility. Free-ranging dogs operating like predators were a problem then, like they are now, and although records are scarce, custom dictates that they were treated accordingly. As the dog and human populations increased, the battle against wolves intensified for they, more than marauding dogs, embodied wild, unpredictable nature.[9]

The domestication of Nature motivated this war on wolves and wild predators, on Indians, on wetlands and rivers that could be drained, channelized, or dammed. The goal was to "civilize" Nature and improve on it scientifically.

EIGHTEEN
Where Did That Dog Get Its Breeding?

*Good blood, good breeding—if not for you, then
for your dog, to vouch for your social status. The
schism between working dogs and dogs for show and
dogs for sport and the mass of dogs mimes caste and
class in the human world. Or whose dog is it?*

Tragically, the process of replacement of indigenous dogs and people in all its blood and gore and tears was on display in the conquest and colonization of the New World in the sixteenth through the nineteenth centuries, when the American West was finally subdued—brought under the plow or domesticated with virtual extirpation of freely migrating bison and the introduction of domestic cattle, and horses. For native dogs, the depopulation was close to total, and for the indigenous people it was not much better. When the wildlife slaughtered for food, hides, fur, feathers, sheep, "predator control," and sport is factored in, the magnitude of the loss of life becomes mind-boggling, with numbers reaching into the tens of millions—more than can be fully known or measured.

Individuals in each new wave of immigration brought what dogs they could from their home countries, along with a dog culture—that of the nobility as well as that of yeomen, peasants, tavern owners, drovers, butchers, and traders. Along the expanding frontier, Anglo-European immigrants and dogs replaced their native counterparts with varying degrees of miscegenation, often despite laws prohibiting Indians from owning Anglo-European dogs. The Indians apparently found the English hounds more tractable than their wolflike dogs, while the colonists feared that if the Indians obtained their dogs, especially their mastiffs, they would gain additional advantage in hunting and in warfare. The colonists also thought that the Indian dogs were worthless livestock killers. In any event, although the degree of admixture is unknown, the result of all the crossbreedings were the American version of the English "dogs of a coarser sort," described by Caius as the "Shepherd's dog, defending dog, and tynker's dog."

They were curs or "curdogs," pronounced as one word—yellow, ginger, merle, brindled, black, or black and white and tan, sometimes with blue eyes so pale, they were clear as glass, with ears of every sort from prick to lop. Nearly ubiquitous on the frontier and on small farms, they were tough generalists expected to hunt game of all sorts, to guard, and sometimes to herd, whether cattle or pigs and sheep was their choice. Local, regional familial lines of cur existed, like the spotted leopard curs of the Gulf of Mexico coastal region, who hunted Florida's feral scrub cattle for the lucrative trade with Cuba, the inland but still southern blackmouth cur, various mountain curs from the Alleghenies, yellow dogs, and the like.

The exemplar of the hard-hunting American frontiersman and indifferent farmer of the early nineteenth century was David Crockett, the inveterate tale teller and bear hunter from Tennessee. While he was in the United States Congress in 1834, Crockett agreed to have John Gadsby Chapman paint a full-length portrait of him dressed for the hunt, his rifle nestled in the crook of his arm, three hounds gathered at his feet. Crockett rounded up three cur dogs from the streets of Washington to use instead of Chapman's blooded hounds, explaining to the painter that they looked more like his bear dogs back in Tennessee.[1]

In the American slave-owning South, some wealthy plantation owners and professional hunters of runaway slaves had mastiffs or a Saint Hubert bloodhound or a Cuban bloodhound, a fell mix of mastiff, wolfhound, and greyhound designed to terrorize, if not maim, only runaway slaves, the notion being that the dog was bred to despise black people. Wealthy planters with connections had their own lines of hounds for foxes or bears or whatever brought them status in the world of the hunt. The dogs were characterized by how they took the trail, whether they ran nose up or nose to ground, whether they ran silent or sounded all of the time or only when they treed. They were also identified by owner or breeder, or place of origin. For lack of money or desire, many owners did not have full packs. They ran the blooded dogs at the head of their packs of curs for the show because in most cases the curs performed better from the start. In the South, slave hunters kept packs of dogs that they used only for pursuing runaways, fearful that if they let the dogs pursue more traditional game, like deer and foxes, they might quickly come to prefer it to the brutality of slave hunting.[2]

The dog was nearly everywhere in the seventeenth and eighteenth centuries, as an indispensable assistant, energy source, beast of burden hauling everything from milk to rags and cinders, in addition to its more traditional roles, even while its position in human society was shifting. Unfortunately, it was shifting toward extremes of praise and condemnation. Stories appeared regularly in the broadsheets and magazines extolling the loyalty, tenacity, and sagacity of the dog—its ability to think and solve problems, to communicate even with strangers. Its virtues frequently exceeded those of the people in whose care it landed by accident of birth or circumstance. Such accolades usually went to the farm collie or "coally," so called either for its black color or because of the black face of the coally sheep that it worked in Scotland. Also the shepherd's dog or shepherd's cur in general had multiple varieties who shared a reputation as the wisest and most intelligent of dogs.

Yet for everyone who attributed intelligence, emotion, consciousness to dogs, there were those who followed the seventeenth-century French mathematician and philosopher René Descartes in declaring that only humans could possess those qualities. Dogs and other animals were, to him, merely unfeeling, unthinking biological machines. Widely accepted until the past decade or two by many people, including scientists, who otherwise claimed to like dogs, Descartes's mechanistic formulation provided a powerful rationalization for the atrocity of vivisection—live dissection of dogs and other animals, especially cats, that were often stolen and sold to hospitals and individual doctors. In this view, the dog was tolerable because it was useful. When its utility ended, so should its life.

Hardcore behaviorists also view the dog as a biological stimulus-response machine subject to the automatic release of certain neurotransmitters and enzymes reacting to specific stimuli. They believe that people are not fundamentally different. Without launching a long argument, it is fair to say that anyone who has ever stared directly into the eyes of another animal for any length of time knows that it feels and thinks, that it is a sentient creature.

The third voice in this trio belonged to those who feared and loathed dogs—or at least believed dogs should be kept under strict control when in mixed company because they represented threats to human health and public safety if allowed to run free. The same packs of dogs that regularly harassed and killed livestock being driven into city stockyards in eighteenth- and nineteenth-century New York and other cities also attacked and stampeded wagons and carriages. In those other cities, however, that problem did not attract as much attention, although the annual summer rabies panic sure did. New York and other cities passed ordinances requiring dogs in the city to be restrained, muzzled, or confined during the rabies season—June to November—or risk being picked up by the authorities. Owners had to pay a fine to free them, or they were killed—or sold to researchers.

What is important from the standpoint of the continuing domestication of the dog or wolfdog or dogwolf is the level of human control exerted over the animal. For much of human and wolf history, even with the first separation event, the attempted control has varied by culture in intensity and effect. Degrees of engagement with dogs vary widely even within cultures and between types of dogs and people, including that ever mysterious chemistry between them. Lack of that chemistry is a primary reason dogs stop working with or for a person, be it a hunter, Frisbee player, shepherd, or police detective, and the obverse. That is why some years ago, I started adding "for me" to the phrase, "This dog won't hunt." Indeed, the dog might perform brilliantly for someone else—providing it is capable of acting.

I would like to say that dogs will not work for people who abuse them, that eventually, given the opportunity, they will flee or bite the hand that strikes them—a justified act that, unfortunately, has resulted in the death of many of them—but that is not always true. Dogs have long been ill served by people, their putative best friends—neglected, abused, and tortured. They have long been beaten or cowed into submission, which has led many people to call them innately submissive. But just because a dog or person can be forced into submission does not mean it is by nature submissive.

For all their failures and limitations, dogs and people do come together for companionship, entertainment, hunting, tending to livestock, helping victims of disasters, and saving people from catastrophes, as they did repeatedly along the American frontier. A democratization of dog ownership occurred there, as the heirs to Anglo-European peasants and poachers became freemen who carved their farms out of the wilderness, surviving on their wits, their hard work, their skill and that of their dogs as hunters, protectors, and, if necessary, drovers. That was not the case everywhere. Patterns of land grants and plantation ownership forced non-slave-owning farmers in the American South into piney woods with their acidic soils, and not much but their dogs and rifle.

The narrative that mattered was of the sagacious, helpful, intelligent dog. Whether a hunting dog or a shepherd dog sat atop the heap depended on the human's needs. In another of those ironies that make history appear to have its own volition, dogs were as interwoven into the fabric of the Anglo/European/American culture as they were for Native Americans—perhaps more so in some areas. Then the Western World went through an upheaval that would ultimately change every feature of every society, including the dog-human relationship.

Particularly after the restoration of the English monarchy in 1660, the rising mercantile class had close to a consensus desire for legitimacy and social standing in the land of inherited rank and privilege, which increasingly they subsidized. They could not buy rank outright, since those titles were inherited, but they could buy all of the trappings of those titles—the manor houses falling to ruin, the forests and the fields, and the blooded livestock and purebred hunting dogs that they bred themselves. By proving they had achieved the godlike ability to improve on Nature, they showed their superiority, if not to the deity, at least to his self-appointed elite. They showed that inheritance could indeed be changed, although it was a proof that they were reluctant to act upon or advertise for fear of rousing in Britain the sort of revolutionary zeal that convulsed the colonies and Europe.[3]

Advances in textile manufacture that drove the Industrial Revolution triggered the expansion of sheep husbandry in the British Isles, Europe, America, parts of Asia, Australia, and New Zealand. Demand for shepherd dogs increased accordingly, with countries following their own traditions or adapting those of the United States, Australia, and

New Zealand, which followed the English model of the active herding dog, with no guard dog. By the time of the French Revolution, France boasted seventeen different herding and guarding dogs—most did both—each adapted to the terrain, livestock, and people of its home region. Germans had a number of regional variations on their wolfdogs and rough versions of schnauzers, Rottweilers, and Great Danes—all used as stock dogs.

The Industrial Revolution also prolonged the life of the plantation slavery system in the American South. The racialist justifications of chattel slavery were given a scientific sheen, which ultimately was transferred to discussions of dogs, the purity of their breeding, and the characteristics that devolved to them by virtue of that.

The end of the eighteenth century brought the development of the shotgun, the ideal weapon for killing upland birds, waterfowl, and any large animal at close quarters. Setters and spaniels already existed for hunting birds, and they were adapted to serve the new weapon, but development of new classes of dog—retrievers and pointers, the gundogs—is as significant in the drive to bring the dog fully into the human orbit as the capture of the genetic mutation for smallness—perhaps more so.

Shotguns and gundogs opened a largely unexploited domain, uncontrolled by nobles, for perfecting one's skills as a hunter and breeder of dogs. The actual kennel work was done by someone else, but no matter. This was a new type of hunting for a new kind of game. Birds were caught in nets with the aid of spaniels and setters or shot with rifles, but not even together could they match what a single man with a shotgun and a good retriever could cart home in a day. Farm fields were excellent for bird hunting, especially if properly baited. Waterways were fine for waterfowl, and no one had to worry about cost and bother of chasing hounds. The retriever, more even than the pointer, who could be seen as an obsessive perfectionist, became the working class star, responsible for bringing back the bird wherever it landed, whatever its condition, and doing so again and again. The pointer was flash and style; the retriever was tenacity and substance.

Establishing a breed of dog or cat or livestock required writing out a standard, describing its physical and behavioral characteristics, and maintaining a studbook showing the pedigree of each animal in its direct lineage. These practices were sufficient to establish an animal's "purity." In 1859, the first recorded dog show was held in England. The Kennel Club itself, the first in the world, was organized in 1873 to bring order to the Fancy, as it was known, and the American Kennel Club followed in 1874, but the mythologizing of breeds was already well under way. Official breeds are cultural and biological entities born of acts of imagination grounded in a few facts about the origin of a particular breed. Because these narratives provide a frame for the breed standard, their historical accuracy has mattered only if it has become untethered from facts all together.

Recently genetic analysis has been added to and, in many cases, reinforced, the breed narrative. Thus, the Japanese Akita is classified as an ancient breed based on analysis of DNA from American Akitas. Descended from dogs brought to the United States by servicemen returning from Japan following World War II, a time when the breed had been so imperiled by fire bombing, that it had to be reconstructed from dogs who had been sequestered in mountain refuges. The Japanese Akita club insists that the American Akita represents a different breed and should be designated as such, whereas the American breed club, violating its own code that a breed is defined by its standard and registry, refuses to recognize a difference. It would be interesting to test the two breeds genetically to see whether they are indeed the same.

As breeds were formed through consolidation of several existing but similar types of dog or by splitting a select group of preferred animals from a larger population purely because they fit the description better than the rest, the parent stock was demeaned. Writing in the May 1872 issue of the *Atlantic Monthly*, Charles Dawson Shanly recommended that people wanting to see "one of the most pastoral as well as sagacious of the canine family" should visit Central Park before dawn when Scotch collies would bring their stock into the yards through crowded streets, walking across the backs of the sheep, if necessary, to rescue a stray. But he also cautioned his readers to be careful not to watch mongrel collies who were not up to snuff.[4]

Conventional wisdom held that any crossbred collie was worthless as a herder and was probably a sheep-killing cur, which now became not a particular kind of roughly bred dog but a hazard, a killer, a low-born wretch that no proper farmer should tolerate. The dogs of the urban immigrant poor were the worst kind of low-born curs to be found. Thus, cur became nearly fully synonymous with mongrel, with mixed-blood, impure, a term of derision applied to dogs and people.

The total bankruptcy of this assessment was exposed in World War I when British Army Major Edwin H. Richardson set up his service's first dog unit relying heavily on farm collies and crossbred collies, Airedales, retrievers, and lurchers, small and fast crossbred greyhounds. Richardson avoided purebred show collies as mentally and physically deficient, hounds because they followed their noses, and poodles and fox terriers because they were too frivolous for words, much less work.[5]

The call to arms for U.S. military dogs specified "farm collies" for the same reasons Richardson wanted them in the British Army. Unfortunately the lesson was forgotten, if ever learned, by men returning home. In the United States, they wanted families, new homes, new appliances, and purebred dogs. Up until that point, the price of a purebred dog was more than the cost of Model T Ford or a year's salary for most Americans. On the eve of the war, purebred dogs accounted for only about 5 percent of the American dog population; curs and crossbreds were 95 percent. By my calculations, purebred dogs, including those their owners never registered, now account for more than half of the dogs in America.[6]

Numbers alone fail to tell the story of this rush to pedigree. According to estimates by Melissa Gray and her colleagues, in Robert K. Wayne's evolutionary biology laboratory at UCLA, the initial divergence of dog from dogwolf resulted in roughly a 4 percent loss of genetic diversity, a small number reflective of a minor shift that set the stage for a major transformation thousands of years later. Since the advent of "scientific" breeding—meaning here the extensive use of favored sires and inbreeding—the loss of diversity has risen to 38 percent. More than four hundred genetic ailments have been cataloged in America's purebred dog population, most of which sort by breed.[7]

With mass urbanization beginning in the nineteenth century and continuing to the present, dogs were moved into cities and apartments where their freedom of movement was sharply curtailed and their reproduction regulated. In France, the United States, and Great Britain at least little companion dogs and some larger gentleman's terriers were given extreme brachycephalic heads, while others were made to look like perpetual puppies. The broad point is that many of these breeds have been turned into little more than adornments, much the way those first, early little dogs were adornments, bio-jewelry. They are supposed to do nothing but be submissive and devoted to their people. The danger we face in our ahistorical age is having people forget that these animals are not like the ones who came to our forebears forty thousand or more years ago and set up camp.

The phenotypic change in pedigreed dogs is often hard to miss, since much of it has occurred since World War II. More significant may be the behavioral changes that began with the era of purebred dogs two hundred years ago, said Kenth Svartberg, a comparative psychologist studying dog behavior at the Swedish University of Agricultural Sciences, in the journal *Applied Animal Behaviour Science* in

2006. Breeds that do well in the show ring, he found, tend to lack any behaviors associated with "inquisitiveness," including "playfulness," which is highly desired in working dogs and dogs sought as pets. Instead, show dogs score highly in "social" and "nonsocial fearfulness." Pets are wanted to be "playful" and "sociable," Svartberg said. Working dogs should score high in "aggression" and "boldness," defined as a combination of "playfulness" and "curiosity/fearlessness," but few breeds are used for work anymore. The mistake people make is in thinking that the behaviors associated with pets and showdogs today are reflective of past behaviors or their history—they are not necessarily.[8]

At their best, dogs and humans have managed to work together in ways that grant the dog the independence it needs to act.

Imagine a farm spread across rolling hills where a sheep-herding competition is held. The morning was for novices, and a mix of dogs showed up, all from herding breeds. A beautifully bred kelpie took his turn and did nothing but watch his handler encourage him to pay attention to the sheep rather than her. Good Luck. D.W. said the problem is that the kelpie was trained to work to his human's direction as a search and rescue dog—work at which he excels—but it has made him handler conscious. After a break for lunch, it was time to collect the flock of sheep being used in the trial. D.W. asked the kennel club's official to send his Best-in-Show, herding trial–certified Belgian tervuren lying at the entrance to the field where the sheep grazed four hundred yards sway. Carrying his shepherd's crook, the official commanded his dog's attention in a firm, authoritative voice. The dog raised his majestic head, looked at his master, blinked, and put his head back down. Laughing, explaining to me that the tervuren was mental, D.W. walked into the deep shade of the paddock and released a chain holding her little border collie, Bam, a dog from one of her litters. "Guy showed up with his son and begged me to sell him a dog, promised, 'We will take care of him and train him.' They chained the dog to a tree and left him for six months so that by the time I got him back, I figured just having him was a bonus. He's my best sheepdog now, doesn't need any instruction."

She clicked her tongue to her cheek and threw her arm toward the sheep. Bam left at full speed and never looked back. He made a wide sweep of the sheep from right to left and left to right, stopping near the center rear of the flock, where a big ram, having come through a hole in the fence, turned to challenge Bam. The little border collie feinted a charge and snapped his teeth fast and loud. The ram charged again, but this time Bam dodged and then grabbed his cheek, pulling out wool. The ram turned and, with flock in tow, set off for the paddock. There the ram was taking aim at the hapless tervuren when Bam intervened and forced him into a side chute where D.W. was standing, having opened a gate, but she said not a word to Bam.

In Svartberg's study only three breeds of putative working dogs retained the personality traits—especially the boldness and aggression—associated with work of any sort: malinois, border collies, and working kelpies (to distinguish them from a line of show kelpies in Australia). Those characteristics also often persist in all-purpose dogs, in the curs and feists, and in some other breeds, but even they are being subjected to breeding practices that promote traits other than those needed for work, including, and especially, playfulness and curiosity. It is paradoxical that at a time when society desperately needs dogs to perform certain tasks, like detecting explosives contraband or assisting people with disabilities, or serving as guards and companions, it has difficulty finding enough that are sound of mind and body to meet its needs. Partly the professionals looking for dogs are constrained from finding them by adherence to breed histories that are, and may always have been, inaccurate. They need to cast a larger net.

The most bewildering breed in this regard is the Labrador retriever. It is no mistake that the Labrador retriever is perennially the most popular dog in the country and one of the most popular in the world—a big dog beating little dogs at their own game. In its original state it appears to have been a curdog from Newfoundland, with a mix of just about every dog that has landed on that Grand Banks weigh station for at least five hundred years, largely aboard fishing boats from Europe, but perhaps with some older Native American dog contribution. British breeders refined the rough water cur, which has black, yellow, and brown coats, and shipped it back to America. It is perhaps the best all-around purebred dog—in many regards one of the all-around best dogs—when bred for performance, structure, and temperament. Poorly bred, it can be a disaster.[9]

Curiously, given the present number of these dogs in North America, the most popular large dog breed in the nineteenth century was another Newfoundland native, the eponymously named Newfoundland dog, a big, robust animal owned and celebrated for its courage, loyalty, and sagacity. Lord Byron memorably mourned his Boatswain while declaiming against the injustice of claiming that humans have souls but dogs do not. Meriwether Lewis's Seaman accompanied the Corps of Discovery across the continent and back. John James Audubon considered his Plato "a well trained and most sagacious animal."

Nearly simultaneously with the promotion of the virtues of purebred dogs, public health agencies and animal welfare groups—joined after the formation of People for the Ethical Treatment of Animals in 1979 by animal rights groups—began drives for leash and fence laws to restrain dogs in order to curb an epidemic of dog bites and control zoonotic diseases. With fence laws came an expansion of animal shelters to pick up and find homes for or euthanize stray and free-ranging dogs.

By the 1970s and 1980s, an estimated twelve million unwanted dogs were being killed in shelters annually in the United States, and campaigns to spay and neuter dogs, including higher licensing fees for sexually intact animals, were launched.

The number of dogs in American households has more than doubled since then, to approximately seventy million, the vast majority of them confined in homes and fenced yards. The number of euthanized dogs has fallen by 75 percent, which still amounts to an unacceptable three million dogs a year.

This process of restricting freedom, controlling reproduction, and determining whether the animal lives or dies is domestication in the fullest sense, and for dogs and humans it remains a work in progress, proceeding in fits and starts with more than a little ambivalence and outright distress over the directions it sometimes takes.

Demands to regulate breeding more tightly are intended, at one level, to end the abuses of commercial breeders who mass-produce dogs without regard for their well-being or health, but their effect would be to bring every aspect of the dog's life under human control in the final act of full domestication. Legitimately concerned about the suffering of animals, some groups have moved abroad with campaigns to spay/neuter free-ranging dogs (and cats) in developing countries where their living conditions are often squalid. A few of those groups recognize the need to understand dogs and people in their time and place and take action from there rather than go in and declare the dogs ownerless, unwanted carriers of disease, scavengers to no purpose. The fact is that people treat each other as poorly as they treat dogs, which is the source of an age-old complaint in every language—"You treat the dog better than you treat me" or "You treat me like a dog."

That is not high praise. At the same time that these attempts are being made to bring the dog more fully under human control or perhaps because of it, scientists are probing all aspects of the dog's genome, psyche, and physiology, hoping to study everything from early puppy development and psychological disorders to the effects of domestication. Many of the tests used are designed to measure the animal's attentiveness to a human handler such that it follows her pointing to or gazing at a hidden object. The idea behind these experiments is to see whether a dog's attentiveness to humans is more similar to that of a child than that of a wolf. As predicted, it is closer to that of a child, according to Brian Hare at Duke University, who believes dogs were chosen and bred for their attentiveness to humans. No one seems to have tested the ability of humans to follow their dog's gaze. Ádâm Miklósi of Eötvös University in Budapest, Hungary, and his research group have argued that the transformation of wolf to dog involved changes in communication, sociability, and cooperation. Still, other researchers have focused on the dog's ability to understand human language, and found that it is better than most humans' understanding of dog language.[10]

More than generating specific results, the tests speak to the broader drive to complete domestication of the dog, to bring it more securely into human society through breeding and training. The underlying supposition is that the dog exists in a healthy fashion only within human society, but that is a limited view that denies the dog its true niche in the border zone where the human meets the natural. The dog roams there with one eye looking forward, the other back, one on each world. In that guise it is a companion, guard, and guide, an ambiguity and a paradox who completes us in myriad ways. Attempts to make the dog a milquetoast, a biological doll who waits all day in a steel crate for the objects of its desire to come home at the appointed hour and take it to the dog park, following the daily drill, deny the dog its freedom. Producing purebred dogs with known debilitating diseases and disorders disrespects dogs and people.

The impetus behind scientific breeding was a desire to improve on nature. Arguably it has failed to meet that goal, which should be rethought. People crossbreeding dogs, searching for animals with intelligence, with the ability and desire to learn and to act—whether to play Frisbee or ball or search for victims of disasters or explosives or otherwise devote their talents to a satisfying task—present the outline of a different approach to breeding and raising dogs, one that seeks to honor and set right our ancient relationship.

ACKNOWLEDGMENTS

Among the many people and animals who contributed to the making of this book, my wife Gina Maranto stands first. Without her unwavering support, there is nothing. Alice Fried Martell is an agent from the old school of publishing, which is to say, indispensable. Special thanks go to Cameron Davidson and Bruce Stutz for their photographs and Chris Hanson for his maps. Bill Walker and his staff at the University of Miami Library provided invaluable advice at a crucial moment as the book neared completion. Marc Bekoff has been a stalwart friend and sounding board. Over the years, Bob Wayne has graciously answered questions about the genetics of the dog, as has Elaine Ostrander. Darcy Morey provided an archaeological perspective. Dave Mech is the source book on wolves. Karen Overall has always shared her vast knowledge of dogs—and their people. Aaron Schlechter first approached me with the idea of the book and set the process in motion. Stephanie Gorton became editor in medias res and saw the book through to completion. Patricia K. Nicolescu provided the copyediting. Peter Mayer and The Overlook Press brought it into print.

The dogs and people who over the years have tried to educate me are too numerous to name, but two of the dogs stand out. They are the intrepid kelpies, Harley, who succumbed to a brain tumor while the book was being copyedited in mid-November 2010, and Katie, the Kate, who returned from a near-death experience to see this book through to the end.

Everyone, named and unnamed, who has helped me grapple with the mysterious paradox that is the dog shares the credit for whatever of merit adheres to this book. Its flaws and errors are strictly my own.

NOTES

PART I

1. Deborah Bird Rose, *Dingo Makes Us Human: Life and Land in an Aboriginal Australian Culture* (Cambridge: Cambridge University Press, 2000).

CHAPTER ONE

1. The Bradshaw INORA Newsletter #42: "Chauvet Cave: Results of the Interdisciplinary Studies," 2006; Paul Mellars, "A New Radiocarbon Revolution and the Dispersal of Modern Humans in Eurasia," *Nature* 439 (February 23, 2006): 931–35

2. Deborah Bird Rose, *Dingo Makes Us Human: Life and Land in an Aboriginal Australian Culture* (Cambridge: Cambridge University Press, 2000).

3. John Paul Scott and John L. Fuller, *Genetics and the Social Behavior of the Dog* (Chicago: University of Chicago Press, 1965); John Paul Scott, "The Evolution of Social Behavior in Dogs and Wolves," *American Zoologist* 7, no. 2 (1967): 373–81; Konrad Lorenz, *Man Meets Dog* (Baltimore: Penguin, 1964).

4. Carles Vilà et al., "Multiple and Ancient Origins of the Domestic Dog," *Science* 276 53/9 (June 13, 1997): 1687–89.

5. Jun-Feng Pang et al., "mtDNA Data Indicate a Single Origin for Dogs South of Yangtze River, Less Than 1630 Years Ago, from Numerous Wolves," *Molecular Biology and Evolution* 26, no.12 (2009): 2849-64.

6. *Ibid.*

7. George Caitlin, *North American Indians,* 2 volumes (Philadelphia: Leary, Stuart and Company, 1911), vol. 1, 258.

CHAPTER TWO

1. Raymond Coppinger and Lorna Coppinger, *Dogs: A Startling New Understanding of Canine Origin, Behavior, and Evolution* (Chicago: University of Chicago Press, 2002).

2. Dmitry K. Belyaev, "Destabilizing Selection as a Factor in Domestication," *Journal of Heredity* 70, no. 5 (1979): 301–8. Lyudmila Trut, Irina Oskina, and Anastasiya Kharlamova, "Animal Evolution During Domestication: The Domesticated Fox as a Model," *Bioessays* 31, no. 3 (March 2009): 339–60.

3. Susan J. Crockford, *Rhythms of Life: Thyroid Hormones and the Origin of Species* (Bloomington: Trafford Publishing, 2006).

4. L. Boitani, F. Francisci, P. Ciucci, and G. Anddreoli, "Population Biology and Ecology of Feral Dogs in Central Italy," in *The Domestic Dog: Its Evolution, Behaviour, and Interactions with People,* James Serpell, ed. (Cambridge: Cambridge University Press, 1995), 218–44.

5. Svetlana S. Gogoleva et al., "Kind Granddaughters of Angry Grand-mothers: The Effect of Domestication on Vocalization in Cross-bred Silver Foxes," *Behavioural Processes* 81, no. 3 (July 2009): 369–75.

6. Jerome W. Woolpy and Benson E. Ginsburg, "Wolf Socialization: A Study of Temperament in a Wild Species," *American Zoologist* 7, no. 2 (May 1967): 357–63.

CHAPTER THREE

1. The Grateful Dead. *Truckin'*, by Robert Hunter and Jerry Garcia (1973).

2. Abi Tamim Vanak and Matthew E. Gomper, "Dietary Niche Separation Between Sympatric Free-Ranging Domestic Dogs and Indian Foxes in Central India," *Journal of Mammalogy* 90, no. 5 (2009): 1058–65. J. E. Echegaray and C. Vilà, "Noninvasive Monitoring of Wolves at the Edge of Distribution and the Cost of Their Conservation," *Animal Conservation* (2009): 1–5.

3. Rolf O. Peterson and John A. Vucetich, *Ecological Studies of Wolves on Isle Royale: Annual Report 2001–2002* (Houghton: Michigan Institute of Technology, 2002).

4. Dawn N. Irion et al., "Genetic Variation Analysis of the Bali Street Dog Using Microsatellites," *BMC Genetics* 6, no. 6 (February 8, 2005).

5. *Ibid.*

PART II

1. *Journals of the Lewis and Clark Expedition,* Guy E. Moulton, ed., 13 volumes (Lincoln: University of Nebraska Press, 1983), vol. 4, 60.

CHAPTER FOUR

1. Wang Xiaoming et al., "Phylogeny, Classification, and Evolutionary Ecology of Canidae," in *Canids: Foxes, Wolves, Jackals and Dogs: Status Survey and Conservation Action Plan,* C. Sillero-Zubiri, M. Hoffmann, and D. W. Macdonald, eds. (Geneva: IUCN, 2004).

2. Dinesh K. Sharma et al., "Ancient Wolf Lineages in India," *Proceedings of the Royal Society, London* B (Suppl.) 271 (2004): S51–S4.

3. Bienvenido Martinez-Navarro et al., "The Large Carnivores from 'Ubeidiya' (Early Pleistocene, Israel): Biochronological and Biogeographical Implications," *Journal of Human Evolution* 56, no. 5 (May 2009): 514–24.

CHAPTER FIVE

1. Adam Brumm et al., "Hominins on Flores, Indonesia, by One Million Years Ago," *Nature* 464 (2010): 748–57. Johannes Krause et al., "The Complete Mitochondrial DNA Genome of an Unknown Hominin from Southern Siberia," *Nature* 464 (2010): 894–97.

2. Marta Arzarella et al., "Evidence of Earliest Human Occurrence in Europe: The Site at Pirro Nord (Southern Italy)," *Naturwissenschaften* 94, no. 2 (2007): 107–12. Joan Madurell-Malapeira, David M. Alba, and Salvador Moyà-Solà, "Carnivora from the Late Early Pleistocene of Cal Guardiola (Terrassa Vallès-Penedès Basin, Catalonia, Spain)," *Journal of Paleontology* 83, no. 6 (2009): 969–74. Paul Palmqvist et al., "Tracing the Ecophysiology of Ungulates and Predator-Prey Relationships in an Early Pleistocene Large Mammal Community," *Palaeogeography, Palaeoclimatology, Palaeoecology* 266. nos. 1–2 (August, 2008): 95–111.

3. Helmut Hemmer, "Out of Africa: A Paleoecological Scenario of Man and His Carnivorous Competitors in the European Pleistocene," *ERAUL* 92 (2000): 99–106.

4. M. Sotnikova et al., "Dispersal of Canini (Mammalia, Canidae: Caninae) Across Eurasia During the Late Miocene to Early Pleistocene," *Quarternary International* 212, no. 2 (February 1, 2010): 86–97.

5. J. R. Blasco, "Who Was the First? An Experimental Application of Carnivore and Hominid Overlapping Marks at the Pleistocene Archaeological Sites," *C. R. Palevol* 8, no. 6 (September 2009): 574–92.

CHAPTER SIX

1. Wolfgang Schleidt and Michael G. Shalter, "Co-evolution of Humans and Canids: An Alternate View of Dog Domestication: Homo Homini Lupus," *Cognition and Evolution* 9, no. 1 (2003): 57–72.

2. Mary C. Stiner, "Comparative Ecology and Taphonomy of Spotted Hyenas, Humans, and Wolves in Pleistocene Italy," *Revue de Paleobiologic Geneve* 23, no. 2 (December 2004): 771–85. Paul Palmqvist et al., "Tracing the Ecophysiology of Ungulates and Predator-Prey Relationships in an Early Pleistocene Large Mammal Community," *Palaeogeography, Palaeoclimatology, Palaeoecology* 266, nos. 1–2 (August 2008): 95–111.

3. Alois Musil, *The Manners and Customs of the Rwala Bedouin* (New York: American Geographical Society, 1928).

4. Jiang Rong, *Wolf Totem* (New York and London: Penguin Press, 2008).

5. Nira Alperson-Afil et al., "Spatial Organization of Hominin Activities at Gesher Benot Ya'aqov, Israel," *Science* 326, no. 5960 (2009): 1677–79.

6. Brigitte M. Holt and Vincenzo Formicola, "Hunters of the Ice Age: The Biology of Upper Paleolithic People," *Yearbook of Physical Anthropology* 137, Suppl. no. 47 (2008): S70–S99.

7. Ronald Nowak, "The Original Status of Dogs in Eastern North America," *Southeastern Naturalist* 1, no. 2 (June 2002): 95–130.

8. Dennis A. Etler, "The Fossil Evidence for Human Evolution in Asia," *Annual Review Anthropology* 25 (October, 1996): 275–301.

9. Konrad Lorenz, *Man Meets Dog* (Baltimore: Penguin, 1964). Rolf O. Peterson and John A. Vucetich, *Ecological Studies of Wolves on Isle Royale: Annual Report 2001–2002* (Houghton: Michigan Institute of Technology, 2002).

CHAPTER SEVEN

1. Helen Pringle,"Primitive Humans Conquered Sea, Surprising Finds Suggest," *National Geographic* Daily News (February 17, 2010): http://news
.nationalgeographic.com/news/2010/02/100217-crete-primitive-humans-mariners-seafarers-mediterranean-sea. Accessed November 28, 2010.

2. Wolfgang Schleidt and Michael G. Shalter, "Co-evolution of Humans and Canids: An Alternate View of Dog Domestication: Homo Homini Lupus," *Cognition and Evolution* 9, no. 1 (2003): 57–72. Maryléne Patou-Mathis, "Neanderthal Subsistence Behaviours in Europe," *International Journal of Osteoarchaeology* 10 (2000): 379–95.

3. Sankar Subramanian et al., "High Mitogenomic Evolutionary Rates and Time Dependency," *Trends in Genetics* 25, no. 11 (October 15, 2009): 482–86. Carles Vilà et al., "Multiple and Ancient Origins of the Domestic Dog," *Science* 276, no. 5319 (June 13, 1997): 1687–89.

4. Schleidt and Shalter, "Co-Evolution of Humans and Canids." M. Sotnikova et al., "Dispersal of Canini (Mammalia, Canidae: Caninae) Across Eurasia During the Late Miocene to Early Pleistocene," *Quarternary International* 212 (February 2010): 86–97. Vilà, *"Multiple and Ancient Origins."* Alan R. Templeton, "Out of Africa Again and Again," *Nature* 416 (2002): 45–51.

5. Valerius Geist, "Neanderthal the Hunter," *Natural History* 90, no. 1 (January 1981): 26–36.

6. Preston T. Miracle et al., "Last Glacial Climate, 'Refugia,' and Faunal Change in Southcentral Europe: Mammalian Assemblages from Veternica, Velika Pécina, and Vindija Caves (Croatia)," *Quaternary International* 212, no. 2 (February 1, 2010): 137–48.

7. Richard E. Green et al., "A Draft Sequence of the Neandertal Genome," *Science* 328 (2010): 710–22.

8. That would put the time and place for the first miscegenation of eighty thousand years ago, when Neanderthals retreating south ahead of glaciers ended up in the Levant, the old world's premier mixing ground, near the Sea of Galilee, where some might have found shelter in caves occupied by *Homo sapiens*.

Part III

Chapter Eight

1. Mietje Germonpré et al., "Fossil Dogs and Wolves from Paleolithic Sites in Belgium, the Ukraine and Russia: Osteometry, Ancient DNA and Stable Isotopes," *Journal of Archaeological Science* 36, no. 2 (February 2008): 473–90.

2. Pat Shipman, "The Woof at the Door." *American Scientist,* vol. 97, no. 4 (July–August 2009): 286.

3. Germonpré, *Journal of Archeological Science,* 2008.

4. Jun-Feng Pang et al., "mtDNA Data Indicate a Single Origin for Dogs South of Yangtze River, Less Than 1630 Years Ago, from Numerous Wolves," *Molecular Biology and Evolution* 26, no. 12 (2009): 2849-64; available as Savolainen-236-manuscript doc.

5. Bridget von Holdt et al., "Genome-wide SNP and Haplotype Analyses Reveal a Rich History Underlying Dog Domestication," *Nature* 464 (April 8, 2010): 898–902.

6. Nathan B. Sutter et al., "A Single IGF1 Allele Is a Major Determinant of Small Size in Dogs," *Science* 316, no. 5821 (April 6, 2007): 112–15.

7. Tovi M. Anderson, et al., "Molecular and Evolutionary History of Melanism in North American Gray Wolves," *Science Express.* www.scienceexpress.org/5 February 2009/page 2/10.1126/ Science 1165448. Accessed February 5, 2009.

8. Adam Powell et al., "Late Pleistocene Demography and the Appearance of Modern Behavior," *Science* 324, no. 5932 (June 5, 2009): 1298–1301. Chris Stringer, "Coasting out of Africa," *Nature* 405 (May 4, 2000): 24–27.

9. Powell, "Late Pleistocene Demography." Ofer Bar-Yosef, "The Upper Paleolithic Revolution," *Annual Review of Anthropology* 31 (October 2002): 363–93.

10. A. Clark Arcadi, "Species Resilience in Pleistocene Hominids That Traveled Far and Ate Widely: An Analogy to the Wolflike Canids," *Journal of Human Evolution* 51, no. 4 (October 2006): 383–94. Wolfgang Schleidt and Michael G. Shalter, "Co-evolution of Humans and Canids: An Alternate View of Dog Domestication: Homo Homini Lupus," *Cognition and Evolution* 9, no. 1 (2003): 57–72.

11. Sufiak Mohsen, "The Quest for Order Among Awlad Ali of the Western Desert of Egypt" (Ann Arbor, MI: University Microfilms, 1971), 170–72. H.R.P. Dickson, *The Arab of the Desert: A Glimpse into Badawin Life in Kuwait and Sau'di Arabia* (New York: George Allen & Unwin, 1951).

Chapter Nine

1. Taryn Roberts et al., "Human Induced Rotation and Reorganization of the Brain of Domestic Dogs." *PLoS One* 5:7 (2010).

2. W. K. Lamb, ed., *The Journals and Letters of Sir Alexander Mackenzie* (London and New York: Cambridge University Press for the Hakluyt Society, 1970).

3. Deborah Bird Rose, *Dingo Makes Us Human: Life and Land in an Aboriginal Australian Culture* (Cambridge: Cambridge University Press, 2000).

4. Bridget von Holdt, et al. "Genome-wide SNP and Haplotype Analyses Reveal a Rich History Underlying Dog Domestication," *Nature* 464 (April 8, 2010): 898–902.

5. Wei Wang and Ewen F. Kirkness, "Short Interspersed Elements (SINEs) Are a Major Source of Canine Genomic Diversity," *Genome Research* 15, no. 12 (December, 2005): 1798–808.

6. Arion D. Wallach et al., "More Than Mere Numbers: The Impact of Lethal Control on the Social Stability of a Top-Order Predator," *PLoS One* 4, no. 9 (September 2, 2009): 6861. Andrew P. Hendry et al., "Human Influences on Rates of Phenotypic Change in Wild Animal Populations," *Molecular Ecology* 17, no. 1 (January 2008): 20–29. Melinda A. Zeder et al., "The Initial Domestication of Goats (*Capra hircus*) in the Zagros Mountains 10,000 Years Ago," *Science* 287, no. 5461 (March 24, 2000): 2254–57.

7. Jerome H. Woolpy and Benson E. Ginsburg, "Wolf Socialization: A Study of Temperament in a Wild Species," *American Zoologist* 7, no. 2 (May 1967): 357–63.

8. John C. Fentress, "Observations on the Behavioral Development of a Hand-Reared Male Timber Wolf," *American Zoologist* 7, no. 2 (1967): 339–51. Eric Zimen, "Ontogeny of Approach and Flight Behavior Toward Humans in Wolves, Poodles and Wolf-Poodle Hybrids," in *Man and Wolf: Advances, Issues, and Problems in Captive Wolf Research*, Harry Frank, ed. (Dordrecht: Dr. W. Junk Publisher, 1981). Mark Rowlands, *The Philosopher and the Wolf: Lessons from the Wild on Love, Death, and Happiness* (New York: Pegasus Books, 2009). N. A. Iljin, "Wolf-Dog Genetics," *Journal of Genetics* 42, no. 3 (1941): 359–414. Jiang Rong, *Wolf Totem* (New York and London: Penguin Press, 2008). John Paul Scott, "The Evolution of Social Behavior in Dogs and Wolves," *American Zoologist* 7, no. 2 (1967): 373–81. Woolpy and Ginsburg, "Wolf Socialization."

9. Zimen, "Ontogeny of Approach and Flight Behavior."

CHAPTER TEN

1. Rebecca M. Todd and Adam K. Anderson, "Six Degrees of Separation: The Amygdala Regulates Social Behavior and Perception," *Nature Neuroscience* 12, no. 10 (October 2009): 1217–18.

2. Lorna Coppinger and Raymond Coppinger, "Livestock-Guarding Dogs That Wear Sheep's Clothing," *Smithsonian* 13 (April 1982): 65–73.

3. Mark Derr, *Dog's Best Friend: Annals of the Dog-Human Relationship* (New York: Henry Holt and Company, 1997).

4. "Trained Female Wolf Excels in Vienna Police Trials," *The New York Times* (April 30, 1933). "Garden Dog Show Lists Timber Wolf," *The New York Times* (February 9, 1939).

5. Richard B. Lee and Irven DeVore, eds., *Man the Hunter* (Chicago: Alden, 1968).

6. Merryl Ann Parker, *Bringing the Dingo Home: Discursive Representations of the Dingo by Aboriginal, Colonial and Contemporary Australians.* (Ph.D. thesis, University of Tasmania, April 2006).

7. Paul Palmqvist et al., "Tracing the Ecophysiology of Ungulates and Predator-Prey Relationships in an Early Pleistocene Large Mammal Community," *Palaeogeography, Palaeoclimatology, Palaeoecology* 266, no. 1–2 (August 2008): 95–111. Preston T. Miracle et al., "Last Glacial Climate, 'Refugia,' and Faunal Change in Southcentral Europe: Mammalian Assemblages from Veternica, Velika Pécina, and Vindija Caves (Croatia)," *Quaternary International* 212, no. 2 (February 1, 2010): 137–48. Mary C. Stiner, "Comparative Ecology and Taphonomy of Spotted Hyenas, Humans, and Wolves in Pleistocene Italy," *Revue de Paleobiologic Geneve* 23, no. 2 (December 2004): 771–85.

CHAPTER ELEVEN

1. L. E. Stager, "Ashkelon's Dog Cemetery," *Near Eastern Archaeology* 68, nos. 1–2 (March–June 2005): 14–15. Darcy Morey, "Burying Key Evidence: The Social Bond Between Dogs and People," *Journal of Archaeological Science* 33, no. 2 (February 2006): 158–75.

2. Peter U. Clark et al., "The Last Glacial Maximum," *Science* 325, no. 5941 (August 7, 2009): 710–14.

3. Miroljub Milenkovic "Skull Variation in Dinaric-Balkan and Carpathian Gray Wolf Populations Revealed by Geometric Morphometric Approaches," *Journal of Mammalogy* 91, no. 2 (2010): 376–86.

4. Nathan B. Sutter et al., "A Single IGF1 Allele Is a Major Determinant of Small Size in Dogs," *Science* 316, no. 5821 (April 6, 2007): 112–15.

5. Dawn N. Irion et al., "Genetic Variation Analysis of the Bali Street Dog Using Microsatellites," *BMC Genetics* 6, no. 6 (February 8, 2005). Bridget von Holdt, et al., "Genome-wide SNP and Haplotype Analyses Reveal a Rich History Underlying Dog Domestication," *Nature* 464 (April 8, 2010): 898–902.

6. Mohanad Alhabi, personal communication (May 19, 2007).

CHAPTER TWELVE

1. Juliet Clutton-Brock, "Origins of the Dog: Domestication and Early History," in *The Domestic Dog: Its Evolution, Behaviour, and Interactions with People,* James Serpell, ed. (Cambridge: Cambridge University Press, 1995) 8–20. Raymond Coppinger and Richard Schneider, "Evolution of Working Dogs," in *The Domestic Dog,* 21–47.

2. Stephen Jay Gould, "Mickey Mouse Meets Konrad Lorenz," *Natural History* 88, no. 5 (May 1979): 30–36. John Hunter, "Observations Tending to

Show That the Wolf, Jackal and Dog Are All the Same Species," *Philosophical Transactions of the Royal Society of London,* vol. 77 (1787): 253–66.

3. Coppinger and Schneider, "Evolution of Working Dogs." Lyudmila Trut, Irina Oskina, and Anastasiya Kharlamova, "Animal Evolution During Domestication: The Domesticated Fox as a Model," *Bioessays* 31, no. 3 (March 2009): 339–60.

4. Mark Derr, *A Dog's History of America: How Our Best Friend Explored, Conquered, and Settled a Continent* (New York: North Point Press, 2004).

5. Abby Grace Drake and Christian Peter Klingenberg, "The Pace of Morphological Change: Historical Transformation in the Skull Shape in St. Bernard Dogs," *Proceedings of the Royal Society, B: Biological Science* 275, no. 1630 (2008): 71–76.

6. V. I. Bazaliiskiy and N. A. Savelyev, "The Wolf of Baikal: The 'Lokomotiv' Early Neolithic Cemetery in Siberia (Russia)," *Antiquity* 77, no. 295 (March 1, 2003): 20–30.

7. Melinda A. Zeder et al., "The Initial Domestication of Goats (*Capra hircus*) in the Zagros Mountains 10,000 Years Ago," *Science* 287, no. 5461 (March 24, 2000): 2254–57.

8. Brigitte M. Holt and Vincenzo Formicola, "Hunters of the Ice Age: The Biology of Upper Paleolithic People," *Yearbook of Physical Anthropology* 137, Suppl. no. 47 (2008): S70–S99.

9. Nathan B. Sutter et al., "A Single IGF1 Allele Is a Major Determinant of Small Size in Dogs," *Science* 316, no. 5821 (April 6, 2007): 112–15.

10. A. R. Boyko et al., "A Simple Genetic Architecture Underlies Morphological Variation in Dogs," *PLoS Biology* 8, no. 8 (August 2010). Paul Jones et al., "Single-Nucleotide-Polymorphism-Based Association Mapping of Dog Stereotypes," *Genetics* 179 (June 2008): 1033–44.

11. Sutter, "A Single IGF1 Allele." Jones, "Single-Nucleotide-Polymorphism-Based Association."

12. Sutter, "A Single IGF1 Allele." H. Parker et al., "An Expressed *Fgf4* Retrogene Is Associated with Breed-Defining Chondrodysplasia in Domestic Dogs," Sciencexpress (July 2009): 4.

13. Lorna Coppinger and Raymond Coppinger, "Livestock-Guarding Dogs That Wear Sheep's Clothing," *Smithsonian* 13 (April 1982): 65–73. Lorna Coppinger and Raymond Coppinger, "So Firm a Friendship," *Natural History* 89, no. 3 (March 1980): 12–26.

14. S. K. Pal, "Parental Care in Free-Ranging Dogs, *Canis familiaris,*" *Applied Animal Behaviour Science* 90 , no. 1 (2005): 31–47.

15. Leigh Dayton, "Tracing the Road Down Under," *Science* 302, no. 5645 (October 24, 2003): 555–56.

16. Thorstein Veblen, *The Theory of the Leisure Class* (New York: Macmillan, 1899). Melissa M. Gray et al., "Linkage Disequilibrium and Demographic History of Wild and Domestic Canids," *Genetics* 181, no. 4 (April

2009): 1493–505. Kerstin Lindblad-Toh et al., "Genome Sequencing, Comparative Analysis, and Haplotype Structure of the Domestic Dog," *Nature* 438 (December 2008): 803-19.

17. Bruce Fogle, *The Encyclopedia of the Dog*, (New York: Dorling Kindersley, 1995).

18. Monique A. R. Udell et al., "What did domestication do to dogs? A new account of dogs' sensitivity to human actions," *Biological Reviews* 85 (2010): 327-45.

19. Mark Derr, *Dog's Best Friend: Annals of the Dog-Human Relationship* (New York: Henry Holt and Company, 1997).

20. Miho Nagasawa and Mitsuaki Ohta, "The Influence of Dog Ownership in Childhood on the Sociability of Elderly Japanese Men," *Animal Science Journal* 81, no. 3 (June 2010): 377–83.

PART IV

1. W. G. Sebald, "A Day and Night, Chalk and Cheese: On the Pictures of Jan Peter Tripp," in *Unrecounted*, Michael Hamburger, trans. (New York: New Directions Books, 2009), 85–102.

CHAPTER THIRTEEN

1. M. V. Sablin and G. A. Khlopachev, "The Earliest Ice Age Dogs: Evidence from Eliseevichi I," *Current Anthropology* 43, no. 5 (2002): 795–99.

2. Mietje Germonpré et al., "Fossil Dogs and Wolves from Paleolithic Sites in Belgium, the Ukraine and Russia: Osteometry, Ancient DNA and Stable Isotopes," *Journal of Archaeological Science* 36, no. 2 (February 2008): 473–90.

3. Frederick Zeuner, *A History of Domesticated Animals* (New York: Harper and Row, 1963).

4. Juliet Clutton-Brock, "Origins of the Dog: Domestication and Early History," in *The Domestic Dog: Its Evolution, Behaviour, and Interactions with People,* James Serpell, ed. (Cambridge: Cambridge University Press, 1995), 8–20.

5. *Ibid*.

6. Evren Koban et al., "Genetic Relationship Between Kangal, Akbash and Other Dog Populations," *Discrete Applied Mathematics* 157, no. 10 (May 2009): 2335–40.

7. Ted Goebel et al., "The Late Pleistocene Dispersal of Modern Humans in the Americas," *Science* 319, no. 5869 (March 14, 2008): 1497–502. Connie J. Kolman et al., "Mitochondrial DNA Analysis of Mongolian Populations and Implications for the Origin of New World Founders," *Genetics* 142, no. 4 (April 1996): 1321–34.

8. David Gordon White, *Myths of the Dog-Man* (Chicago: University of Chicago Press, 1991). Mark Derr, *A Dog's History of American: How Our Best*

Friend Explored, Conquered, and Settled a Continent (New York: North Point Press, 2004).

9. Yuichi Tanabe, "Phylogenetic Studies of Dogs with Emphasis on Japanese and Asian Breeds," *Proceedings of the Japanese Academy of Sciences,* series B 82, no. 10 (2006): 375–87.

10. Mary E. Prendergast et al., "Resource Intensification in the Late Upper Paleolithic: A View from Southern China," *Journal of Archaeological Science* 36, no. 4 (2009): 1027–37.

11. Tamar Dayan, "Early Domestic Dogs of the Near East," *Journal of Archaeological Science* 21 (1994): 633–40.

12. Juliet Clutton-Brock and N. Noe-Nygaard, "New Osteological and C-Isotope Evidence of Mesolithic Dogs: Companions to Hunters and Fishers at Star Carr, Seamer Carr and Kongemoae," *Journal of Archaeological Science* 17 (1990): 643–653. Clutton-Brock, "Origins of the Dog." Preston T. Miracle et al., "Last Glacial Climate, 'Refugia,' and Faunal Change in Southcentral Europe: Mammalian Assemblages from Veternica, Velika Pécina, and Vindija Caves (Croatia)," *Quaternary International* 212, no. 2 (February 1, 2010): 137–48.

CHAPTER FOURTEEN

1. Jennifer Leonard et al., "Ancient DNA Evidence for Old World Origin on New World Dogs," *Science* 298, no. 5589 (November 22, 2002): 1613–16. Paul S. Martin, "Pleistocene Overkill," *Natural History* 76, no. 12 (December 1967): 32–38.

2. Ted Goebel et al., "The Late Pleistocene Dispersal of Modern Humans in the Americas," *Science* 319, no. 5869 (March 22, 2008): 1497–502.

3. Charles Darwin, *The Voyage of the Beagle* (London: P. F. Collier and Son, 1839).

4. Alana Cordy-Collins, "An Unshaggy Dog Story," *Natural History* 103, no. 2 (February 1994): 34–41. Glover M. Allen, "Dogs of the American Aborigines," *Bulletin of the Museum of Comparative Zoology* 63, no. 9 (March 1920): 439 cf.

5. Marion Schwartz, *A History of Dogs in the Early Americas,* (New Haven, CT: Yale University Press, 1997). Christine P. White et al., "Isotopic Evidence for Maya Patterns of Deer and Dog Use at Preclassic Colha," *Journal of Archaeological Science* 28, no. 1 (January 2001): 89–107. Mark Derr, *A Dog's History of America: How Our Best Friend Explored, Conquered, and Settled a Continent* (New York: North Point Press, 2004).

6. *Journals of the Lewis and Clark Expedition,* Guy E. Moulton, ed., 13 volumes (Lincoln: University of Nebraska Press, 1983), vol. 4, 54.

7. Samuel A. Hearne, *A Journey from Prince of Wale's Fort in Hudson's Bay to the Northern Ocean: Undertaken by Order of the Hudson's Bay Company for the Discovery of Copper Mines, a North West Passage, &c., in the Years 1769, 1770, 1771, and 1772* (New York: Da Capo Press, 1969).

8. Glover M. Allen, "Dogs of the American Aborigines."

9. Danny N. Walker and George C. Frison, "Studies on Amerindian Dogs, 3: Prehistoric Wolf/Dog Hybrids from the Northwestern Plains," *Journal of Archaeological Science* 9, no. 2 (June 1982): 125–72.

10. Maximilian, Prince of Wied. *Travels in the Interior of North America,* Reuben Gold Thwaites, ed., Hannibal Evans Lloyd, trans. (Cleveland: The Arthur H. Clarke Company, 1905).

11. Mark Derr, *A Dog's History of America: How Our Best Friend Explored, Conquered and Settled a Continent* (New York, Worth Point Press, 2004).

12. C.F.C. Klütsch et al., "Regional Occurrence, High Frequency but Low Diversity of Mitochondrial DNA Haplogroup d1 Suggests a Recent Dog-Wolf Hybridization in Scandinavia," *Animal Genetics* (2010).

CHAPTER FIFTEEN

1. Priscilla S. Turnbull and Charles A. Reed, "The Fauna from the Terminal Pleistocene of Palegawra Cave," *Fieldiana Anthropology* 63, no. 3 (June 1974): 81–145.

2. Wolfgang Haak et al., "Ancient DNA from the First European Farmers in 7500-Year-Old Neolithic Sites," *Science* 310, no. 5750 (November 11, 2005): 1016–18.

3. Zhang Chi and Hsiao-chun Hung, "The Neolithic of Southern China—Origin, Development, and Dispersal," *Asian Perspective* 47, no. 2 (Fall 2008): 299–329.

4. David Rindos, *The Origins of Agriculture: An Evolutionary Perspective* (Orlando, FL: Academic Press, 1984).

5. Alan K. Outram et al., "The Earliest Horse Harnessing and Milking," *Science* 323, no. 5919 (March 6, 2009): 1332–35.

6. Loukas Barton et al., "Agricultural Origins and the Isotopic Identity of Domestication in Northern China," *Proceedings of the National Academy of Sciences* 106, no. 14 (April 7, 2009): 5523–28.

7. *Ibid.*

8. Dinesh K. Sharma et al., "Ancient Wolf Lineages in India," *Proceedings of the Royal Society, London,* B (Suppl.) 271 (2004): S1–S4.

9. Abi Tamim Vanak and Matthew E. Gomper, "Dietary Niche Separation Between Sympatric Free-Ranging Domestic Dogs and Indian Foxes in Central India," *Journal of Mammalogy* 90, no. 5 (2009): 1058–65.

10. *Ibid.*

PART V

1. Mark Derr, adaptation, Homer, *The Odyssey*

CHAPTER SIXTEEN

1. Confucius, *The Book of Rites,* volume 4 of *The Sacred Books of China,* volume 24 of *The Sacred Books of the East,* James Legge, trans. (1885). www .sacred-texts.com/cfu/liki/index. Accessed November 4, 2010.

2. Nobuo Shigehara, "Morphological Study of the Ancient Dogs from Three Neolithic Sites," *International Journal of Osteoarchaeology* 8, no. 1 (January–February 1998): 11–22. Yuichi Tanabe, "Phylogenetic Studies of Dogs with Emphasis on Japanese and Asian Breeds," *Proceedings of the Japanese Academy of Sciences,* series B 82, no. 10 (2006): 375–87.

3. A. Higham et al., "An Analysis of Prehistoric Canid Remains from Thailand," *Journal of Archaeological Science* 7, no.2 (June 1980): 149–65.

4. *Ibid.*

5. L. E. Stager, "Ashkelon's Dog Cemetery," *Near Eastern Archaeology* 68, nos. 1–2 (March–June 2005): 14–15.

6. M. Zedda et al., "Ancient Pompeian Dogs—Morphological and Morphometric Evidence for Different Canine Populations," *Anatomia, Histologia, Embryologia* 35, no. 5 (October 2006): 319–24.

7. L. Junius Moderatus Columella, *L. Junius Moderatus Columella of Husbandry: in Twelve Books and His Book Concerning Trees,* 13 vols. (London: A. Milla5, 1745). Henry Rowe Schoolcraft, *Journal of a Tour into the Interior of Missouri and Arkansaw, from Potosi, or Mine a Burton, in Missouri Territory, in a South-West Direction, Toward the Rocky Mountains, Performed in the Years 1818 and 1819,* (London: Richard Phillips and Company, 1821).

8. Adam R. Boyko et al., "Complex Population Structure in African Village Dogs and Its Implications for Inferring Dog Domestication History," *Proceedings of the National Academy of Sciences* 106, no. 33 (August 18, 2009): 13903–8.

CHAPTER SEVENTEEN

1. Chao-chou Ts'ung-shen, sped2work.tripod.com/chao-chou.html. Accessed October 26, 2010.

2. Mark Derr, *Dog's Best Friend: Annals of the Dog-Human Relationship* (New York: Henry Holt and Company, 1997).

3. John Manwood, *A Treatise and Discourse of the Lawes of the Forrest,* (London and New York: Garland, 1978; reprint of 1598 edition).

4. Catherine Smith, "Dogs, Cats and Horses in the Scottish Medieval Town," *Proceedings of the Society of Antiquaries, Scotland* 128 (1998): 859–85.

5. A. Zinoviev, "Study of Medieval Dogs from Novgorod, Russia (X–XIV century)," *International Journal of Osteoarchaeology.* Published online in Wiley Interscience, 2010. www.interscience.wiley.com.

6. Johannes Caius, *A Treatise of Englishe Dogges, 1576* (Amsterdam: Theatrum Orbis Terrarum: reprint New York: Da Capo Press, 1969).

7. *Ibid.*

8. Mark Derr, *A Dog's History of America: How Our Best Friend Explored, Conquered, and Settled a Continent* (New York: North Point Press, 2004).

9. *Ibid.*

CHAPTER EIGHTEEN

1. Mark Derr, *A Dog's History of America: How Our Best Friend Explored, Conquered, and Settled a Continent* (New York: North Point Press, 2004). Mark Derr, *The Frontiersman: The Real Life and the Many Legends of Davy Crockett* (New York: William Morrow, 1993).

2. Mark Derr, *Dog's Best Friend: Annals of the Dog-Human Relationship* (New York: Henry Holt and Company, 1997). Derr, *A Dog's History of America.*

3. Harriet Ritvo, *The Animal Estate: The English and Other Creatures in the Victorian Age* (Cambridge, MA: Harvard University Press, 1987).

4. Charles Dawson Shanly. "New York Dogs," *The Atlantic Monthly,* May 1872.

5. Lieutenant-Colonel Edwin Hanleville Richardson, *Forty Years with Dogs* (Philadelphia: David McKay, n.d.)

6 Derr, *A Dog's History of America.*

7. Mellisa M. Gray et al., "Linkage Disequilibrium and Demographic History of Wild and Domestic Canids," *Genetics* 181, no. 4 (April 2009): 1493–505.

8. Kenth Svartberg, "Breed-typical Behaviour in Dogs: Historical Remnants or Recent Constructs," *Applied Animal Behaviour Science* 96, nos. 3–4 (February 2006): 293–313.

9. Derr, *A Dog's History of America.*

10. Brian Hare and Michael Tomasello, "Human-like Social Skills in Dogs." *Trends Incognitive Sciences* 9 (2005): 439-44. József Topal et al., "Differential Sensitivity to Human Communication is Dogs, Wolves, and Human Infants." *Science* 325 (2009): 1260-71.

INDEX

1 oz 7-10% cut
140 - 14 = 26 lbs